THE SHORE DIMLY SEEN

THE SHORE DIMLY SEEN

by

ELLIS GIBBS ARNALL

J. B. Lippincott Company

PHILADELPHIA AND NEW YORK

COPYRIGHT, 1946, BY

ELLIS GIBBS ARNALL

PRINTED IN THE

UNITED STATES OF AMERICA

THIRD IMPRESSION

To My Son and Daughter

Alvan and Alice

With the hope that when they grow up the shore will be seen more clearly.

CONTENTS

1. The Paradox That Is the South — 11
2. Exporting Illiteracy — 29
3. Demagogues in the Dark — 39
4. Experiment in Democracy — 51
5. Land Laid Waste — 62
6. 13,000,000 Americans — 83
7. The Ingredients of Fascism — 107
8. Prophets of Doom — 123
9. A Six-Point Program — 141
10. Our Common Country — 150
11. Our Colonial Regions — 165
12. The Monopolist's Nightmare — 186
13. Making Free Enterprise Work — 208
14. The Role of the States — 225
15. A Modern State Constitution — 247
16. Jobs and Government — 259
17. Peace and Public Opinion — 272
18. "Our Realization of Tomorrow" — 289
19. The Shore Dimly Seen — 306

THE SHORE DIMLY SEEN

"I could never believe that Providence had sent a few men into the world ready booted and spurred to ride, and millions ready saddled and bridled to be ridden."—Richard Rumbold, on the scaffold, 1685. Macaulay, *History of England,* Vol. I, Chap. v.

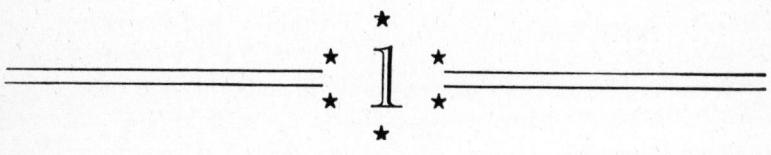

THE PARADOX THAT IS THE SOUTH

THERE IS A mountain where Tennessee and Georgia meet. If it is a clear day and your eyes are good, you can stand and see from a single spot seven States that formed the heart of the Southern Confederacy and that today are the South as the rest of our country knows it. It is a land fabulous and romantic, somewhat akin to the Forest of Arden or the Seacoast of Bohemia.

I was born in this South and its past colors my dreams, as it must color the dreams of all those who were born to see Spanish moss hanging from great water oaks, or tall pines shimmering in the light of a hot August sun, or to hear the nostalgic voices of the Negroes on the wharves of Savannah, Memphis and New Orleans.

Each man must survey our common country from the spot where he stands and look at it through his own eyes and not through the eyes of another. But all of our looking at it must be very like that of Francis Scott Key peering through the dim dawn of a new day from the quarter-deck of an alien vessel; it is not always the reality we see, but a reflection cast upon the stream. It is the shore dimly seen, but a shore much loved.

It is difficult to picture for the rest of America the paradox that is the South. How can such intense egalitarianism be united with such disparity in wealth between the prosperous and the poor? How can a fierce individualism be a part of the heritage of a section that has but one political party? In the midst of so much natural wealth, so gracious a climate and such an abundance of potentially comfortable living, can there exist the most squalid slums of America and the most grinding poverty that any large number of Americans have ever known?

And what are the relations of the South to the rest of America? Has it yet a contribution to make to the ways of American living; is it to turn toward the main currents of American thought, profoundly affecting them; or is it to stay outside the life of the Nation like some placid backwater?

Newnan is a quiet town, with a Courthouse square in the middle and stores facing it on all four sides; and some cotton mills, off to themselves in the background. Its citizens were born in Coweta County or the adjoining counties. When I was a boy the outside world was represented by an Italian family engaged in the wholesaling of fruits and vegetables, a few Greeks, who operated a café, a Syrian conducting a merchandise business and the ubiquitous Chinese laundryman, who did not come from Canton, however, but from somewhere in California, probably was the sole representative of an American-born Newnanite who did not originate within a day's ride of the town.

There were differences in the income of the people of Newnan, but the town was exceptional among Southern cities of its size only because there was a larger, more firmly established middle class than in most communities that were farm and textile centers.

It was typical of the South. You could explore its history and its mind, bringing to light the layers of its years as an archaeologist lays bare the foundations of more than one city upon a single site. You could trace its history from the opening of the Indian country to settlers, through the years when yeoman farmers grew grain and plantation owners grew cotton on the rich land. Then came the shock of war and reconstruction and the sudden enthusiasm for progress, spelled always with a capital, and constituting faith in the efficacy of growing more cotton and building more cotton mills, whether the land was impoverished by the crop or whether the cloth could be sold profitably on a market from which Southern products were excluded, as nearly as possible, by an enormous domestic tariff.

Newnan was the South in microcosm. Every poignant paradox that is the South is there: the fierce pride and loyalty, the shivering gentility, the blundering paternalism combined with a graciousness that saves it from the curse of Babbittry and dogoodism.

To understand the people of the South, you must look at their origins. There are English in Virginia, Huguenots in Charleston, French and Spanish in New Orleans, and Salzburgers in Georgia; but the great mass of the South, especially the Southeast, is Gaelic.

It is not literally true that, to the average Southerner, no battle, except Kings Mountain, intervened between Bannockburn and Shiloh. But a glance at the telephone directory of almost any Southern city except Richmond and Atlanta will show the predominance of Scotch names. They are all there; every name in the ballads; every name that Highland and Border knows: Bruce, Douglas, Hays, Campbell, Gordon, Jackson, Stewart, McAlpin, and MacIntosh. Yes, and MacGregor too, a name that once, on the other side of the Atlantic, no man might bear and live.

In simple truth, the Southeast was the final haven for the wandering Gael, the fierce men of Ulster, the Scotch-Irish.

Subtly their thoughts color the thoughts of the South. Strange Pictish demons walk through the swamps and pine forest of Georgia and of the Carolinas, wailing their exile from the highlands and the moors. The little people make fairy crosses and leave them scattered in their rings in the Southern uplands. The involuted talk of the Scot has left its mark upon the Southern idiom, where every kinsman is a cousin. The loyalty to tribe and clan and family, to stream and hill and sky, is as fierce and enduring as on the day when the Bruce hurled his gillies against the proud Edward's Norman and Saxon chivalry and broke it as a man does a rotten stick for the fire.

It is small wonder that witch-doctors of the South resorted to the fiery cross of the clansmen as the symbol of their sheeted parody. And the rhetoric of the South, somehow, is endowed with a Gaelic fire that sometimes burns brightly without illuminating any object about it. At its best, it would inspire the backwoodsman to stand firm against Tarleton's invincible Redcoats; at its worst, it can inspire a mob to smash the doors of a jail.

Nowhere is Southern thought more curiously paradoxical than in the field of civil rights. During the War Between the States, when Burnside was imprisoning citizens casually without warrant and for inexplicable personal whim, James Louis Petigru could speak freely for the Union and against the Confederacy on the streets of Charleston, and, dying, could be accorded the rites of a hero.

One afternoon a friend and a Georgian expressed to me his profound horror at undertaking a trip to New York and Boston. He felt unsafe there, he declared, because of the absence of even rudimentary safeguards for personal liberty. Was it not true that in New York a man had no right to a trial before a regular jury but might at any moment be confronted with "a Jeffreys jury"? And was not there always open season on fishmongers and cobblers in the Bay State, with no Appellate Court of sufficient jurisdiction to right the wrongs inflicted by a hanging judge?

It is possible that my friend, who combines a puckish spirit with a great zeal for fighting all the wrongs of all the underdogs, felt a great shock when the Nation's most populous State turned its back on a thousand years of judicial progress to establish the harlequinade of a "blue ribbon jury" to satisfy the needs of a political prosecutor. He may have felt more keenly the judicial lynching in Massachusetts than those in the East, who were more engrossed in the economic and ideological aspects of the case than in the fundamental question of the guilt of the victims. But this anecdote illustrates the disparity of thought between the sections of our Nation.

The South, in the frenzied years of the turn of the century, enacted none of the weird statutes against aberrant political and social thinking such as led to persecutions in the Middle West. Indeed, the only statute ever passed in Georgia that sought to interfere with freedom of thought and speech was held unconstitutional by a Georgia jurist, when, after fifty years on the statute books without a prosecution, it was brought to light and an indictment returned under it.

But the Angelo Herndon case is never cited by those who may be termed professional anti-Southerners. Herndon, a Negro Communist, was convicted under this ancient statute prohibiting the possession or dissemination of subversive printed matter, advocating a fundamental change in the government. His freedom was obtained through a writ of habeas corpus.

Part of the South's paradox is explicable upon the basis of the South's heritage from its pioneer stock. Part can be explained by the curious intellectual heritage of the South, which draws its political philosophy from two divergent sources.

The first source of the South's viewpoint is to be found in the line of empirical philosophers, of whom Berkeley, Hume, and Locke are representative, and who, in turn, drew upon the expressions of absolute liberty developed by the non-conformist sects of the seventeenth century. The profound effect of Roger Williams, Harry Vane, and Algernon Sidney upon the viewpoint of this school of philosophy is obvious. Their influence upon the South is indicated by the fact that Locke was one of the planners of North Carolina, and that the theocratic libertarianism of Williams has dominated Southern religious thought since long before the Revolution. But another source is discernible.

The ideas of the remarkable coterie of Tory writers and philosophers of Queen Anne's day flowed into America. They were profoundly influenced by the Cartesian skepticism of the rationalists. But the humanism of Swift and Pope and Bolingbroke, whatever its source, was to affect American thought far longer and far more deeply than it did the thought of England.

Thomas Jefferson represents the confluence of these two streams of thought. Throughout the many volumes of his papers and letters you may trace the influence of *The Bloody Tenent,* of *A Modest Proposal,* of *Leviathan,* and above all of Locke's treatises on government.

Jefferson is at once the best that the South can offer and its most typical. All the conflicts and all the paradoxes that appear in its people appear in his life and his way of thought. It is to the liberal hedonist of Monticello that the South owes its debt for the formalization of its political and philosophical doctrines.

I do not imply that they have sustained no change. The impact of the long political quarrel over the slave issue, which inevitably produced certain schizoid traits among the people to whose history and ideology slavery was instinctively abhorrent, and the calamitous aftermath of the longest military occupation in modern history upon its economy, modified the fervor if not the dogmatism of Southern beliefs.

Moreover, the Southern scene contains, and the Southern mind, at times, is obsessed with, the Negro. He makes up a third of the Southern population and half of the Southern poverty. His presence is not a problem, for a problem assumes the existence of a solution. He is profoundly an American phenomenon and obviously typical of the paradox that is the South; for his presence represents both asset and liability to the social organism.

Generalizations about the Southern mind are possible. Indeed, it is a common viewpoint that binds it together; for economic and social disparities between different areas of the region can be discerned at a glance. Not only does the Southwest differ so greatly from the Southeast as to constitute, geographically and economically, a wholly different region, but the Southeast itself has no basic homogeneity except in mind, in viewpoint and in community of exploitation.

For example, Virginia is a part of the border continuum that includes Kentucky, Missouri, Southern Ohio, Maryland, Delaware and Pennsylvania. The difference is enormous between, on the one hand, North Carolina, Tennessee and Georgia, where the yeoman farmer is predominant to such an extent that even among the Negroes he makes up a third of the agricultural population; and, on the other, Arkansas and Mississippi, where the plantation system continues to chug along like an outmoded vehicle patched together with haywire. Nor is there more ready comparison between Birmingham and Atlanta, on the one hand, and Charleston and Memphis, on the other. There are many Souths, and it is easy to write about any of them if you have no special regard for accuracy.

There is the South of magnolia blossoms and spacious white verandas; of houses like transplanted Greek temples; of fields white with cotton where gay workers pick the fleece as they sing happy but plaintive melodies; of mocking birds having no moment to stop from their song even to catch the early worm. There is the South of squalid unpainted tenant shanties on eroded nonproductive acres; of once splendid hills where forests have been leveled by the axe to turn into gully-ridden desolations; of rivers running red as blood with the soil from ruined farmlands.

Somewhere in the South great mansions exist. Very few of them, I fear, are heritages from the Old South; but belong, rather, to wintering Easterners or to the sons of the men who built the earlier Southern textile mills. Somewhere, too, the shanties exist. Lamentably there are a good many of them in the soil-depleted portions of the old cotton belt. But neither mansion nor shanty, Marse Chan nor Jeeter Lester, julep-sipper nor turnip-gnawer, is actually representative of the South. These are confined to the antithetical clichés born of the romantic sentimentality of the South. And the romanticism of Hopkinson Smith and of Faulkner derive from common sources; the Colonels, Carters and Sartoris, are brothers under their skins.

The South is not even a "cotton empire." Certainly Georgia, Tennessee, North Carolina and Florida no longer rely exclusively upon cotton as the chief cash crop. Georgia was the last of these to break with the cotton tradition, but last year almost forty cents of each farmer's dollar came from livestock against thirty-two cents from cotton. The threat of eventual mechanization of cotton production hangs so heavily over the old belt, where yeoman farmers again are becoming predominant, that the trend to other crops is overwhelming.

Many of the Southeastern States can make the transition from one-crop agriculture without prolonged dislocation of their economic system or personal calamity to the families displaced. But the mechanical cotton picker may mean temporary catastrophe to many tenants and sharecroppers in Alabama, Mississippi and Arkansas, and other resources of these States must be developed to provide employment for the displaced agricultural workers.

In view of the riotous exploitation of Southern timberlands and the retarded position of Southern mining, the outlook for many areas is not bright. Efforts to provide employment, through a combination State-and-local subsidy for manufacturers and the maintenance of subnormal wage scales, present no hope to the economy of the South or the people affected by the revolution in agriculture.

But the picture is not altogether bleak. The textile industry will tend to become wholly Southern. Heretofore, at a great loss to the South and to the Nation, mills below the Potomac have been precluded from the manufacture of finer fabrics because of an internal tariff.

In the new decentralization of American industry, the manufacture of all classes of textiles will center in the Southern States. For example, it is obvious that America's woolen mills must be largely rebuilt. All are outmoded and inefficient by world standards. Their reconstruction may be delayed because even submarginal mills can operate at a profit until full production is resumed in France, Britain, and Germany; but to attain a competitive position upon the world market in normal years the industry must be almost completely rebuilt. Much of the woolen industry will move to the Southeast.

Most of the wartime industries that came to the South were temporary. The great modern plants built by the government went to sections already overindustrialized. But the production of synthetic rubber was concentrated in this section, and, since most of the tire fabric is a product of Georgia and Alabama mills, a gradual transplantation of this industry will result. New industries that rely upon wood pulp and plastics will center their production in the South, unless artificial barriers to their development are erected.

The industrialization of the South is a certainty in the next two decades. The form it will take depends upon the national policies that are adopted in the next few years and upon the course of our diplomatic and economic relations with Latin America.

If trade with the republics of South America is to be important to the United States, the harbors of the Southern States must be utilized for shipping, and Southern industry must be expanded, especially in the fields of textiles, appliances, light-metal products, ceramics, and other consumer goods that can be exchanged for the fibers, vegetable oils, lumber, fruits, and ores that will be imported in exchange. Industrialization of the South depends, in part, on South American commerce; but trade with South America must involve the South if it is to be profitable to the Nation. Much depends upon the diplomatic policies of the future, and upon whether the relationship with South America associated with Hull's "good neighbor policy" is continued or is displaced by a proposed system of imperialism.

The vision of an industrialized South has been received by Southerners with mixed emotions. There is bitter disagreement below the Potomac on the subject. To one group, industrialization means progress; and neither industrialization nor progress is spelled without a capitalization that suggests to the mind of the dissenting Agrarian the erection of a graven image in the form of a machine. The cult of Industry is served by many who have no hesitation in proposing to turn the already exploited South into a mechanized slum, although there is force in their retort to the Agrarians that cotton farming, especially in the one-crop areas, is a form of outdoor mass production indistinguishable from widget-making. It is true that the Southern Agrarians live in the never-never land, that their imaginary farmers bear less resemblance to the depressed sharecropper or the flourishing yeoman farmer than to the Dresden figurines of shepherd and shepherdess; but they have scored some points in the debate.

The South will not become, of course, either a single great factory or the habitation of thirty million cheerful peasants engaged in subsistence farming. Neither idea has attracted the Southern mind, which rebels instinctively against either form of monotony. The South is one of America's last remaining frontiers. Its development is consequential not only to the millions who live there but to the other hundred and ten million Americans who are fellow citizens in a common country.

I have tried to give you a glimpse of the Southern mind, the Southern scene and the Southern problem, as a prelude to presenting some suggestions about a course that Americans must take if our country is to escape the multiplied perils that await it in the next generation.

For any man to profess to speak without either prejudice or bias is for him to assert that he grew up without contact with other men, with life, with the world that surrounds him; it is to assert that he is formed of different clay from his fellows and cast in a finer mold. I have told you about the South, about the little town of Newnan with its modest Courthouse square and its Confederate monument and its merchants and farmers and textile workers, because it is from that vantage point that I see the world. It is with their eyes that I look at a changing America. It is with their emotions that I feel pain and hope and sadness and joy. I do not profess a detachment that I have not; only those who have been uprooted and left to dry in the noon sun are truly detached.

But Newnan and Georgia and the South are a part of the great experiment that is America. It is important to all of us that the experiment succeed. Too many lives, too much treasure, too much work and too many dreams have been expended upon it for it to be abandoned.

I am convinced that the experiment should go on, in the Nation, in each of forty-eight States, in the thousands upon thousands of communities that together sum up the population of our country. Though this optimism may derive from nothing but the ebullient romanticism of my Georgia neighbors, I am convinced that somehow we can make an America free of fear and want. And keep it free from boredom and monotony, too.

The first needful thing, of course, is to regard the United States as a common heritage for all its citizens, wherever they were born and wherever they live. The exploitation of whole regions, under a colonial system more wasteful than that practiced by the most greedy of European powers in Africa or the Pacific, must end. Our natural resources, which are not so great as they were before they were depleted in winning two wars, must be conserved. The oil reserves of the West, the copper and lead of the Mountain States, the very soil of the South, must not be wasted.

Our human resources must be conserved. Oil and copper will store in the earth, but the time wasted in unemployment cannot be used some later day. A program for the utilization of the highest skill of every American worker, all sixty million of them, is imperative. That it must involve guarantees by all of society to each member of society is inescapable.

The right of the individual to make his own choices must be kept free. Individualism has taken much criticism, as a creed, in recent years, because ineluctably it is the defense of the greedy when confronted with their own anti-social conduct. But it is obvious that society as such has no rights except those that are the sum total of the rights of the individuals who compose it. Individual initiative is a phrase of contempt in the mouths of those who advocate one or another form of authoritarianism. To answer them, it is not necessary to resort to any argument from ethics, faith in which seems to have been displaced since the apparent triumph of first century intellectualism over the ideas of the eighteenth century intellectuals; authoritarianism, whether fascism, communism or the dreamed-of "military republic," is not consistent with the mores of America.

The surest safeguard, at least economically, that can be adopted on behalf of individual enterprise—"free enterprise" if you like that phrase better—is the rigid enforcement, by society in self-protection, of statutes against monopoly.

Conservation of human and natural resources, preservation of individual liberty, and protection of free enterprise cannot be obtained by writing them down on paper. These three phases of economic liberty will not stand alone. Distasteful as the word "implement" has become, it must be employed: We must implement these statements of an economic creed.

The discriminations against the Southern and Western regions of our country must be abated, both in the freight rate differentials that prevent their normal industrial development and in the distribution of Federal funds for highways, education and public health. If these injustices are not remedied, the people of the South and of the West will become no more than hewers of wood and drawers of water to imperial masters in the East. Federal funds must be distributed on a basis of need and not on a basis of ability to "match."

Control over the economic life of the Nation through monopolistic conspiracies, or through monopolies attained through misuse of the patents granted by the government as a reward for inventive genius, must be ended.

Industry in America must be decentralized. Enforcement of the present inadequate and ineffective laws against monopoly would do much in this direction, but more positive action is needed. Both to attain nationwide prosperity and as an essential element in national defense, industry must be field-sown in the United States instead of crowded together in an Eastern hothouse.

A public works system, embracing every region and community of the country and admitting of immediate activation in case of need, must be prepared and ready for any economic emergency. This is an expensive counterbalance to the free enterprise system in industry. It will be less needful as decentralized industry eradicates the economic plague spots of America.

Control over corporate enterprises must be restored to ownership. The most dangerous present menace to American business is not a handful of pinkish dissenters from our economic orthodoxy, but the erection of an irresponsible bureaucracy of management, more involuted and pernicious than any governmental bureaucracy ever to haunt the nightmare of a High-Tariff Republican.

Attention must be given to farm problems. The medication of subsidies and allotments was an unavoidable necessity during the depression illness, but some less drastic draught ought to keep the patient in health hereafter.

The enumeration of needs appears to be entirely upon the economic side. There is no specific mention of civil liberties or of States' rights. The answer is that the civil liberties of our people are in no immediate danger of violation; they risk only the erosion incident to poverty and the political weakness that accompanies it. As for States' rights, I shall have to insert a Gargantuan parenthesis.

The States of our Union, as geographic divisions, neither possess nor have ever possessed any rights. As political units, they have possessed for some 170 years enormous powers; as independent States, as participants in the first loosely knit Union, as members of the United States. Undoubtedly some of their authority was wheedled from them by Federalist politicians; some was diverted by too clever legalists on the Bench; much disappeared somehow over the borderline that divided Federal from State power, a borderline that, until the advent of the New Deal and the change in the membership of the Supreme Court, was a growing limbo threatening to devour the effectiveness of both major units of government.

It is the duty of a loyal Democrat in campaign years to point out the unrighteous destruction of States' rights by the followers of Hamilton, Marshall, Clay and Hoover; it is also a pleasure. But in somber reality, the States divested themselves of their rights by the same method that a middle-aged athlete divests himself of his muscles; the diagnosis could be atrophy through non-use.

The forty-eight States have the power to experiment, for example. It is possible in this country, and almost nowhere else, to conduct simultaneous experiments in government and to seek the best. It is safe to do so, because even a serious mistake on the part of one State could not cause disaster, even to its own citizens. But experiment by the States is infrequent; Nebraska is testing a unicameral legislature; Minnesota has a promising budgetary system; Georgia is experimenting with placing education in the hands of independent constitutional boards, free of the Legislature and the Governor. And that is about the sum of the experiments, and none of them is earth shaking.

This want of experimentation by the States would be explicable and defensible if there were any uniformity in their governments, or even any pattern in their want of uniformity. You might then say that the experiment was finished; the result discovered; the best attained. But such perfection is not discernible.

Moreover, the States have enormous powers that can be used for the protection of their citizens. A reference to the "Kentucky Resolutions," protesting the invasion of civil liberties, will disclose, at least in part, the background for Georgia's suit to protect its citizens from unfair freight rates, which we charged were the result of monopolistic practices. The right of a State to plead in the Supreme Court is in the Constitution; its status as protector of its citizens is recognized in our laws; the freight rate issue had been much alive since the establishment of the Interstate Commerce Commission. But in all those years, no Southern or Western State had taken any action; and the issue had become reduced to set phrases in the orations of candidates for office, all of whom condemned with voluble vigor a condition about which they did nothing.

The States can regain their rights, if the people believe that their problems can be solved on the State level. It would be desirable to see a rapid movement by all State governments to assume increasingly greater responsibility and thereby move government a little nearer to the people. But even a native optimism does not encourage me to believe that, for some years to come, "States' Rights" will be used except as an excuse for delaying action on major problems.

Whether economic freedom for the people of our country is a legitimate corollary to the doctrine of political freedom is a question that each individual must answer according to his viewpoint, his prejudices and his personal philosophy. Doubtless there are still those who believe that hunger and freedom are in no wise incompatible. They never met a sharecropper in the winter of 1931 and asked him if he was free.

There also may be those who do not very genuinely care whether the sharecropper or anyone else is free. These are short-sighted individuals, who believe themselves safe from typhoid because the slum in which it is raging is across the city, although that is where their kitchenmaids return home after work.

Most men know better, whether in Newnan or Newark or Nogales or Nome. They know that wherever hunger is, hunger is master. And they know, too, that nowhere in all the world can any man be free until everywhere all men are free.

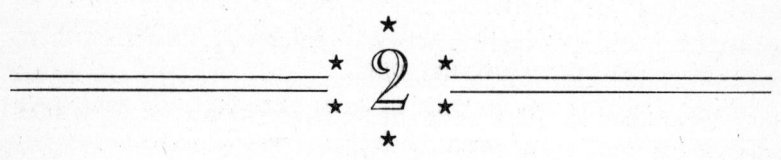

EXPORTING ILLITERACY

IN THE SOUTH politics is a lifetime career. You enter it when you are young and you remain in it until the undertaker or the voters intervene. I entered politics at the appropriate age; six, to be exact.

It came about this way. There was a Hallowe'en party for the first grade of the Newnan grammar school and Miss Maggie Brown thought it might inspire her pupils if they drew fortunes out of a wishing-bag. She had the more agreeable occupations written out on small slips of paper in a neat Spencerian hand: banker, fireman, lawyer, preacher, merchant; I do not recall that any slip was labeled "sharecropper"; but Miss Maggie was a romantic, an optimist, and a Southern gentlewoman. My slip said: "Governor, you will be." I would gladly have exchanged it for that which predicted the more gallant and hazardous career of a fireman, but with the fatalism that inhibits the Southern mind, I accepted my unknown lot.

I took it home to my mother, who was appropriately pleased

and who explained what a Governor was and that Mr. Atkinson, whose house was not so far away and whose son, Bill, was the most engaging younger man of my acquaintance—he is a State Supreme Court Justice now and still the most charming man in Georgia—had been Governor once.

From that time on, in spite of some preoccupation with football and girls in prim summer dresses, I was a politician. When I got out of college, just over twenty-one, I ran for the Legislature from Coweta County and the people elected me because they liked my father, and my uncles and my aunts and my numerous cousins.

It seemed to me that it would be a good thing to run for Speaker *pro tempore* of the Georgia House of Representatives. It appeared reasonable that the way to get elected was to visit every member of the Legislature in his home town, and shake hands with him, and tell him what a fine man he was and what a fine man I was and how, because of that, he should vote for me. Sometimes in a battered jalopy that had served in the last year of college and for evening rides on the quiet roads around Newnan, and sometimes hitchhiking, I visited every county in Georgia, all 159 of them. The members of the House were very amused and very kind, and if they laughed at a brash boy who wanted to be an officer of the Legislature, they also agreed to vote for me; and with the good humor and tolerance of men in politics they did vote for me the next January.

My folks didn't like the expedition too much. The ones who were wealthy, by virtue of owning some stock in one of the cotton mills, thought the jalopy a little outrageous even for 1932, when jalopies had become somewhat commonplace on the roads of rural Georgia. My mother was always concerned that I might get my feet wet or eat something that was not really good for me—the argument that I had the digestion of a razor-back hog did not appeal to her—and my account of spending the night in a barn near Darien contained no element of humor.

But, admittedly there was very little for a young lawyer to do in tranquil and nonlitigious Coweta County in the autumn of 1932, and my father did not think that a lesson in Georgia geography could do any great harm.

So I saw Georgia at firsthand while I visited all the county seats and the members of the Assembly. I had never seen Georgia before. Its hills were beautiful with their masses of frost-painted leaves. Its coastal plains had harvested the crops, and Georgians, white and black, could be found on the banks of every little creek catching suckers and catfish. There were plenty of Georgians to talk to, for the depression had arrived and there was leisure for conversation.

They told me about the steady slump in the price of tobacco, about the ruinous losses of the cotton farmers who saw no way to settle with the supply men. They talked about the schools where the teachers were being paid in scrip that only the hardier merchants in the town would redeem, and about the schoolhouses that had not been repaired since the cotton depression of 1920 and the devouring invasion of the boll weevil. They talked about the man who was running for President and who promised a new deal for people like themselves.

They told me how some Negro turpentine hands had broken into a chain-gang enclosure in one county, and concealed themselves, and gone out daily with the prisoners to work on the roads; and how the Warden had winked at his volunteer convicts and allowed them to enlist because he knew that with bankruptcy sweeping the Naval Stores industry, the boys were hungry and the camp was a well-fed one without too much work. It was a very funny story.

Somehow out of all that, I learned more than geography about Georgia. I discovered the fierce desire in the people of Georgia to educate their children. I think that is part of their Scotch heritage; wherever a Presbyterian preacher settled, back in the early days before the forest had been cut, he set up a little school. Georgia was the first State, in all the Union, to charter a State University. It was one of the first to provide for State support of the common schools. Its colleges frequently were little more than academies and its school buildings often were only one- and two-room shacks of unpainted pine, tended by teachers who had less claim to literacy than to zeal. But how was democracy to be a living thing unless the men and women could read, and write and cipher?

At the time I was riding briskly from one county seat to another over the length and breadth of Georgia, the South was making an heroic but seemingly futile fight against illiteracy. Of the twelve States that stood lowest in education, ten were in the Southeast. Yet in terms of sacrifice, the South was pouring more of its money into education than any other part of America. With less than twelve per cent of the Nation's wealth, the Southeast was expending twenty per cent of the total granted by State governments for higher education and even a larger percentage of the total for common schools.

Never had people a greater thirst for the magic of the written word than the people of Georgia, both white and Negro; and never had such thirst been so ill gratified. The explanation is simple, the South had more children of school age than any other section and far less wealth with which to pay teachers and build school buildings.

That there were any schools at all in many communities was due to the perseverance and the community effort of the people who actually built the inadequate frame structures with their own hands so that their children might go to school. And it required real heroism to be a teacher in the South. Teaching was not a profession; it was a vocation; the Lord had to call you to it or else you could not have withstood the poverty that accompanied it. The average annual salary of a teacher in Georgia in the year that the depression first struck was $546. Since salaries in Atlanta and a few other large communities approximated the national level, the income of the rural teacher fell far below the average; it would be fair to estimate the annual pay of a rural white schoolmarm at $360; a Negro teacher, with the same classes, made $210, a disparity usually representing a shorter term for pupils in the Negro schools.

In many a town, in the South in 1932, property tax collections were negligible and the school system faced virtual bankruptcy. Scrip was the medium for paying salaries, and only the sympathetic and good-humored willingness of merchants to accept the seemingly hopeless risk kept the teachers from becoming universal victims of swindling speculators.

The struggle against illiteracy in the South is continuing. In Georgia, during the era of the WPA, the State Department of Education launched a terrific campaign to teach adults. Many of the teachers, especially among the Negroes, undoubtedly were ill qualified for the task; many of the buildings that were used were not classrooms at all; many of the textbooks were so antiquated as to suggest their resurrection from attic junk heaps. But 335,000 adult Georgians learned to read and write during the WPA days.

I leaned against a drugstore counter in Thomasville one day, late in the summer of 1934, and heard men talk about the adult education program.

"I got to buy a present for my cook," the man in the seersucker was saying. "She gets some kind of certificate next week for being able to read and write. You ought to've heard her reading about the Billygoat and the Ogre to my little girl the other night, out of the Third Reader. She gave it sound effects."

They both laughed. It was nice laughter; with, I think, a little pride in it.

The South does not have much money to spend for public services. But what little it has is spent on education. North Carolina is spending more money on Negro common schools annually than it spent on all schools in 1900. Georgia devoted more than half its State income, after reserves for debt retirement, to education in the last fiscal year. Almost five per cent of the total income of the people of the South goes into education.

But it is not enough. To maintain adequate standards of pay for the teachers, to provide for the transportation of children in the rural sections on school busses, and without any expenditure for new buildings badly needed throughout the State, Georgia requires an additional fifteen million dollars annually above the maximum that the State, the counties and the municipalities can provide. The only alternative appears to be for the Federal government to provide some kind of educational equalization fund that will permit the Southern States to meet the problem.

From the standpoint of the rest of the country, it might be a wise investment. The South has long been the victim of economic discrimination, and has been driven to the exporting of its irreplaceable natural resources in the form of soil-depleting crops, minerals and forest products. But it is exporting, all over the Union, one other product: illiteracy.

For the Southeast is the seedbed of America. The birth rate of both races is higher than the average for the Nation. The Southern population has remained stationary for twenty-five years. The missing Mississippians and Carolinians and Georgians are to be found all over America. It would be a prudent national investment to provide them with sound educations.

The most tragic lines in Howard Odum's *Southern Regions* speak of America's greatest waste "reflected in the vast potential power of millions of youth, undeveloped and untrained, moving through life without sensing their abilities or maturing their capacities, oblivious of the wide reaches of opportunity."

In the South this is reflected by the low ratio of value added by manufacture to the raw materials processed and by the lower wages paid to Southern workers. Lack of technological skill, of course, is only one of the various factors involved, but it is a consequential one. In the prewar years, the South provided 13.2 per cent of the industrial workers of the nation, but the increased value of goods through manufacture stood at 9.1 per cent.

The wartime industrial expansion demonstrated that Southern workers could be trained rapidly for any of the skilled occupations. In spite of the fact that the superior machine tools were concentrated in the Eastern industrial area, the production record of Southern workers compared favorably with the average for the Nation.

The efforts of the Southern States to utilize education as a means of changing their economic statuses have borne fruit. In many particulars, Southern educators have been more willing to experiment than others in the Nation, especially in the fields of vocational training, where there is a maximum acceptance of the objective and a minimum impact upon the prejudices of the public.

That Georgia has been restored to the position of a general-crop State, which it occupied before the War Between the States, and is no longer in complete bondage to a cotton-tobacco cash-crop economy, is primarily the work of the teachers associated with the Vocational Education Division of the common schools and the Extension Service of the University. The speed of the transition can be indicated by the fact that, when Odum published his monumental *Southern Regions* in 1936, more than half the cash income of Georgia farmers derived from cotton, while income from the production of livestock was a negligible item upon their cash budgets. This was true in spite of the gradual decline of cotton production in the State in a twenty-year period, which resulted in Georgia cotton sales dropping fifty per cent, with the 1914 record production of 2,718,000 bales shrinking, in 1931, to 1,395,000 in the face of an increased national production of the lint.

As a result of the vigorous educational drive in the rural areas, Georgia, which had shown a decrease in the production of cattle, hogs and chickens in the decade 1919-1929, increased tremendously its productivity in this field. In 1945, cotton was ousted by livestock of all types as the greatest single cash crop of the State. Cattle, hogs and poultry provided 38.5 per cent of the cash income of the State's farmers. A similar pattern is discernible in Florida, Tennessee, parts of Alabama and the Carolinas.

The living standards of the South have been improved enormously by the efforts of the educators. The school cannery has become a community cannery, where rural housewives not only receive instruction but find the equipment and facilities necessary to can their garden crops. The school workshop often serves adults as well as children of school age.

That this training program already had been imagined, shaped and made to function, before the war imposed upon the South the obligation of mobilizing its labor for the defense industries, was of the greatest value to the country as a whole. The speed and success of the mobilization, and the statistical evidence that in vocational rehabilitation training of the handicapped the Southern States, especially Georgia and Texas, were far in advance of the rest of the country, proved that the Southern regions were making rapid progress in adult education.

The comparison does some injustice to other sections of America. There is no essential difference between the training of an adult worker and the retraining of an adult worker, except in the mind of a certain type of educator. The Southeast had been engaged in eliminating adult illiteracy for almost a decade when Pearl Harbor came. It had developed techniques, facilities capable of expansion, and an educational force more alive to the problem than was to be found elsewhere.

The findings of wartime are suggestive. It is probable that the schools of America will be called upon in the future to provide retraining programs for adults upon a scale never considered possible in the past. It is probable that the entire approach to vocational education in the curriculum will require fresh examination. It is even possible that it will be discovered that much more time can be expended in the common schools upon cultural subjects, with an acceleration of vocational training as adulthood is approached.

To treat such a problem as regional, in a day when transportation is simple and migrations of workers commonplace, is to disregard the problem. As long as the South supplies so large a segment of the population of other sections, the problem of financing educational efforts in the region must take on a national aspect.

Yet much of the opposition to Federal assistance to education centers in the South. A great deal of this can be attributed to the suspicion by Southerners that Federal aid will be associated with an intolerable interference, a suspicion not entirely allayed by the lapse of four decades since a New England Senator last proposed extending civilization into the South at the point of a bayonet. Another source of opposition is the absentee owner of Southern industry, who is concerned with maintaining a surplus of tractable labor; it is he who largely inspires the demagogic outbursts in Congress that have delayed enactment of any reasonable and generally acceptable measure.

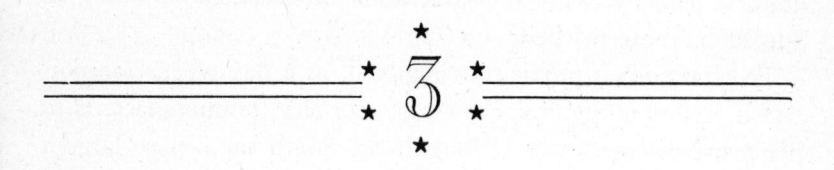

DEMAGOGUES IN THE DARK

It is not sufficient that schools be financed adequately and that teachers be assured of decent retirement incomes; many a lie has been perpetuated in pretentious cathedrals of learning; many a full belly has accompanied a heart long tired with half-truths and expedient evasions. Education's purpose is to set men free, it is intended to help the individual lead a useful and happy existence. Its purpose is distorted and debased if it is otherwise. Our philosophy of citizenship assumes man's basic and inherent right to self-government; that man has the capacity, both mentally and morally, to exercise that right. We believe that our institutions are proof against attack, so long as our people are trained to examine facts, to recognize truth from falsehood by their examination of the facts, and reason clearly from the facts presented to them.

That is a very fine language. It expresses the belief held by every American, a belief that seldom prompts any specific action. So long as stones are cheaper, there will be those who offer them in lieu of bread; but there will be those, too, who will seek to become bakers.

Free tuition does not mean free schools; free lunches for tenant farmers' children cure but one kind of tyranny. It is only where education is free to teach facts, and educators are free to challenge the mind of youth with the truth as they see it, that freedom exists for the schools. In the South, I think this is better understood than in the rest of the Nation. It may be that this is an echo of the intense individualism of the South, where prejudice combats prejudice, sometimes with blows and sometimes with debate. It may be a vestigial remnant of the Southern egalitarianism: whatever the social and economic distinctions, the white tenants' children attend the same schools as the plantation owners'; private schools, with their delicately phrased snobbery of religion and money embodied in the neatly worded phrase "select clientele only," rarely exist in the South.

And yet the Southern demagogue can no more leave the educational system alone than can his European equivalent. It is the nature of the demagogue. Reading and writing are the two enemies that he fears the most; they appear in his dreams, no doubt, in the likeness of Gog and Magog, brandishing annihilating weapons; they appear at the polls with the equally annihilating ballot.

The South has had its share of demagogues. They can be divided into three species. The first, and in the South the most common, is a charlatan, dedicated to the interest of absentee overlords; he is a Quisling; he is like those sheep trained to lead the lines of his fellows to the slaughter pen. The second is merely avid for power; usually a former member of the current political hierarchy, he seeks to build himself an individual and personal following by painting upon his face the symbols of a painful and righteous indignation and stomping like the dickens. The third deserves sympathy; he begins as the honest, sincere, well-intentioned politician who wishes to right obvious wrongs, and who fails to awaken the interests of the people by a simple assertion until, finally goaded to despair, he utilizes the tricks of trade of the mountebank and attains to power; sometimes he dies of a broken heart, sometimes of an assassin's bullet, and sometimes of drunkenness upon the power that he had bought at a price his conscience regards as somewhat excessive.

To whichever group he belongs, the demagogue is recognizable by three obvious traits. He promises a vague utopia in which milk and honey shall flow more opulently than in the New Jerusalem. He is flanked by a company of jackals who pluck the corpse of the State's treasury to dry bones. He selects as an object of attack some religious or racial group that is weak and relatively defenseless and loads upon its back the sins of the people, preparatory to driving it into the wilderness as a sacrificial goat.

To a demagogue on the Pacific Coast, the scapegoat very likely will be the Nisei. When he lived in Germany, before he put a bullet through his brain, his scapegoat was labeled "Jew"; his soul goes marching on in Boston where he suppresses books, and overturns the monuments in graveyards, and writes filth on the walls of synagogues, and waylays little Jewish paper-carriers on their way home at evening. If he lives in the South he hates "niggers."

But wherever he lives he fears schools and colleges and teachers and students. He feels that they are engaged in a single gigantic conspiracy against his rule, his person and his way of thought. His instinct is both sure and accurate; they are.

But he is a good showman, whether at Nuremberg before a youth congress, or in Georgia at a political barbecue. He knows the tricks of the ham actor, the gestures, the tones of voice that can arouse passions. Always he dresses himself up as the little man, the common man come to life, grown to Brobdingnagian stature and become the "Duce" or the "Leader" or, maybe, "Ploughboy Pete."

In 1941 a considerable calamity overtook the oldest chartered state university in America. Through the whim of the incumbent Governor of Georgia, Eugene Talmadge, who purged from the Board of Regents a number of distinguished citizens and appointed his own relatives and henchmen to the vacancies created, the University System, with its twenty institutions, had fallen into the bad graces of the accrediting associations.

Although the war was breaking in the Pacific, the repercussions were felt everywhere throughout Georgia: in the larger places, on isolated farms where more prosperous tenants were struggling to send a girl to normal school or a boy to the college of agriculture, on every campus and in every college town.

I decided to run for Governor, promising to free Georgia's educational system, common schools and colleges alike, from every vestige of political interference.

I had learned something in the ten years that had intervened since my optimistic journey from county seat to county seat, running for Speaker *pro tempore* of the House. I now knew that the odds were very great against my election. The incumbent governor had possession of all the patronage in the State. He had authority to dismiss any State employee, even in the independent agencies, without giving a reason. He was an experienced campaigner, with eight statewide campaigns under his belt. He had an almost bottomless war chest, and an alliance with most of the local political machines in Georgia.

But I had not been politically idle. In the interval I had become Attorney General. Between bringing successfully the first antitrust action ever filed in a United States court by a State government, carrying on the routine duties of the Law Department, providing opinions officially and unofficially for almost every unit of government, and speaking at school exercises over the State, there had been many occasions for making political contacts in every county—and I had made the most of them. As Attorney General of Georgia, I brought a suit to recover damages under the antitrust laws in the instance of a conspiracy in the sale of roadbuilding materials to the State Highway Department. In that case, the Imperial Wizard of the Ku Klux Klan, Dr. Hiram Wesley Evans, had acted as "agent" for almost all companies selling asphalt in Georgia and had made bids upon a noncompetitive basis exceedingly costly to the State and quite profitable to himself. The defendants won the first round, when the District Court of the United States held that a State was not a "person" and was unprotected by the antitrust laws. The Supreme Court, however, determined in Georgia's favor, and the defendants were compelled ultimately to disgorge. The precedent was extremely far reaching in determining that political entities enjoyed the same protection given individuals and corporations.

I do not believe in luck; I pick up pins because I am thrifty, elude ladders because they are hazardous, avoid travel on Friday because it is near the end of the week, and throw salt over my shoulder when it spills to test the condition of the shaker. So I accepted it as an augury when, on the Fourth of July, 1942, traditional date for opening a Georgia campaign, the skies in Newnan were blue and there was even a little breeze to make the day more pleasant. Moreover, in Moultrie, where my opponent was opening his campaign, a sudden rainstorm devastated the fried fish and hush-puppies and left the assembled faithful in an unhappy and unenthusiastic frame of mind. The barbecue at Newnan was good, and the Brunswick stew was the best that West Georgia had eaten in many a campaign.

The portents of the weather were confirmed by the reports of political observers. Into Moultrie had flowed a steady stream of trucks, provided by highway contractors, and many automobiles bearing State employees impressed into service as a cheering section. Aside from the rain, the program had been organized with the meticulousness of a dramatic spectacle; complete even to the boys in trees, to caution whom not to fall in their emotional exuberance, the orator must pause at the appropriate point in his speech. The henchmen and the bunting and the bands were on hand; but the average voter was not.

On the other hand, into Newnan had poured 12,000 people from West Georgia and delegations from each of the communities where a Georgia college is located. They were genuine voters, and their enthusiasm, though not rehearsed to insure spontaneity, was more sanguine.

Following the Fourth, the campaign began in earnest. It was tobacco marketing time in South Georgia, and I visited each of the towns where the huge warehouses held the bright leaf that had replaced cotton as the cash crop of the section. In each warehouse I shook hands with every farmer who stood beside his piles of tobacco. Every day I made two or three speeches from the stump and at least once each week reported on my campaign through a radio hook-up that covered the entire State.

My opponent's endeavor was to play the role of indulgent elder statesman, amused at the efforts of a negligible contender. But it soon became obvious to the State machine that here was revolution; the women's clubs, the parent-teacher groups, the newspapers, the students themselves canvassing house-to-house in many Georgia towns and farm-to-farm in most of Georgia's 159 counties, constituted a menace to things as they were for a highly conservative administration with close Eastern affiliates. There was but one last resource.

"Nigger, Nigger," they cried. "All teachers is nigger-lovers. All newspapers is subsidized by nigger-loving Yankees."

It is a cry that the South had heard before. In Mississippi, in Texas, in North Carolina. The liberal educator is usually rather naïve; he is an easy butt for jokes; he tells hard truths, and there are many who prefer to listen to gaudy lies.

There was a day in the South when the educator was assailed for heresy, but after Poteat of Wake Forest challenged the bigots and summoned the shade of Roger Williams to his defense, that form of attack lapsed. But the racial brand of demagogic attack continued and, in a sense, the educators fostered it by suggesting eradication of hookworm, typhoid, tuberculosis and syphilis among the Negroes. Since the educator deals in a circumambulatory terminology, too often understandable only by his colleagues, it is easy for the demagogue to accuse and almost to prove him to be an advocate of miscegenation upon the basis of a recommendation that Negroes be provided with sanitary privies.

Let me engage in a long parenthesis of educator-baiting myself. The science of semantics includes being understood as well as being definite, and a great many volumes offered by educators contain a professional jargon uninterpretable by the layman. I do not challenge the right of the candidate for a doctorate to write his thesis in doctorese, or in Lithuanian, Flemish or Hittite if he desires. I will defend to the death his right to do so; but he would save his defenders a considerable amount of inconvenience if for popular publication he translated his work into English.

Seizing upon some of the professors' harmless statements torn from their context and a few misquotations that were unintelligible enough to be exciting, my 1942 opponent flayed the educator and the Negro with almost equal zeal and with equal want of effect. When the ballots were in he had lost by eighty-nine counties to sixty-nine, with a tie in one; and by a three-to-two margin in popular votes. And I had inherited twenty colleges that had lost their accredited status with the educational world.

Georgia's Legislature undertook in the next January an experiment in liberating the institutions of higher learning, and the common schools as well, from every vestige of political control. A constitutional Board of Regents for the University System and a constitutional Board of Education for the common schools have complete control and direction of education. The Governor cannot remove members of these boards, nor can the Legislature dismiss them except through impeachment.

This is an experiment, which will depend for its success upon the flexibility of mind of the boards' members. For the average educator, however, it guarantees freedom to teach and places a buffer between him and the devouring demagogue.

The real bulwark for academic freedom is to be found, however, in the people. Intellectual integrity is not the possession of the educated alone; liberty is not served exclusively by those who can define its meaning in clear, and sometimes curtailing, language. The average Georgian was aware that freedom of discussion was associated closely with academic freedom. He may have been conscious also that the loss of accredited status would affect the professional standing of his son or daughter, but that never became either the issue or the main concern of the voter.

The Georgia University System was readmitted to the Southern Association of Schools and Colleges at the Association's meeting in Memphis, Tennessee, early in December, 1942.

America has been caught for a generation in an educational theory that is abhorrent to its traditional mores, the theory that education should be specifically utilitarian. Unquestionably education should include many types of training that make it easier for the individual to become a self-sustaining economic unit. The acquisition of mechanical skill is very important, both to the worker and to industry. But emphasis upon vocational training as an end in itself is dangerous in a democracy.

Upon the surface the trend toward the "practical" in education appears to be a triumph for those who believe that the stratification of American society into classes is both inevitable and desirable. The Marxian is not alone in regarding man as, primarily, an economic animal; the extreme Right borrows the theory if not the terminology of the extreme Left. The creation of a large labor force, educated for work but uneducated for citizenship, seems to be the objective of many educational systems in America.

This is especially obvious in those States where the sons and daughters of prosperous or privileged families are consistently withdrawn from the public school systems and provided with educations of an altogether different type and quality. The tendency in those States, most of which are in the East, is to create a social pattern in which one group is trained for leadership in the "old school tie" tradition and a larger group is trained for exploitation.

This factor and others that escape statistical indices in the records of American education suggest strongly that the conventional opinions expressed about the quality of educational facilities in different American regions are fundamentally erroneous. Observation would suggest that the quality of common school education is best in the Corn Belt, with the Pacific Northwest's urban schools second and rural New England third. In spite of the inadequacy of facilities for Negroes in the Southeast and for Mexicans and other minority groups in the Southwest, both of these sections have public school systems less conducive to class distinctions than is the cleavage between public and private schools in the East and the industrial Mid-West.

The position of higher education is widely different. The South possesses few graduate schools of merit and almost no provision for suitable professional institutions for Negroes. While professional training for Negro students is made available by Southern States through payment of tuition for students in established Negro professional schools, the result is unsatisfactory, since physicians, dentists and lawyers trained outside the South show little interest in returning to small towns or rural areas and remain in the East or enter their professions in the larger Southern cities. Since the need for Negro physicians and dentists is acute, the Southern States are confronted with the necessity of seeking some other solution to this problem.

Higher education tends to center in the East, because of the presence of many heavily endowed universities there. In general the antisocial trends of education in the East have been limited to the public schools; the colleges and universities of the East maintain a liberal tradition, though there is talk of a "quota system" among the old gentlemen of the Ivy League.

That the functions of education must be broadened, that schools must not be regarded as enterprises serving as caretakers for children but as service agencies for all age groups of citizens, is apparent.

Despite its poverty, Georgia has conducted some educational experiments that are suggestive. One has been in the field of rehabilitation. The clients trained and placed by the Division of Vocational Rehabilitation numbered 2,771 in 1944, and their average earnings of $1,770.60 were far in excess of the average earnings of Georgians or other Southerners.

Almost all of the clients of the agency are adult; very few are illiterate. In general, a training period of six months is adequate to insure successful placement of a handicapped person in a suitable job.

This suggests that adult vocational education is a desirable function of our school systems; that it is a needed service to the public, repaying the relatively high cost by increasing the earnings of workers; that a retraining program and refresher courses for industrial workers, especially those making changes in occupation, is a legitimate function of State-supported schools.

It also suggests that the experience of vocational teachers throughout Georgia, who have taught farmers and housewives in various community classes, might point the way to some improvements in our educational systems.

For the primary functions of the common schools, as they serve the children of a community, are to teach them the elementary means by which one person communicates with another, the venerable "Three R's" of the little red schoolhouse; to provide them with habits of rational thought and to inculcate the rules of reasoning; to let them acquire for themselves the cultural background that alone makes it possible for them to participate intelligently in making collective decisions as part of the body of citizens.

America professes to believe that its citizens can direct every phase of its government; that the collective intelligence of the Nation is wise enough to control our society, our economy and our relationship with other nations. That belief presupposes not only native intelligence but a considerable training in logic and a wealth of information. The schools and colleges must be enabled to provide those fundamentals if we are not to abandon our experiment in popular control over public affairs.

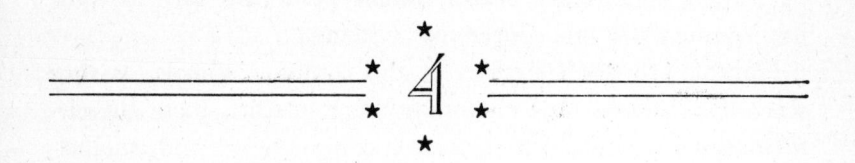

EXPERIMENT IN DEMOCRACY

IN THE CAMPAIGN of 1942, many young people under the age of twenty-one took an active interest. They drew the fire of the spellbinders stumping for my opponent. The young men and young women in the colleges of Georgia were aroused by the loss of accredited status of the institutions. Many of them already were in uniform; many men were waiting calls from their draft boards; but between their interest in the war and their class work, they found time to canvass thousands and thousands of Georgia homes and ask neighbors and relatives and friends, and strangers they had never seen before, to vote for me and rebuke the demagogues who had attacked education.

As the campaign neared its close even the educator and the Negro found themselves supplanted, as denunciatory objects, by the "irresponsible young jackanapes and painted-faced little girls who think they know how to run Georgia." Worse names were used in private. Somehow it never occurred to the experienced and versatile management of my opponent's campaign that these young people were the sons and daughters of Georgia voters, that they were an intelligent and highly articulate group even if they could not vote, and that the attack was upon the future of the State. Perhaps the opposition was too engrossed in planning bigger and better mass demonstrations in an attempt to counteract the larger crowds that were attending the rallies of our side.

I knew that I owed much to the audacious and vigorous campaign of Young Georgia. I knew that they represented an element in public life that deserved, somehow, to be recognized. But it was not until the campaign and the party convention were over that their real place in the political system occurred to me.

A young man, a student at Georgia Tech, who had worked hard in the campaign and shown exceptional interest in spite of his nineteen years and his disqualification as a voter, came to my office to tell me goodbye. He was being inducted into the service and expected to be stationed soon in New Mexico.

"Well, I guess I am old enough to help with the Japs, even if I can't vote," he said as he was leaving.

My young friend was old enough to fight, but he was not old enough to vote. It set me to thinking and to examining the precedents. It was easy to discover that the idea of letting a citizen of eighteen vote was not really new in America; the State of Franklin established that precedent one hundred and fifty years ago. Moreover, in England and France, the age of eighteen was a conventional age for attaining a majority, being the age at which youths normally might receive knighthood. It was the age of full citizenship in many jurisdictions in Greek and Roman days. It was the age at which women might lawfully contract marriage without parental consent. It was the age at which a boy might shoulder a rifle or flash through the sky in an airplane to defend his country. It was an age at which both boy and girl ceased to be a "dependent" for income tax returns of parents.

In my message to the General Assembly of 1943, a proposal to reduce the voting age from twenty-one to eighteen was recommended. The idea was embodied in a constitutional amendment and attained the two-thirds majority of each branch of the Legislature for submission to the people; and in the summer of 1943, we went into a campaign to get the amendment ratified by the voters of Georgia.

The political organization that was defeated in 1942 was still alive. It singled out the "teen-age amendment" as its object of attack. Though there were many other amendments on the ballot that year, including those establishing academic freedom and removing control of clemency from the Governor's office, it was the question of youth suffrage that attracted the most attention. It was a lively campaign. In a radio talk on the amendments, I challenged the belief that American parents had failed to rear honorable and intelligent sons and daughters and defended the theory of youth suffrage by saying:

"The additional experience that these young men and women will obtain through extension to them of the right to vote will equip them better to serve their country as citizens, whether officeholders or not, throughout their lives.

"We need the idealism, the candor, the unselfishness of these young people's influence in our public affairs. We need more, I say, of the 'starry-eyed enthusiasm of youth.'

"I quote that phrase to you because the cynical, the overwise who have plunged the world through their disbelief in ideals into the flaming tormented chaos of war that has overtaken us all, have twisted that phrase. They have made many believe that the 'starry-eyed enthusiasm of youth' is an indecent, an undesirable, a worthless thing, instead of what it is: the finest and most generous thing in the world, the proof of good rearing in a happy home which led these young people to the belief that folks were good and kind, honest and decent, as they are themselves.

"I have no tolerance for this brand of cruel cynicism. I have no faith in those who posture and prate about the value of not having ideals, and who scoff at those who do have them.

"This amendment's ratification will affirm that we believe in the honor and patriotism of our daughters and the courage and loyalty of our sons."

The people of Georgia responded to that plea with an overwhelming vote in favor of the amendment, a vote of slightly more than two to one. And Georgia became the first of the forty-eight States to lower the voting age to eighteen.

That younger citizens have brought something into political life in Georgia that has been long needed is agreed by most observers. Eighteen is an excellent age for a citizen to begin the assumption of public responsibility, since it is the age at which most young men and women have just completed high school. If the continuity of their education is interrupted or they do not attend college at all but seek employment, the three-year interval between their interest in public affairs incident to school attendance and their lawful participation in government may result in their eventual failure to become voters. Reducing the voting age is essential if the United States is to indulge in peacetime conscription; to permit military training to be forced upon a group below voting age is to invite military domination of the United States and its conversion into a "military republic."

It is a recognition of the new responsibilities assumed by American youth and of the place of young men and women in the national life that has led President Truman to urge that, throughout the Nation, they be given the right to vote. It seems to me to be an inevitability if political democracy is to retain its dynamic quality in our country.

Lowering the voting age to eighteen brought to the fore in Georgia an issue that was unexpected. Georgia had a poll tax, levied upon all male citizens above the age of twenty-one and below that of sixty, and upon such women of that age as registered for voting. The poll tax in Georgia was not originally designed, as many suppose, to limit the right of suffrage. Almost from the establishment of the State and until 1933, Georgia had required the payment of all taxes as a prerequisite to voting. This was not the practice in the typical "poll tax State."

But the younger voters were exempt from taxation under the new amendment, and the voters above the age of sixty had been exempt from poll tax since its establishment. More than half of all Georgians were free of the tax; its retention was ridiculous.

The 1943 Assembly had authorized revision of the Georgia Constitution by a commission that was to report its findings and recommendations, and if desirable, a new Constitution, to the 1945 Legislature. The Revision Commission recommended that the poll tax, as a prerequisite for voting, be eliminated. In the meantime, I prepared to ask the Legislature to abolish the tax, which was permitted by the existing State Constitution but which was not required.

There was long debate in the 1945 Assembly over abolition of the poll tax, although, even among its opponents, there were few who endeavored to turn the debate into a discussion of racial problems. Ultimately, after one defeat in the House and a successful move for reconsideration, the repeal measure was adopted. Local officeholders had little complaint against repeal; the few who had worked against it discovered suddenly that not only was the measure popular with Georgians but that it had created about 500,000 new voters overnight, whose votes they desired most earnestly in the next campaign. These former opponents became publicly the most fanatical converts to the wisdom and virtue of the measure.

The poll tax continues to be a topic of heated debate. As a prerequisite for voting, it is confined entirely to the South, today, but once was found everywhere in America. Originally it was a revenue device; today it is either an anachronism or a device for the disfranchisement of citizens whose ballots deserve to be counted in an election.

The South's present championing of the poll tax is based more upon irritation than anything else. I know this is true because hundreds of Georgians have told me that they are glad to be rid of the nuisance of the poll tax but that they resent Federal interference on the subject.

If the issue were reduced in every Southern State to the one drawn in Georgia: "No man ought to have to pay for the right to vote," removal of the poll tax would be easy except in two machine-dominated States; but zealous self-designated liberals persist in using the poll tax as an excuse for bitter attacks upon the South. Some of them are ill informed and cannot distinguish between conditions in any two Southern States; others of them are deliberately irritating at the behest of Southern Bourbons and the special Eastern interests that they serve.

The poll tax unquestionably has been a means of disfranchisement of many voters, utilized deliberately for that purpose. In Tennessee, with the imposition of the tax, the percentage of voters to the number otherwise eligible declined from seventy-two per cent to less than thirty per cent. In North Carolina, when the tax was removed, the number of voters actually casting ballots increased eighteen per cent, but registration figures increased even more rapidly. In Georgia, where registration stood at about 600,000 before the tax was removed, it was approaching the million mark a year later, with every indication that it would exceed that figure within a few months. This increase was of course due, in part, to the lowered voting age.

Registration is a better indication of the blighting effect of the poll tax than is the actual figure of the vote cast. Elections differ in popular interest, in issues involved, in the element of a psychological negative vote cast by staying away from the polls when none of the contestants have genuinely popular appeal.

It can be expected, on the basis of comparable experience in Georgia and North Carolina, that the increase in the exercise of the right of suffrage will be more rapid in those states where the poll tax has been in existence for many generations than in those in which the poll tax was a deliberately intended curb upon some class or group of voters.

In North Carolina the short-lived poll tax was a device to curtail voting, and an incident in the fight between Regulars and Populists in the years around the turn of the century. North Carolina, indeed had been the first of all the States to eliminate property qualifications and the payment of taxes for its voting citizens. While it curtailed the vote eventually by about thirty per cent, it never affected it to the degree common in many states, and its removal did not result in such a flocking to the registrars' offices as has occurred in Georgia.

Many States preserve some restrictions on the ballot. Georgia requires a literacy test, though it is somewhat less stringent than that imposed in New York. A literacy test is almost an essential in a democracy, and, obviously, the kind of test required must vary with the State. For example, in bi-lingual States such as New Mexico, an ability to read either English or Spanish would be adequate, because the voter has a choice of publications in either language; in Georgia, where less than one citizen out of ten is not native born and where the language is universally English, a requirement to read, speak and understand that language is reasonable.

Georgia today has the broadest electoral base, not only of any Southern State but of any State in the Union. Every literate citizen above the age of eighteen is eligible to vote. There is no poll tax. Registration is simpler than in almost any other State. Adequate provision, under the most liberal measure in the Nation, has been made for voting by those in the armed services.

There are a few improvements needed. Georgia's "open primary," in which any citizen can vote without party registration, could become a dangerous tool of reaction if a genuine two-party system ever became established in the State; voters of the rival party could then invade a primary and disrupt party unity. Provisions for permanent registration leave on the voting list the names of too many voters who have changed their residence, as well, often, as names of those who have died. These are trifles compared to the enormous expansion of the right to vote.

The removal of the poll tax by all States is necessary to the proper functioning of democracy. The continued existence of our political system depends upon widespread participation of all citizens in determining the course of government. If one citizen's voice is missing in an election, the counsels of government are incomplete to that extent. It was this argument that we presented to the people of Georgia and to the General Assembly when my Administration sought removal of the poll tax. It is an argument that is effective. There are few, outside the ranks of those who admit frankly their preference for some kind of dictatorship, who are willing to deny to any man the right to participate in his own government.

In the South there exists in some States the device of the "white Democratic primary" to bar Negroes from any actual participation in democratic government. In recent decisions in cases arising in Texas and Georgia, these devices have been held unlawful by the United States Supreme Court. In a majority of Southern States—ultimately in all of them except perhaps Mississippi, Arkansas, and South Carolina, where conditions have not favored the Negro's becoming economically independent as an individual, literate and a real part of the community in the sense that prevails elsewhere—there will be a ready acceptance of the court's decision.

There was a tremendous amount of political pressure applied to my Administration to call an extraordinary session of the General Assembly to enact laws that would permit barring the Negro voters from the Democratic primary. The issue was seized upon by the usual type of politician seeking to capitalize upon racial tensions. But the great mass of Georgia citizens displayed little concern. They supported overwhelmingly my determination not to call such a session of the Assembly, and the State Executive Committee of the Democratic party went forward with plans to permit participation of Negro voters in the primary.

Of course, the mail on the subject was heavy, and some of the letters and telegrams that I received during the weeks when the subject was being discussed in the press and on the stump were mildly abusive in nature; a few were more violent. But most of the mail approved my stand, and, unexpectedly, most of the letter-writers expressed agreement with the views of the Court. The number of Georgia citizens who think that the Negro, if he is literate enough to understand the issues presented to the electorate, is unfit to be a voter was surprisingly small.

When it is considered that the Negro was admitted to suffrage in the South, immediately after the War Between the States, with no experience in public affairs and in a completely illiterate condition, and became the unconscious tool, first of the carpet-baggers and then of the equally sinister Bourbons who took over public affairs after the iniquitous "deal of '76," by which Tilden was deserted to obtain concessions to certain Southern groups, the existence of some prejudice against Negro participation in politics could be expected. There is, however, a great difference between the conditions of 1866 and those of 1946, and both races are aware of the change.

At any rate, it has given me some satisfaction that Georgia has eliminated every unreasonable restriction upon voting during my Administration, and established legitimate safeguards about the ballot boxes. This experiment in broadening the base of democratic participation in government will be helpful to every State of our Union.

Georgia's experiment in democracy, as it affects younger voters and as it affects a minority race, again is evidence that "States' rights" is a matter of assuming obligations and responsibilities. The issues of youth suffrage and of the poll tax are somewhat unlike, since the former has national aspects involving the very grave moral problem of utilizing in the armed services those not entitled to the most elementary safeguard of citizenship. But both issues can be solved on the State level, if State governments are willing to regard themselves as something more than casual tax collectors and transfer agents through which Federal funds trickle down to local levels, something more than patronage machines, something more than lines drawn on a map, something more than convenient references in a postal guide.

There are such differences in viewpoint in the many regions that make up our common country that local and regional autonomy is needed. But in every region, there are racial, religious, or ethnic minorities whose relationship to the rest of the population must be solved. These relationships can be solved only by mutual understanding, by adherence to the basic laws of the land, by democratic processes, by solution of the underlying economic problems that aggravate the plight of the various minorities, by an appeal to the inherent good sense and good heart of all men of good will.

There is nothing wrong with government today that a good dose of democracy will not cure.

5

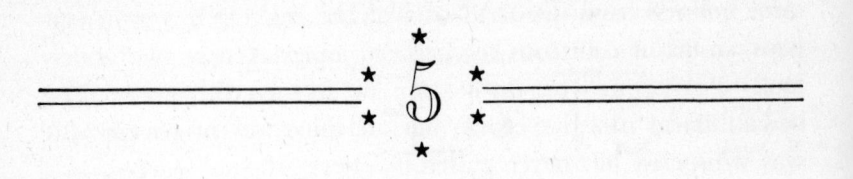

LAND LAID WASTE

I HAVE TRIED to remember something about the lady who appeared one Sunday as teacher of the junior boys' class at the Newnan Baptist Church. She was a visitor to the town, I think, impressed suddenly into service that late summer morning, for I do not remember that I saw her again. Sometimes she seems to have been a rather large person dressed in black, with a pink cameo brooch at her throat. At other times, my memory describes her as older and slighter and more fragile, and the cameo brooch on the neat black taffeta frock is white as her hair. She is remembered because her voice was somehow an impressive and resonant whisper when she read to the junior boys' class about how Moses encountered the Presence in the Burning Bush. That whisper accompanies the passage whenever I read it now: "Put off thy shoes from off thy feet, for the earth whereon thou standest is holy ground."

The logical processes of childhood are as convolute as those of an adult, and the imagination of childhood can erect hypotheses to explain any bewilderment. But why, I asked myself, must Moses take off his shoes? Was it that he might draw to himself some holiness from the earth whereon he stood? Or was it, perhaps, an act of courteous recognition, undertaken as one undertook to raise one's cap to a lady one met on the street? The bewilderment passed speedily, but the music of the phrase as it was whispered has never passed.

One day, in Southwest Georgia, it came to my mind again, as I looked into the deep chasm of the Providence Canyon. I saw the perverse beauty of the great cut across the face of nature: the mosaic of colors, as one layer after another of clay was revealed. Where once there were fields of cotton and corn, was this great chasm. Within a generation, the unprotected land had been despoiled of its richness, then swept away, until there was a nothingness panelled in red and yellow and cream and a score of variations of these colors.

The United States Parks Service has called the canyon the most remarkable and most beautiful natural phenomenon east of the Mississippi. It may be. Certainly the colors are striking enough and the gorge is big enough.

To me, however, it was almost the ultimate in horror, unsurpassed except by Copper Hill, which resembles nothing so much as one of the scenes Doré imagined to illustrate the *Inferno* in the gold-embossed edition that some book salesman had inflicted upon my Uncle Alvan. At Copper Hill can be found the same twisted and leafless trees that featured the infernal landscape, trees that seem to be in a torment and a terror that never ends because they have been frozen forever in the endless chill of Hell's winds. There is no grass. No flower interrupts with a whisper of hope the monody of despair. The red barrenness of burned clay alone surrounds the watcher. The dogs whimper in the pitiless sun, or crouch despondently under doorsteps, for there is no shade in this land where every green thing has been destroyed.

The day I saw Ducktown and Copper Hill, the phrase ran once more through my mind: "The earth whereon thou standest is holy ground." The wantonness of the sacrilege made me afraid; for here the earth had been desecrated, its holiness mocked, and a horror set up as, thousands of years ago, men might have crept to the wilderness in perverse madness to set up an altar to the Abomination of Desolation. Here men have denied Earth, from whom they were born, and have been pitiless with her in their denial, and written their hatred of her goodness in cruel wounds.

The earth is holy, wherever men stand. It is their home. It is the breast from which their food and drink is poured. And they have repaid that goodness with cruelty in their unwisdom.

Once as I walked over some submarginal Middle Georgia cotton lands where erosion had eaten away the top soil to a thin layer that would hardly sustain the weight of the plants and where the fertility depended upon ever-increasing amounts of guano, I heard some talk about the shiftlessness of the tenants on the place. My friend had lately bought it, in the hope that it could be converted into good grazing land, but our other companion still put his trust in cotton and little trust at all in the tenant farmers who grew it.

"Most of the good small white farmers in these parts have sold out and gone somewhere else," he told my friend. "The best nigger tenants have moved away. All we have around here is sorry niggers and po' white trash that you can't beat for shiftlessness. They won't make enough on a place to pay their supply bill. They have to be carried all winter, and they grumble all the time wanting things they see in the mail-order catalogs. Last winter three families half tore down their houses to get firewood, when they could have cut all they wanted a mile off."

We went on in silence, inspecting the rusted strands of barbed-wire fence and the sorry soil.

"Just shiftlessness. Worth nothin'. No 'count folks, but all you can get. Imagine a man tearing down his house and burning it stick by stick," he went on, as we walked across the final field.

The land that we saw that afternoon had suffered long. It lay in one of the earliest-settled counties of the State. Soon after the Revolution, which laid Georgia waste and destroyed more than half the farm homes in the new State, families from Virginia and South Carolina had moved into this newly opened land. In general, they acquired large acreages. In most instances, they were accompanied by slaves. The farm that lay before us had been cleared in 1790, while General Washington was President of a newly organized government.

And by 1850 the land had been worn out; within the lifetime of a single man, men through folly had destroyed the fortunes of their children. The rich hillsides grew cotton and corn more profusely than the white soil of the flat country. The hardwood was cut off the hills. The fields were planted to row crops. The rains washed gullies. Soon the soil was exhausted. But the supply of land seemed never to end. More slaves banded the trees and felled them on more hillsides, and more land was planted with cotton while the first fields lay untended.

Finally, about 1850, the owner removed himself from the worn-out land and took his slaves to the new Texas fields. Many of his neighbors went to South Georgia; others tried Arkansas or Mississippi.

Pine replaced the hardwood that had been cut. A little of the fertility of the soil was regained. In 1885 or thereabouts, the pine was cut for sawmills, and the hillsides were turned back to cotton again. But the earth rebelled against this cycle of misdeeds. Only in exceptional years did landowner or tenant wring a living from the soil.

My friend was buying the farm from the son of the man who had bought it in the year after the pines were cut. The father had never been able to support his family on the land, and about 1900 had moved to town and gone to work to support the land. Every year, the son said, there had been a small loss in operations and there had been taxes to pay. When he inherited the property, on his father's death, he had made the best bargain he could with tenants for nominal rentals and moved to a large city where he could earn his living. A few years before, immediately after a two-year period of good crops in the section, he had found a man willing to rent the entire property for a little more than the taxes. The renter, in turn, placed his own sharecroppers on the land and supplied them. Though the man had a bad name for dealings with his cotton hands, though he was notoriously a sharp trader in dealings with merchants and supplymen, he failed. Now the land was turned back to its owner, and he was glad to sell it to my friend.

During the period when America believed itself most prosperous, when the vision of a boom lasting forever dazzled the eyes of everyone, during the magic decade of the foolish twenties, the county, in which my friend now thought to plant kudzu on the slopes to check erosion and to fatten cattle presently in redeemed meadows, might have given indication enough that all was not well in America. Thirty-five per cent of the people left the county, unable to obtain even a subsistence from cotton lands that had worn out completely. A fourth of the whites and almost half of the Negroes fled from poverty and its accompanying hunger. They fled from soil that had been the richest in the State a century and a half ago. They fled as the slaves and the slaveowners had fled seventy years before them.

I do not know where they went. There have been statistical summaries of the journeyings of the dispossessed, but they do not tell the actual story. They are not banded like migratory birds. Some of them came to the cities and were successful and became skilled workers or joined the white-collar class. Some of them came to the cities and went on relief rolls. Some of them became migrant workers, voyaging about the Nation from crop to crop in battered automobiles held together with baling wire, sleeping in miserable shacks and often in the open. Some of them died of broken hearts. Some of them refused to take root in alien soil and like vines torn up and replanted, they faded, yellowed and died; they could no longer draw to themselves the holiness of the earth, for its goodness had fled and it no longer brought forth crops in its season but was sterile and bare because virtue had gone out of it.

You can see some of them, or their like and kin, on any highway of America any late afternoon. Their obsolete cars are piled high, almost buried, with the scant and worn household goods that they carry with them wearily. They look out over and past the highways of America at fields that are not their fields, at houses that are not their homes; and there is something in their eyes, in the eyes of each of them from the worn grandmother in faded bonnet to the little grandchild in hardly anything at all; and the thing that is in their eyes is the sight of an apocalypse remembered:

"And there followed hail and fire mingled with blood, and they were cast upon the earth; and the third part of trees was burnt up, and all green grass was burnt up."

There are many of them on the chief routes of the Nation. We were early for a speaking engagement in Brunswick, so Thad Buchanan, my confidant and helpful friend, pulled up and we offered to help the two men who were trying to change a tire without benefit of a jack that would work. Something had gone wrong with theirs, so that it would not lift. We took ours out and they accepted the loan. The travellers were two men, apparently brothers, with their womenfolk and children; all of these stood quietly some distance away from the car in that silence that is traditional in the presence of menfolk. The piled belongings included a dismembered stove and a small hickory rocking chair. One of the children presently detached the rocking chair from its retaining ropes and set it on the grass beside the road for the oldest woman.

The soft Southern drawl has an infinity of regional variations. I thought I caught the tongue of Southwest Georgia.

"No, but not far away," the elder brother said. "We used to live out from Eufaula 'bout twenty miles across the Alabama line. But my brother worked a place in Macon County for two or three years."

"Are you making out all right now?" Thad inquired.

"Not too well, with gas so hard to get. We been down in the beans, and there ain't much money in them."

"Where are you going now?"

"Well, I guess we'll try the tomatoes for a while."

"Things never have been right since the boll weevil came when I was a boy," the younger brother said as he handed back the jack.

As we drove off, I could hear the oldest woman singing as she rocked:

> Blessed assurance, Jesus is mine;
> Oh, what a foretaste of glory Divine;
> Working and waiting . . .

America for this family had become a land divided into beans, potatoes, cotton, tomatoes and oranges. The highways did not link towns nor pass through States; they led from a bean farm to a tomato acreage.

They did not know where they had wandered, across a continent perhaps; from Florida to Maryland to California, for all they knew. Their life has been spent in fields or upon asphalt highways, crowded into a car loaded with all their possessions. They may have been among the fortunates among the migrants, those who are seldom really hungry for more than a few weeks at a time. But they must keep moving. Perhaps some day there will be a job that is permanent, a place that is home with a bare swept yard and a few flowers and a garden of greens. They are seeking something.

"*And the Lord brought us forth out of Egypt with a mighty hand, and with an outstretched arm, and with great terribleness, and with signs and with wonders. And He hath brought us into this place, and hath given us this land, even a land that floweth with milk and honey.*"

They do not come from the Southeast alone, these wanderers.

They come from all over America, from every section where the land has been abused by men, and, where in turn the land has rebelled and cast men off. They come from Kansas and Missouri, from Texas and Michigan, from the Carolinas and Kentucky, from Oklahoma where the billowing dust drove them in a migration that has given their name to all the displaced of America. These are the Okeies, the people without homes, the sharecroppers and tenants and small farmers of yesterday who have no roof today. During the war years many of them found temporary shelter, found jobs in the shipyards and in the shops, put on a uniform to defend a home that is not their home. At the first sign of a depression, they must take to the roads again, a little wearier and a little more beaten.

"Call out the deputy-sheriffs. Don't give them any credit, they won't pay you even if they have the money. Give them a little gas, for Christ's sake and let them get out of town. Here comes another family of those damn 'Okeies.'"

There are at least 150,000,000 acres of eroded land in the United States today. Almost seventy-five million acres of this land is in the Southeast. But it is extending into other areas. There is a growing area of erosion in the Northwest spreading over many acres in Washington, Oregon and Idaho. The land destruction is increasing in Illinois, Iowa, Indiana and Ohio.

In some parts of Georgia, the Carolinas and Alabama, as much as fifty per cent of the farmlands have been denuded of their topsoil. In some sections half the land once under the plow has been withdrawn from cultivation. Throughout these regions, if any crop is to be made, commercial fertilizers must be applied lavishly. Sixty per cent of the fertilizer used in America goes to the Southeast to assist the production of cotton and tobacco. But the tonnage required by the Middle States is increasing year after year, an indication that the wastage of the soil is not limited to any single part of America.

Erosion is generally thought of as the result of washing, but another major cause is wind. Much land in the Southwest, which was turned to cotton, has sustained serious wind erosion. Great acreages in the Middle West, that should have been left in grass for cattle ranges, were converted unwisely into grain farms, and these have been scenes of dust storms and are rapidly being robbed of all fertility. Aside from erosion, much land is rendered useless in the Southeast by the silting up of streams, with a resultant overflow.

To a considerable extent the typical areas of erosion in the United States, and the areas in which land waste represents the most serious economic and social loss, are the basins of the Missouri and of the Tennessee. In the second of these, a serious and tentatively successful effort to rebuild an economy, while developing the tremendous waterpower potential of the area, is going on. I say "tentatively successful," because there is no certainty when the same sinister forces now blocking the Missouri Valley Authority may succeed in altering the objectives or interfering with the program of the Tennessee Valley Authority.

The economic loss to the Nation through erosion can be pictured statistically. In normal prewar years, the Southeastern States purchased 5,500,000 tons of fertilizer at a total cost of $161,000,000 annually. Yet annually there was taken from the land by erosion 20,000,000 tons of potash, nitrogen and phosphoric acid, with a value above $600,000,000. In many areas, Southern farmers were not engaged in agriculture; they were mining their soil, not in the metaphorical sense employed by those who think of the waste inherent in the system that dooms the South and West to colonial position in the Nation, but in an actual and physical sense. Every year the average Southern farmer puts $2.71 worth of fertilizer back in the soil, and sweats in the sun, chopping cotton to produce the money to pay the supplyman; and during that year the rains wash from his soil nine dollars' worth of the same elements.

It is true, however, that earth is merciful, and that with kind treatment the soil of these acreages can be restored. It is necessary only that the farmer of the South forget the one-crop system and turn to the other crops that his soil will produce. These are many. Oranges will grow in the South, for the climate permits. Barley, the grain that ranges farthest north, can be produced in the South. Every small grain, legumes, hay, potatoes, peanuts, vegetable truck, many of which aid to restore the fertility of the soil, can be grown in the South. And by parallel, in the dust-bowls of the Southwest and Middle West grass could cover the threatened land and they could be turned back to the production of cattle. All this can be done. In one place it is being done.

As you drive through the area that the Tennessee Valley Authority is redeeming for America, you cannot escape the sight of the great engineering accomplishments. Dams have been built that dwarf all architectural fantasies of the past. Work is still in progress, and you can see the latest mechanical monster toiling at its task; you can watch the parade of dump-trucks if you enjoy such parades, or look while a giant bulldozer performs. You can stop at one of the great electrical plants and hear the throb of the machinery and learn how many millions of horse-power these installations produce, and watch some employee flip a switch that sends them in some other direction to turn the spindles of mills or to heat the smelters that produce aluminum. It is impressive.

But if you ever saw any part of the Tennessee Valley before TVA came, or if you are familiar with any similar area, such as the far less despoiled Alabama-Coosa basin, your eyes will not be upon the accomplishments of the engineers too long. They will turn toward the land, where earth's wounds have been healed in part, though still some of the scars can be seen. David Lilienthal, one of the men who dreamed the dream of restoring this countryside, has written the epic of TVA, and like every good epic, the volume has its lyrical interludes. He thus describes the scene where land is being rebuilt:

> The many wounds yet to be healed are by their contrast eloquent evidence of what a decade's work in restoration has accomplished. The cover of dark green, the pasture and deep meadow and upstanding fields of oats and rye, the marks of fertility and productiveness are on every hand. Matting and sloping, seeding and sodding have given protection to eroded banks on scores of thousands of acres. Ditches to divert the water and little dams to check it, hundreds of thousands of them, help control the course of the water on the land, hold it there till it can soak down and feed the roots of newly planted trees and grasses. . . . One would not recognize these rich pastures and fields today as those same sedge-covered, eroded slopes.*

They have planted trees, a hundred and fifty million seedlings, that will remake hundreds of thousands of acres. They are cutting the timber wisely, employing eight per cent of the workers in the valley in industries built upon the forests; they have made

---

* From: *TVA: Democracy on the March,* copyright 1944 by David E. Lilienthal; published by Harper & Bros.

the woods the basis for a $112,000,000 industry. They are using the farmlands kindly, and the production of meat, eggs, milk, and dairy products has increased by half. Millions of acres of land have been terraced. The straight furrow, invitation to erosion, has been supplanted by contour plowing. The number of livestock in the region has more than doubled.

Hunger has been driven out. The yield of the land has increased. In many instances land that, at the time of TVA's establishment, was regarded as definitely submarginal and suitable only for retirement and public purchase, has been restored to such condition that it supports good crops and hearty families.

And because families are hearty, they are no longer fleeing from the Tennessee Valley. The fever of migration has been checked, not by treating the people but by treating the land that they love; by giving the land new hope, their own hope is restored. But there are other areas in America where migration was not unchecked, and a map of the areas of loss in population would coincide very closely with a map disclosing the waste of the land. Population losses in Georgia, for example, during the decade 1920-1930, corresponded very closely with the areas of the worst soil depletion.

In those years, despite a birth rate higher than the national average, Georgia did not have an increase in population. Though the State sustained neither dust storms nor floods, and therefore little in the way of mass migration, here and there a small crossroads community was shuttered up, a farm went to sedge and small pine-seedlings. The roof of a country church fell in and the graves in the churchyard went untended, because the people had gone, somewhere.

The eroded areas, the areas in the South where the land has

been despoiled and has become submarginal, are explanatory of the entire subject of erosion in the Nation and of the migrations that land-destruction have caused. In general, the ruined areas in the South follow two patterns and represent two different types of inhabitants.

One area of erosion follows the hill-country. This is an area of small yeoman farmers. They are the proudest people in the South, a section of the Nation never noted for an insufficiency of pride. Their great-grandfathers came out of the hills in 1780 to meet the finest force of British regulars engaged in the attempt to suppress the Revolution. At King's Mountain the hillsmen and the Redcoats faced each other, squirrel gun against musket, long knife against bayonet, and when night came the Revolutionists had won the decisive battle of the war and the retreat of Cornwallis to the Yorktown peninsula was inevitable.

Yes, proud these people were, and fierce, and independent. So that they seceded from North Carolina and established themselves an independent State of their own and invited the new United States to admit them as members. The State of Franklin possessed the most democratic Constitution of any early American commonwealth, a Constitution that breathed the undying individualism of the people of the hills.

Their descendants are to be found in Tennessee, in North Georgia, in North Carolina, in the hill regions of Kentucky. They are still yeoman farmers. But the soil on the hillsides is washed thin, and the sawmill has stripped much of the land of the trees that held back the waters. Through the area in which they live, through the uplands of these States, there has been increasing poverty.

Some of these people wander from their hills to the cotton

mills. But seldom, if ever, do they part with the land they own. It is left to be tended by some relative or neighbor, and ultimately most of them return to the hills from the mill villages, with enough money saved from their wages to buy a pony and a cow and to resume life again in its familiar pattern. To their group belongs a preponderant part of the families that TVA has helped to find a new prosperity.

The other section of the South where the land has been laid waste is the Black Belt. It is the section that extends across part of the Carolinas, Middle Georgia, part of Alabama and even into Texas. It is the section in which the plantation system existed before the end of slavery; a plantation system which bears no resemblance to that of the Delta or of the regions in which mechanized farming has turned the agricultural worker into a mass producer indistinguishable from the man working on an automobile assembly line.

The ills of this area are to be traced back over a hundred years. Much of the land was abandoned temporarily around 1840, and put back into cultivation in 1865 when the temporary high price of cotton made submarginal cotton lands valuable for a three-year boom period.

This is the land of the true sharecropper. The word is one used loosely, applied at times to a class of workers who are no more than wage hands paid in kind, or, more precisely, wage hands who share the risk of farming with their employer but who share to only a limited extent in the profits. Such a system of sharecropping is exceptional in the Southeast, though common in parts of Mississippi and Arkansas.

The genuine sharecropper has no easy life; neither does the tenant farmer just above him in the caste system, nor the renter who has his place at a fixed payment in cash or cotton; nor the small farmer, nor the plantation owner, for that matter. All of them are caught by the tentacles of the one-crop system, and squeezed of their labor, their vitality, their lives. Even today, when a considerable part of Georgia has been freed from the one-crop system, when livestock has supplanted cotton as the greatest dollar producer for the Georgia farmer, these sections of the State still are tied to a cotton economy. And no matter how high the price of cotton, they never are prosperous. It is a lucky sharecropper who has money left after paying for his supplies, his share of the cost of guano and calcium arsenate to fight the boll weevil; it is a fortunate plantation owner whose place is unmortgaged and who does not lose a little money on each sharecropper on his place.

Cotton and corn are the greatest robbers of the Southern soil; but corn and cotton these sharecroppers must plant apparently until either Gabriel's trumpet blows or there is a revolution in the agriculture of the South: corn to feed the mules that plow the cotton that sells for cash to buy the fatback and corn meal and syrup that is the standard diet of the region.

A little more than half the people who live in the Black Belt area are Negroes, about a sixth of whom are small independent farmers, in contrast to approximately the third of Negro farmers who own their own land elsewhere in Georgia. Only about a fourth of all farmers, of both races, are land-owners, but perhaps an additional tenth are cash renters and another fourth are tenants who supply their own livestock and receive from two thirds to three fourths of the products of their lands.

These people are leaving the land, too; but not in the same pattern that is disclosed by the people of the hills. For, if they own the land, they sell it and never return. If they were tenants, they leave and never come back. The land does not seem to have for these people the same attraction that it has for the men of the hill country, whose hearts are left behind when they essay the adventure of spindle or loom in the lowlands.

You would think that the hillfolk, who are among the most intelligent people of the Southeast, would establish small home industries to give employment to their people; that they would carefully replant for themselves the hillsides with trees as TVA is doing for them in one area; that they would diversify not only their crops but their employment, so that some members of the family would be industrial workers while others tended the farm. Indeed, that is the precise pattern that TVA is developing for them; it is the pattern that has raised their income in those sections where TVA operates, from the lowest in the South to a point well above the Southeastern average.

And you would think that the people of the Black Belt, whites and Negroes alike, would limit their plantings of cotton, that they would plant more soil-building crops, that they would put in more livestock on their farms and grow more garden truck.

But it costs money to do this. And it requires technological skill to convert from relatively simple cotton farming to the complexities of producing cows and pigs. Also you must be able to sell your products, and there are inadequate marketing facilities.

The acquisition of technological skill is difficult, but Georgia's educators have persisted under great difficulties and have managed to teach many the how of producing things to eat. The marketing problem can eventually be solved, when the South is accepted as part of the Union, together with the West, and when these two great areas no longer are regarded as colonial appendages to be exploited and drained of all wealth for the support of an Eastern industrial empire. But until that is done, the problem of where the Black Belt farmer will sell his products, other than cotton, cannot be solved.

For the man who buys his cotton, very often the same man that supplies him with fertilizer and fatback, with calcium arsenate and corn meal, is used to handling cotton. It is a marketable crop. It can be stored in a warehouse, and the receipt can be taken to the bank as the basis for a loan. But what would such a merchant do with thirty dozen eggs, or six Duroc-Jersey pigs, or a fat veal? There are limits to the appetite of his family, and he has neither knowledge of grades nor of markets for such products, nor has he the facilities for temporary storage until he can collect enough to ship a full car of such products.

Moreover, where would he ship them? There are no genuine industrial centers near by, with a tremendous appetite to be fed. The industrialization of the South has proceeded in such a manner that it has contributed little thus far to the economy of the farmers of the region, although it has been a stimulus outside the two specific areas that have been described.

Shall he ship them to the markets of the East? He has knowledge of the cotton market, but where in the East would he dispatch a carload of eggs, and how much would the freight be on them? And how would his banker and his Eastern wholesaler react to his trading in such strange products that have no easily estimated cash value?

The result of the one-crop system is a veritable mining of the soil. It is not cotton that the Southeast is exporting to feed the hungry spindles of the world; it is the very soil of the South. Year after year the fields are fed their starvation diet of guano; year after year the rains sweep the hillsides and wash away even greater wealth; year after year the yield of each acre of the tortured land is just a little less. Year after year the owner's profits grow smaller, and the hunger of the sharecroppers mounts.

More and more land is taken from cultivation in this belt each season. Not all of it will be wasted, of course. In some instances the slash pine, which Dr. Charles Herty regarded as the salvation of the South, is replacing cotton as a crop on much of this land, especially in Southeast Georgia and North Florida and parts of Alabama. To the landowner this is economic salvation. But sharecroppers cannot live amidst seedling pines, nor can they wait seven years for them to grow to harvest. They must move on.

This picture of erosion throughout wide areas of the South, both in the Piedmont and other sections, is the real tragedy of the region. It may be the tragedy of America, that and other wastes of the land. For in some parts of the West, where the plow broke soil that should have been left to grass, the desert is encroaching, nibbling off a yard here and an acre there. And in the South, it is nibbling at men's homes; and at their hearts.

Only one thing can save this region from destruction, and that is diversification of its crops, a turning from soil-wasting to soil-building, the making of peace with earth and with the forces of nature. Economic barriers, some of them a century old, conspire with the customs and habits of the region to make this exceedingly difficult. Yet here is the area where the fight must be fought to save the land and to save the people on it. And the fight must be won.

The fight must be won because the people must not be driven from their homes to join the multitude of wanderers about the face of America. There are people in the Middle Georgia counties, for instance, who have never travelled a day's journey from where they were born. They have stayed and fought for the land, while the less courageous or more adventurous of their cousins went away to seek some other place, where living was less of a struggle.

The South cannot solve the problem by itself. Regional methods had to be applied in the Tennessee Valley, which cuts across state lines. National remedies will have to be found for some of the economic ills that burden the sharecropper of the Black Belt and threaten to reduce him, whether white or Negro, to the status of an Egyptian fellah, toiling in the sweltering Nile valley for some overlord in Cairo or Alexandria. It is not only the red clay of Georgia that is pouring into the sea; it is a part of our common country; and all America has a share in solving the problem.

They are patient, these people who live on these eroded Southern acres, and they have a great love for their soil. But they are growing restive; they are dispersing; they cannot bear to see what they have been driven to do to the earth.

One night, and it must have been a Wednesday for Wednesday is the traditional night for prayer meetings in the South, we passed a little unpainted Negro church in one of these counties. The congregation was singing and, since it was a rural church which had not acquired the manner or the songs of the town Negroes, they were singing one of the old spirituals. We slowed the car to listen, as it swelled across the little burying ground toward the road:

> "Go down, Moses!
> Way down in Egypt's land.
> Tell old Pharaoh: 'Let my people go.'"

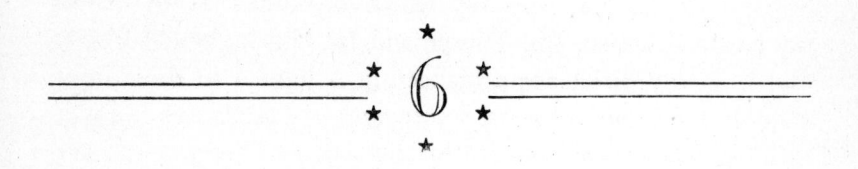

13,000,000 AMERICANS

"THE COLORED MAN, be he Japanese, Chinese, Indian, or Negro, is the natural enemy of the white man, in the same way that the tiger is the natural enemy of the lamb."

I glance at the copyright page of the volume, which is one among the many "hate books" that come to the desk of any man who happens to hold public office. It assures me, and I am not very greatly surprised, that the volume was published by a Brookline, Massachusetts, firm, and that additional copies can be obtained from an address in Boston, America's Tobacco Road. It occurs to me, idly, that I know very few of these people whom the author describes so vividly, at all well.

There have been one or two Japanese waiters in my life. Newnan had one American-born Chinese family for a time. About the Indians, I am immediately uncertain whether he means the people who live in India, and who are chronically short of food. Once, when he was making a personal-appearance tour for the Red Cross, I met Sabu and was impressed that he was a rather tired young person with very white teeth. But perhaps the author means Redskins, of whom I killed thousands before I was eight, and for which bloodshed I am certain my boyhood heroes, Jim Thorpe and Joe Guyon, would forgive me; if so, my direct acquaintanceship is limited to those innumerable Virginians who are descendants of Pocahontas and who speak in definitely clipped accents that suggest Charlottesville and the gracious buildings that Jefferson imagined rather than any tepee or long house. But I know a great many Negroes, because in Newnan they are a considerable part of the population.

I have seen Negroes all my life, and it has never occurred to me that there was anything tigerish about them. Some of those I knew were exceptionally shrewd businessmen, some were teachers, some were sharecroppers, some were prideful farm owners. A few "white man's niggers" I disliked instinctively, in the same way that I dislike scalawags, Quislings, and the stink of cheap moonshine liquor in a Saturday night crowd: they were a little mephitic and a little vulpine as they played the role of Uriah Heep in blackface, but they were not tigerish.

It is difficult to divest oneself of the many Southern attitudes about the Negro. I say many attitudes, because obviously those of William Alexander Percy and of John Rankin are both typical; and those of Clark Foreman and of Virginius Dabney are both typical; and my own is typical; and none of the five coincides. Four of the five of us, it is true, would agree that the Negro is a part of the South's heritage; Congressman Rankin dissenting. Four of the five of us would agree that the Negro is a useful citizen, who has been a valuable part of America's working and fighting forces in two world wars and a part of America's social and economic fabric at all times; Congressman

Rankin dissenting. Three, or a bare majority, would determine that the Negro constitutes a special problem for the South and the Nation; the author of *Lanterns on the Levee* and I dissenting, but, as is so often the case in such matters, for entirely different reasons.

For I am not an aristocratic poet and the owner of an ancient plantation; nor a stump speaker seeking a scapegoat for the economic distress of the people of my Congressional district; nor a social scientist with a brain keen enough to reduce almost everything to statistical data; nor the editor of one of the foremost Southern liberal publications steeped in the history of a State from which I derive my name; I am a Georgian from a cotton-mill town. My viewpoint is colored neither by a love for the music of lazy voices on the levees of the great river; nor by a desire for reëlection to Congress; nor by a concern with the statistics that prove that the world might get better if in the meantime it does not worsen; nor by a belief that presently, all will be well if everyone exercises good taste and moderation, though I think that this might help rather a great deal.

It is sad, for him and for the South, that Will Percy has gone to a place where he can see the sun across the Mississippi only by leaning from the golden bar of Heaven, and where his ears can hear only far off the plunking of the banjo, and the sound of plantation Negroes laughing on Saturday night. I did not know him well, except through others; but I went to college at Sewanee and they remembered him there and I talked to him once when he visited the mountain: a fragile man, with the mouth and hands of a poet, and the heart of St. Francis of Assisi, and the temper of Hotspur leading the charge against Prince Harry's men.

I do not think that the Negroes that Will Percy loved ever lived anywhere except at Trail Lake and in his heart; though surely, wherever he is—and it will be on the banks of the Last River thinking of the fish in it and cracking jokes with Skillet and St. Simon the Cyrenian with even the holy angels not too proud to call him "Mister Will" and do his bidding—there'll be some of them. Every Negro cropper in Mississippi wanted to work on his plantation; half the scamps in his county, black and white, lived at one time or another out of his smokehouse. If every feudal lord had responded to the cry of "haro" from those demanding justice as did he, the world would be a somewhat different world; and the hearts of men would smell as clean as pine woods after a night rain. Nevertheless, I have never seen the careless, laughing, improvident, gentle, and rather triflin' Negro men and women who populated the dream that was Trail Lake.

Nor have I seen the half-apes that populate the nightmare that Congressman Rankin uses to frighten some of his constituents into the vapors. These creatures live in the Rankin heart, just as those of Will Percy lived in his. And sometimes I wonder, with William Blake, at the mystery of heart-making. Perhaps every man makes his own heart and populates it with the dreams of his own devising.

Clark Foreman is from my home State. He has been a remarkable public servant, both in governmental office and in the semi-public life incident to serving various privately established commissions. He is a great economist, a masterful sociologist, and I respect many of his views and agree with a fair number of his conclusions at times. But I rather think that his Negro is so completely an economic creature that he exists, not in the heart as do the Negroes of Percy and Rankin, but somewhere in the mind; or perhaps in a filing cabinet, tucked away with other data.

The Dabney Negro lives in the intellect, too, most of the time, and is somewhat the creature of compromise, because the great Richmond editor is engaged in the difficult task of being a liberal in the South, which is even more difficult than being a liberal elsewhere. There is coming, I think, a day in which the South will be the most liberal section of our common country. The basis for genuine liberalism is to be found here. The people have a natural inclination in that direction, as Mr. Dabney untiringly points out. But liberalism in the South is handicapped by the attitude of a group of critics, who form a coterie of professional liberals, and who can find nothing in America to view with alarm except the atmosphere of the Southern States.

Assailed on the one hand by these, and on the other by native reactionaries, scalawags and demagogues with vocabularies of invective of which "Communist," "traitor to Southern ideals," "fellow-traveller" and "nigger-lover" are the least opprobrious and only the beginning, most Southern liberals search for another tag to wear.

Possessing less hardihood than Virginius Dabney, that is precisely what I am going to do.

Let me label myself, if I must have a label, as a democrat; with a small "d," please. I have known a good many individuals whose political line deviated from my own, some of them radicals and some reactionaries. I do not think that I have ever met a genuine Communist, except once at a press conference. The old-fashioned, Hell-and-damnation reactionary, who was not Fascist-minded like so many of the newer sort, rather charmed me; so did the elderly Socialist, who talked a little, with moistening eyes, about Eugene Debs and made you see the man as he must have appeared to those who loved him so greatly. The Communist, if he was one, was a little brittle, I thought, and perhaps a little tense; but then he may not have been a Communist but only a young man with his mind on something outside the room where the press was asking questions; though, for all I know, his mind might have been on revolution, bombs, and the equation that determines how the surplus value contributed by manufacture shall be divided among Third-Vice-Commissars.

I liked the reactionary and the Socialist very much; they were a little alike, although so different, with one owning a booming voice and the other as quiet spoken as a country parson. I liked them because they believed something, even if it was something that I could never quite believe, whether a perfectly astounding brand of individual initiative that uprooted entire forests, or a vision of a brotherhood of man founded on the ownership of power sites. They were a little quaint, like the illustrations in my mother's third reader; and very American. I have never met a Fascist that I liked; even an incipient fascist, with a little "f," busy with his thoughts of how a Third-Assistant-Vice-President might fare, come the managerial revolution, in the division of the surplus value contributed by manufacture. Most of the young fascists, with a little "f," seem to me to be as brittle as the young man who, quite likely, was a Communist; and both seem to be thinking about the same thing.

About professional liberals, however, I am not so sure. They no doubt acquired their thirst for rye-and-soda in the days of Prohibition, when, if I am informed correctly, Maryland rye was the standard of comparison in the speakeasies. They are great weighers of the value of things, and undoubtedly well intentioned, and prone to organize committees that never meet, and to pass resolutions.

They distrust emotion and approve of a pure style in writing, and are careful of every unimportant little fact, and sometimes are careless about the big facts. During the House and Senate hearings on the Bulwinkle Bill, which would permit the railroads to cut the guts out of the antitrust statutes, they discussed what was the matter with our Bulgarian policy. During the hearings on the bill to provide Federal assistance to education through an equalization fund, they discussed what was the matter with our relations with Ecuador. During the past five years, when some parts of New England have been boiling and seething with the Hell's brew of racial and religious intolerance, they have discussed at great length whether the detention and starving of the Spanish Republicans was or was not more annoying than the affair of the sixteen Poles; but then, Boston is not many miles away from their favorite night spot and they lack the perspective necessary to weigh properly the ifs-and-ands of the question. Though I am fond of many of them personally, I am afraid that, when Gabriel finally persuades the Lord to let him blow, they will be busy with an indignation meeting over rye and soda and will miss the affair at the barricades of Hell.

So let me close this parenthesis by saying that, for the time being, at least, I had rather be called a democrat, with a little "d," please, than to be called a liberal. It is a better label for a resident of Newnan.

There is no Negro problem, although the American of Negro ancestry has a problem. In many respects it is a problem common to all minority groups anywhere in this or any other country. It is an ugly problem for the racial group concerned. It is an ugly problem for the Pole in some parts of New England. It is a doubly ugly problem for the Jew in Boston, where there is negligible police protection. It is cruelest of all for the Mexican minority in the Southwest, the most savage for the third-generation Japanese on the Pacific Coast. It is unpleasant for the Negro in the South, or in Harlem, or in Chicago, or in Detroit. Because the Negro is the largest minority racial group, because he is easily differentiated from all other groups by the oddity of coloration, his problem is the greatest one in volume if not in intensity.

Individually, the Negro has a problem. Collectively, it is an American problem, affecting deeply the great centers of population and the agrarian Southern States that are the seedbed of America. But it is not "the Negro problem," for the Negro is no problem as an individual, as a citizen, as a race; he is sometimes a victim; and occasionally, when he becomes fictionalized, he is an ideological nuisance; and he is a strawman for cheap, loud-mouthed, scalawag demagogues to beat verbally. The Negro is in desperate danger of becoming, in the next depression, the scapegoat, if prompt, energetic measures are not taken to prevent a spread of Fascist philosophy in this country; in that particular, the Negro is less in danger in the South than in those urban centers where he lives in a black ghetto and is subjected to pressures from many different directions.

In the South, the Negro's problem is a part of the general poverty of the section. He shares in the injustices of a socio-economic system that has reduced the South to colonial status, and, since he possessed nothing eighty years ago and still finds himself at the bottom of the economic pile, he gets a shade the worse of what is a bad bargain for all the citizens of the Southern regions. The injustices that oppress the Southern Negro are felt keenly by a preponderant number of his white fellow-Southerners, both those who share his oppression and those who have found some defense against it.

One afternoon in my office, I caught a glimpse of one of the many Southern attitudes toward the Negro. My visitor was an old friend, some twenty years my senior, and the owner of some of the finest farmland in Georgia. Negro farmers of the county in which he lived always tried to get on his place, possibly because he had helped some score of tenants to become landowners. On his mother's side, he was the descendant of one of the great Georgia families; his father had been a man from the Georgia uplands, of yeoman stock. Enough of his younger great-uncles and older uncles had been wounded and killed at Shiloh, Chancellorsville, Gettysburg and Chickamauga to assure the family of a place in Southern tradition. One great-uncle had been helped off the field at Shiloh by his Negro body servant; the armies of Lee and Johnson must have been heavily encumbered with houseboys, messboys, grooms and body servants, to such an extent that deploying was awkward.

I never ascertained precisely what public business he wished to discuss. He was in the kind of fury that novelists describe as a "black rage." It seems that he had brought Eulamae nearly two hundred miles to town to take the train to Philadelphia, where some granddaughter or other who was in the Wacs was spending a leave. Eulamae was my friend's brother's nurse, but before he came along she had graduated into the kitchen. I have eaten Eulamae's fried chicken, which is fit to set before the kings of this world. My friend, his wife, their children, and their two grandsons stand in awe of Eulamae, who wears terrific corsets and square-lensed spectacles over which she looks frigidly whenever a small person is behaving in an unseemly manner; she had never been outside the county but once, when my friend's wife drove her to Macon to have some dental work done.

"We couldn't get any Berth Thirteen for Eulamae," my friend began, somewhat incoherently, referring to the practice of providing transportation in Pullman drawing rooms for Negro travellers whose use of such facilities was too infrequent to justify the operation of separate sleeping cars. "And you ought to have seen the stinking cattle car she had to ride in. It'll half kill her to ride to Philadelphia in that thing. The crummy Yankee railroad owners charge full fare for our colored folks, don't they? Why can't they give them decent cars, then? If I was half the man my grandfather was, I'd take a horsewhip to the nearest railroad president. If the white people in the South don't do something to keep the carpetbagging. . . ."

I must leave him to trail off into voicelessness, because I have no wish to decorate this page with the explosive forms of punctuation from cartoonists' balloons, and I dare not quote him verbatim lest this volume be banned in Boston, where old maids see such words only when they peer through their lorgnettes at the scrawlings on synagogues.

The fiercely possessive attitude of my friend toward every Negro family that has ever been associated with his farms or his household is one aspect of the Southern attitude toward the Negro. I do not share it. To begin with, there are not enough white men like my friend to make it a working system. It is bad in principle, and it deprives the Negro of the sense of self-reliance and responsibility that is a part of citizenship. But it is an attitude far from that often pictured as typical of the cotton belt.

I stumbled into another attitude and another conversation by accident one morning. One of my friends is a man who could play Cat in *Chanticleer* and improvise all of the lines, so neatly does the character fit him. He has very few fixed convictions and a love for argument and a ready imagination for nonexistent facts with which to bolster them. He was engaged in his favorite occupation of baiting one of those people whom he disliked on sight.

"The niggers have got to be put in their place," his victim was saying. "They can't be allowed to associate with white people in any way. There's too much of this fool talk about educating them. All they need to learn is to say 'yes, sir' to a white man and 'gee and haw' to a mule."

"You're thoroughly right," my friend concurred. He had his tongue in his cheek and his fish hooked. "I'd like to see us really have complete segregation. Different stores for the Negroes, run by them. Keep them out of the white section of town altogether. While I don't mind educating them, I think we ought not to have any business dealings with them at all."

"I couldn't go that far," the reply came quickly. "After all a nigger's hand doesn't stink up a dollar. I just want to keep them in their place." The man had shrewd little pig's eyes, and you could tell at a glance that his grandfather had been an overseer, and his father a scalawag, and that he had voted against Al Smith.

There is some of this attitude in Georgia, in every Southern State, in Chicago, Detroit and New York. It is not a regional attitude. It does not arise from any dislike for the Negro, but from a dislike for all mankind. It comes of a desire for power and wealth at the expense of other men, and from cowardice that understands that it is easier to rob a blind man than one who can see and less dangerous to slap the face of a man whose hands are tied. Mrs. Stowe in *Uncle Tom's Cabin* and Erskine Caldwell in *Kneel to the Rising Sun* have drawn pictures of two types of sadistic "nigger-haters." Simon Legree is running a good many plantations for British or American investors in Southern cottonlands; Mister Arch has a fair number of tenants who have yet to be killed or to run away; but Mister Arch and Simon Legree are to be found in many other parts of America; their name is Legion, and they have escaped from the bodies of the Gadarene swine to trouble earth again.

The Negro makes up about a tenth of the population of America. Of the approximate thirteen million Americans of that race, about half live in the Southeast, where they constitute about a third of the population. About two and a half million more live in the Southwest, where they are about a fifth of the total population. The remainder is scattered about the Nation, and, generally, this remnant is concentrated in a few large industrial cities in the East and Mid-West, although numbers of Negroes have gone to the Pacific Coast during the war years.

Within the South there are many differences in the percentage of Negroes to whites. Georgia is almost a precise average for the entire Southeast, with one Negro for two white citizens. In Tennessee, outside Memphis, there are very few Negroes, and the percentage of Negro residents of Kentucky is actually smaller than that of Delaware. Heaviest proportionate concentration of Negroes is in Mississippi, South Carolina and Louisiana. The

Mountain States and New England have only occasional Negro residents, mainly city dwellers.

The problem of the Negro's life with white citizens surrounding him is different in the South from the problem in Chicago. It varies in many sections of the South.

For example, in Georgia and North Carolina, there have been serious efforts by FSA and by the local communities to make the rural Negro into a farm owner, and these efforts have been successful. In fact, while many white farmers were slipping into a tenant status, twenty-five per cent of all Negro farmers became landowners. About the same proportion of Negro farmers in Tennessee own their own land, and land-ownership is increasing among Negroes in Northern Florida although not in the citrus and truck-farming areas of that State.

That one Negro farmer in every four in the Southeastern States should have been able to climb from absolute poverty to the position of a landowner within a period of eighty years is evidence of two things: first, that the widely believed stories current throughout America about the lack of thrift of the Negro are untrue; second, that a much greater economic opportunity and more economic justice exist in the Southeast than critics of that region are willing to admit.

The economic status of the Negro in the principal and representative Southeastern States is tied to the economic status of every other resident of the Southeast. If he is a farmer, he is caught to some extent in the trap of a one-crop economy and is not flourishing. His opportunities in industry are few, since the only industries permitted the South before the Second World War, except textiles, were of the cruder types of processing.

In other parts of the South, it is likely that the relationship of the Negro to the economy of the region and to the white residents is vastly different. The large plantations of the Delta, of Arkansas, of the Black Belt, are frequently in the hands of absentee owners, operating through managers whose duty is to supervise the mining of the soil to extract the last possible pound of cotton. There are model plantations here and there, where tenants are treated fairly and obtain incomes higher than the very low standards that generally prevail in the entire South. But these plantations are the exceptions, and many sharecroppers, both white and black, have a dismal life and periodically enjoy the privilege of starving.

The complaint of the Negro in the Southeast, his demands for justice, do not originate out of a sense of economic inequity. His diet of fatback, corn pone, and molasses is the standard diet of the tenant farmer of his section. If he lives in the tobacco belt of South Georgia, or in West Georgia, he is very likely to be a landowner and to fare reasonably well.

His complaint is about other things: poor educational opportunities; deprivation of political rights; occasional interferences with civil liberty. This last is less serious, relatively, than it appears from any examination of specific cases; outbreaks of antiminority feeling are uncommon in most parts of America, and they are uncommon in the South; in general, the basic civil liberties of Negro citizens are respected thoroughly in Georgia.

Educational opportunity for the Negro has been inadequate everywhere in the South. Too little has been spent on schools for both races, although the South has taxed itself more heavily for education than any other section of America. North Carolina and Georgia both, as was pointed out earlier, are spending more money on Negro schools currently than they spent on all schools in 1900, and the basic pay of teachers in the more progressive Southern States is not affected by racial considerations. In Georgia, the literacy rate of Negro citizens is rapidly increasing, although it has been difficult to persuade either landlords or the parents involved that Negro boys and girls should not periodically interrupt their classwork for seasonal farming crises. Indeed, it may be that some solution of this problem must be met by educators in devising a year-round classwork system that will permit farm youth to help at home at periodic intervals.

The higher education of Negroes has been shamefully neglected in the South, to the distress of the region, which needs thousands of Negro physicians, dentists and other professional men, as well as teachers. This, too, is being gradually corrected, and will present no challenge of want of opportunity within a few more years.

But the legitimate aspirations of the Negro to have some share in the government to which he pays taxes, before whose courts he must submit his complaints, for which he must fight every twenty years or so, have confronted a more difficult obstacle.

There is no Southerner, except a crackpot or a dirty-mouthed demagogue, who does not agree that any Negro is entitled to the same precise justice from a court as is accorded a white man. But not every Southerner is willing to grant the franchise to the Negro.

The aftermath of the War Between the States was the longest armed-occupancy of a defeated country in the annals of modern history. By contrast, the occupation of a few portions of Germany after 1918, lasting months instead of years, was a mild affair. Reconstruction brought to the South a good many cranks, who wanted to provide every rural Negro with forty acres and a mule; it would have been a good thing, indeed, if this had been done and the Negroes set on their feet as self-sustaining units in Southern economy; it might have been done, if it had not threatened both to cost money and to interfere with the systematic looting of the section.

For twelve years, until the Bourbon Brigadiers made their infamous "treaty of 1876" with the looters and despoilers of the whole Nation, agreeing to the fraud against Tilden and continuation of the railroad thefts, the Southern States had no political independence of any kind. In the next two decades, the Negro was used as a political tool by miscellaneous scoundrels, until he awakened under the impact of the Populist rebellion. Then, at the very moment when a large portion of the race had fitted itself for participation as voters—which had not been the case in the thirty years preceding—Negroes were disfranchised.

In the more progressive States of the Southeast, this disfranchisement was not accompanied by specific repression, although the status of the Negro unquestionably deteriorated henceforth until the exodus of 1917. In many States, the disfranchisement of the Negro was the expedient by which more than half the white voters of the State also were pushed off the registration lists. But, again, so disparate is the South, broad generalizations are impossible.

Prior to 1917 there had been Negro residents in the East and in the Mid-West. One of the largest colonies, indeed, was to be found in Chicago, which had once been a haven for escaped slaves, manumitted slaves, and freemen and freeborn Negroes from the East. In 1917 and in the years that have followed, the Negro has spread to many parts of the country; and he has found problems awaiting him everywhere.

In the South, a recognition of the relationship of the two races began to grow, partly because the exodus called attention to the value of the Negro as a working force and partly because the era of Reconstruction had passed; it had been two decades since a gentleman from Boston, puzzled how his fellow-citizens of that festering mudpuddle could cause trouble—and not having hit upon the expedient of smearing filth on the windows of kosher delicatessens—suggested civilizing the South with more bayonets. Today I believe that the Southeast rather generally shares my view of the Negro and of his position in the South. And that view is very simple to state.

The Negro is entitled to equal protection under the law. His civil liberties must be guarded as zealously as those of any other citizen.

He is entitled to educational opportunity for himself and his children, and this should not be limited through prejudice or narrow-sightedness to vocational training, but should include opportunity to acquire professional skill.

He is entitled to the rights of a citizen: to vote in the elections, including the primaries of the party to which he belongs, provided he is literate, and the literacy tests should be enforced even-handedly and not made subterfuges to prevent Negro citizens from voting.

Where segregation exists, equivalent facilities must be afforded. Segregation must not be a device for robbing the Negro, as it has become in the instance of some classes of public transportation.

Segregation in the South mystifies those who have never seen it. John Gunther visited Atlanta in his tour over the Nation obtaining material for his book *Inside U.S.A.* On a Saturday night we rode down Peachtree Street to Five Points. The streets were crowded. I asked Mr. Gunther to notice any Negroes he saw. The only Negro he was able to point out to me was the Negro doorman at the Henry Grady Hotel. At Five Points we turned into Decatur Street. There were literally thousands of Negroes on the street, visiting, shopping and fraternizing. I explained to Mr. Gunther that there was no law, no city ordnance, and no prohibition which kept white citizens from going on to Decatur Street. Likewise, there was no prohibition preventing the Negroes from strolling down Peachtree Street. He asked me why it was that they didn't. The only answer that occurred to me was that the whites preferred to window-shop on Peachtree, while the Negroes preferred to visit together on Decatur Street.

Negro citizens are entitled to the same standards of public service that are provided for other citizens, to the same kind of social security, to the same public health benefits; it is exceedingly difficult to induce the typhoid bacillus to observe the rules and to stay in Darktown, and these aspects of fair treatment of the Negro are hardly more than elementary precautions on behalf of the white populace.

Like the other people who live in the South, and to the same extent, and to no greater and no less extent, the Southern Negro is entitled to economic opportunity. In large measure, he has been accorded precisely the same want of economic opportunity that his white neighbors have found facing them. Economic problems so fundamental cannot be solved by legislation such as that proposing a permanent Fair Employment Practices Commission. Undoubtedly there are some well-meaning individuals among the advocates of this measure; but its principal purpose is to serve as an irritant to the South, for Southern citizens, both liberals and conservatives, regard it as a successor to the Lodge Force Bills. FEPC is an example of class legislation; it is indefensible logically. Employment rights might be affected by age, sex and other considerations as well as race. The FEPC has become a political game, useful to reactionaries of both parties as an excuse for embarrassment to liberals in the South. Currently it serves no other purpose; it alleviates no economic distress and promotes no harmony between the races.

Fundamentally, the problem of the Negro in the South is a problem of economics. In a prosperous South, in a South that did not suffer from colonialism and exploitation, the Negro would prosper and would be able to obtain most of the things that he desires. He would find his life, I think, more comfortable in the South than elsewhere, because it has been his home, and he is not easily to be wrenched away by the roots from the soil that he loves and from people who, in the main, are less resentful of a minority group than any other in America.

From a friend who is among the many Georgians who have been exported from the South because of want of opportunity, there came to me recently a report upon a young Negro who wished to return to the South and become a teacher. He was a little sick and fed up with Chicago, where his parents had moved in 1917 from one of those rather exceptional Southern communities where the Negro is frankly repressed.

That kind of town, of course, exists in the South, though it is not representative. In the instance of this community it can be traced to an altercation between a drunken, subnormal Negro and an outlander who had acquired some property in the area and who disliked Negroes intensely; there was an "incident," and the suggestion of a riot; and for a score of years, until the depression hit the section in the fall of 1930, there was a police chief who "knew how to keep niggers down," and there was a good bit of tension. The father of this family was a barber, a profession then almost preëmpted by Negroes. On moving to Chicago, he eventually secured employment as a waiter and did fairly well. The young man who wished to return South was born the year before his parents moved to the great city on the lake. He has known no other home. His parents are somewhat distrustful of the South, on the basis of their experience, and all that he knows about it comes from acquaintances. He thinks, or so he tells my friend, that he would prefer the South to Chicago.

Two reasons were given. First of all, the "Old Settlers," descendants of the Negroes who went to Chicago in the days before the War Between the States or even in the earlier years of the twentieth century, looked down their noses at the new arrivals, loaded them with opprobrious names, and excluded them from their various lodges, churches and social groups. Second, the social sanctions imposed upon the Negro were unregulated by any etiquette between the races, cruelly enforced, and accompanied by newspaper attacks of the utmost virulence. This last surprised me; I had forgotten that the *Tribune* was published in Chicago, assuming that it would long since have transferred itself to the more hospitable atmosphere of Boston.

In the narrative of this young Negro, there is an obvious disparity between what is consciously recognized and the underlying factors that are the true ones. He has overlooked, for example, the congestion of the Negro areas of population, a mere physical congestion that puts a serious burden upon the individual psyche. He emphasized the degree of racial repression evidenced in Chicago, and, I think, somewhat exaggerated it; but he failed to look beneath the veneer and see that the economic opportunity for the Negro was so limited that it formed the basis for most of these complaints.

I have never seen the congested Negro areas of Chicago and New York—"Black Metropolis" and Harlem—but I have seen a portion of the Negro slums in Detroit, and these beggar description. The problem of the Negro in the urban East and industrial Mid-West is the problem of finding living room; it is accompanied by tremendous exploitation, and is associated, in some cities, with alliances between selfish interests and political machines. It is a matter of space, and space for the Negro citizens sells at too high a premium everywhere but in the South. Though the Negro slums of the South are a reproach, they at least provide room for expansion, which the slums of the industrial areas do not.

The want of opportunity for the Negro in all areas of America needs to be overcome. Except by joining in the exploitation of his own race, there is no opportunity for him to obtain land-owning status other than in agrarian areas. Outside the South, apparently, the Negro farmer is unwelcome, which limits his aspirations to own property to becoming a yeoman farmer in the Southeast.

The riots in Detroit, Chicago and New York can be traced very largely to the two factors that I have enumerated, a want of living space and want of opportunity. The bottling up of the Negro in urban slums is dangerous to his welfare, and to the

Nation; for it makes him the obvious scapegoat for some Fascist-minded agitator to view with alarm when the next depression rolls around.

As the individual Negro American ponders his problem, he will find it most readily solved in the Southeast, in spite of economic difficulties. He will find it most difficult in the Southern plantation area, the Black Belt and the Delta. He will find his ultimate status most perilous in the urban areas of the Mid-West and in the Eastern centers, except New York. So far as my observation permits me to judge, the only serious efforts to assist him in solving his problem are being made in New York and in the Southeast. In the former, a real attack is going on, not too successful as yet, upon the grave problem of housing. In the latter, an effort to improve his status as a citizen and his economic position is being made.

In most of the Southern States, the right of the Negro to cast his ballot in both primary and election is now unchallenged. Educational facilities for his children are improving rapidly, and with increasing emphasis upon subjects other than wholly vocational. In Georgia, there has been evenhanded enforcement of the compulsory attendance laws, with a result that there are 249,629 Negro children enrolled in the schools compared to 468,579 white, a ratio almost exactly that of the respective population totals.

Prejudices die hard. They can be kept alive by agitation, by the cheap quackery of demagogues of both races; for the Negroes have developed some of their own. The relationship between Negro citizens and their white neighbors will not be settled in a day. They will not be settled by Bigger Thomas; certainly they will not be settled by Uncle Tom; and it is a commentary on the sound judgment of the average Negro that "Uncle Tom" has become an idiom of reproach among their race, applied to those servile scoundrels who traffic in good-will. They can be solved only by mutual forebearance, by improving the economic outlook of those sections where the overwhelming number of Negroes live, and by developing a national consciousness of the danger of fascism.

If I insist upon recurring to that theme, it is because I apprehend a danger. The Negro is dispersing over America, although his roots remain in the Southeast, where I think he will be safe whatever dangers arise elsewhere. He is an inviting scapegoat for the Fascist to select; scapegoats were usually black, and the black man will do; he can be pointed out easily and found easily.

Even in the South, where Fascist-thinking is not the really serious aberration that it may become elsewhere in America, you can detect a new note in the stump roarings of the demagogues and a new twist to the "racial issue" that they develop. No longer do they speak of the Negro as one not yet fitted intellectually by training and experience to become a voting-citizen, as did their predecessors, but as a creature risen from Hell to be repressed. It isn't taking too well in the South; but it may be a prelude of what will happen someday soon in some other part of America.

Accept this as a personal view, however; all of it. It is a view colored by my knowledge of West Georgia Negro farmers, of Georgia's Negroes in uniform still bewildered at having travelled all over the world and found their way home again to the ice-cream palaces on Decatur Street in Atlanta; and shaped by a belief that the Negro is a part of the South and of our common country and that the problem he faces is one that all America must take a hand in solving.

Other men will have other views, and other solutions. There is a Congressman who suggests sending all the Negroes to Africa and dumping them somewhere to build a new home or starve. There are clever economists and sociologists who have provided ideas drawn from filing cabinets and slide rules. There are well-intentioned liberals, who hope that everything will someday work out well. There was Will Percy; but for him, as for Hotspur, time has had a stop; I wonder what he would have said to the author of the nasty little "hate book" from Boston, with whose quotation I began this.

More than half the problem is a problem of poverty; a problem of the poor South, of two races that must share a half-loaf between them. But it is not all of the problem, for part of the answer must be found within the human heart.

7

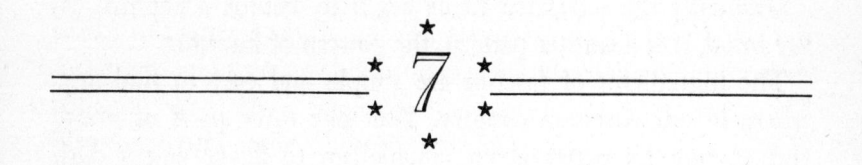

THE INGREDIENTS OF FASCISM

ON THE DESK in front of me is a litter of notes and maps and newspaper clippings that seem unrelated. There is the map prepared by the Senate Committee on Decentralization of Industry, the McCarran Committee: I glance at it and notice that the outline of the depressed areas coincides with the outline of the areas affected by discriminatory freight rates. There is a clipping that someone has sent me, a rather lengthy news story in which the president of a great industrial company says that he does not open his books, under any circumstances, to the investors in the corporation. I recall that instinctively I have a distaste for the word "investors" as a substitute for the word "stockholders." There is a letter from a friend, enclosing some literature passed out by one of the "hate" organizations that seem to flourish somehow and be financed somehow all over America. There is a telegram from a crank, urging that I call a session of the Georgia Legislature to make provisions for sending the Negroes back to Africa. There is a handsome mailing piece from an association with a long and impressive name, advocating repeal of the existing antitrust laws.

Gradually the unrelated items begin to assume a pattern. To my mind, it is a sinister pattern, the pattern of fascism.

The ingredients of fascism are simple and easy to find anywhere in our common country. You take three parts of greed, and enough hypocrisy about colonialism to flavor and a dash of irresponsibility in a world of business where stockholders lose their status and become investors, and two parts of racial hate; let it stew and simmer under cover for a time, and get a demagogue to stir the mess; and when you open the kettle, there it is, the witches' brew.

It is impossible for a democracy to function in a nation hatefully divided along sectional lines, with an imperial domain on one hand and distressed colonial appendages on the other. The centralization of industry invites centralization of political control; and centralized political control in any country will fall either to the organized Right or the organized Left, given time. Political liberty will not outlive economic liberty, in America or elsewhere.

The "hate" organizations are growing. Their nasty little pamphlets, preaching the doctrine that some men must be the enemies of all other men, are distributed all over the Nation. The fantastic flummery of the Ku Klux Klan, the Christian Front, the Camellia, the shirts of various hues, continues to grow. The growth was interrupted by the war, in a sense; it was driven underground, but there it multiplied fivefold. There is not today a section of the country that does not possess its own little regional organization based on hate, and they apparently maintain close contact with each other, for if you examine the publications of one of them, you will find quotations culled from another of the hate sheets somewhere else in America.

"Come let us free America from the Jew," say these sheets, or the Negro, or the Mexican, or the Japanese.

Of course respectable Americans are not taken in by this shrill screaming. There is very little prejudice to be found anywhere in our common country, if you stick your head in the sand and close your eyes by way of added precaution. Those signs on private schools in New York: "Select Christian Clientele Only"; those regrettable small incidents in Boston; the barring from veterans' organizations in the West of those American soldiers of Japanese descent who fought so well in Italy; the arrest in San Francisco of bobby-soxers waiting to hear a generous and pleasant young man who sandwiches in pleas for better understanding of all Americans between the songs he croons; the screaming mobs in Madison Square Garden praising Franco; these are inconsequential. No American anywhere has been taken in by the apostles of hate.

If we say that over and over again, we may come to believe it; but it still will not be true. The hatemongers and their nasty little pamphlets have poisoned many American minds.

There is one more fact that must be taken into account. Tucked under the McCarran map, where I could not see it when I was enumerating the items on my desk, was a report on the increase in one specific mental disorder, schizophrenia. While admittances to mental institutions for other psychiatric ills has continued stable in relationship to the population, the upward curve of the incidence of this form of madness is distressing evidence that the world of the twentieth century, like the world of the first century, is a sick world. The life span may be increasing; many maladies of the body may have been brought under control; new drugs may be discovered more potent than the elixir of life sought by the ancients, but man is still sick.

Confronted with the relative impotence and insignificance of the individual in the modern world, man has taken refuge in neuroses, in psychoid traits of varying degrees of seriousness, in a dissolution of his personality.

This always has occurred when men are haunted by the spectre of any form of authoritarianism. The madmen who crowd the narrative of the Four Evangelists were the product of the degenerate and degenerative philosophy of the first century. The madmen who crowd the institutions of America, the neurotics who seek release upon the couches of the psychoanalysts, the crowds that cheered themselves hoarse at Nuremberg or that storm jails in California and Florida as crowds cheered the puffy-jowled Procurator one Friday morning nearly twenty centuries ago—these are the products of the degenerate and degenerative philosophy of the twentieth century. For the neo-Hegelian of today, whether of Right or Left, whether totalitarian or collectivist, has denied the humanity of man and reduced the individual to inconsequence. The individual in turn has rebelled; but his rebellion has taken the form of flight into a world of fantasy, since the powerful of the world have denied his claims to a place on the earth that was his home.

The little hatemongers of today are the legitimate offspring of Cato the Censor and his sycophants. Even in features, Hitler bears more than a chance resemblance to Caligula. The praise expended upon Hadrian is reminiscent of that lately lavished upon his successor, the man who made a train run on time. We have achieved that worship of order that reduces the human entity to the position of a cog in a wheel, a cog that must be liquidated if it impedes the operation of the mechanical monster.

Remember, I am writing this from the viewpoint of the South, and the South is still pioneer country, and the South is still Gaelic, and the South still taps its feet to the tune of "Dixie." And once an old man in the North Georgia hills, who was quite mad and had fought at Chancellorsville and claimed to be of the Alpins, told me that, come Armageddon, they will play "Dixie" on the pipes. Then, or so he said, they will all come back: Douglas, who flung the Bruce's heart into the battle that he might follow it; and Montrose and Dundee, to ride beside Stuart and Jackson and Gordon; and Wallace, with the mark of Edward's hangman on his throat, will lift his terrible broadsword with both hands and cry the charge to the men of Chancellorsville and Bannockburn, and to those who fell at Flodden and who died on the slopes of Missionary Ridge. Then, so he says, and he claims the secondsight, the red ranks of Hell will waver, and panic will seize them, and they will break, fleeing back to their infernal pit which is defended with such a wall as Hadrian built to protect his legionaries. It may be so; for someday, it seems to me, man must make some final stand in his own defense.

There is a trifle more to the individual than the sum of his determinable parts. There is as much evidence in his conduct that this is so as there was evidence in the gyrations of the planets that such a fellow-traveller as Neptune was somewhere in the sky. Man is not wholly an economic animal, as the Marxists insist, when they differentiate him from all other species by insisting that he alone is impelled by a single, simple motive; man is at least as complex and misunderstandable as the lemming, and seemingly, as bent upon self-destruction. But if he has this passion for death, upon which the Fascist counts heavily, he has also a counterbalancing passion for life. Somehow, in spite of the pressure upon his mind, there is a likelihood that he will survive and outlive such playthings as atom bombs and such leaders as the Duce and Plowboy Pete and such shibboleths as trains-run-on-time; and will build cities, unlike Boston, where the gravestones will not be desecrated.

But if he is to do this, he must combat the trend toward fascism, and Americans must apprehend the serious menace presented by Fascist ideology in our own country today.

The fundamental battle, of course, is against any form of authoritarianism, whatever the color of its shirt or of its flag. But America is less threatened at the moment by the collectivists than by the totalitarians, though it is very difficult to distinguish between their mental processes. They agree on the basic principle that men should be regimented and controlled, that they should be kept busy at "useful employment," that dissidents should be suppressed, that opinion should be limited, that the exploration of the boundaries of the physical universe or of the more expansive universe of the human spirit should be supervised by appropriate authorities. They agree, too, in a humorlessness, a seriousness of purpose mindful of the intentness with which an ant goes about transporting a bit of garbage to his tunnel; and this monotonous seriousness is a graver charge against them than their outrageous assaults upon human dignity.

If this seems unfair, this coupling of the conventional Fascist's mind and the conventional Marxist's mind, it is needful only to turn to the evidence. The condemnation of the radical sectarians, if that described the heterodox Leftist groups that range from Nihilists to Old Bolshies and Trotskyites, follows identical thought patterns, whether it emanates from conventional Communists or from Fascist-minded ideologues. Now with none of these groups do I agree, though the Nihilists at least succeeded in teaching Tsars the elementary fact that they, too, were mortal; but I am amused at the fundamental basis of the criticism levelled at deviators. For it arises, among Fascists and Communists alike, from the dissidents' advocacy of two heretical articles of faith: first, that direction of all affairs should be decentralized; second, that there ought to be something in the nature of a "vagabond's wage" for such fellows as do not desire to engage in productive efforts.

Of the thousands upon thousands of controversial tracts that have been written against the Bakuninists, in the hundreds of thousands of pages of polemics, these are the themes: "How are men to be kept in their places if controls are not centralized?" and "Would anybody work if starvation were not the penalty for idleness?" Lawrence Dennis and C. V. Foster find themselves completely in agreement on the question of whether the common man has any right to live his own life, to order his own way of living, or to choose the field of opportunity in which he shall engage. And the neo-Fascist, the advocate of irresponsible management of industry, concurs speedily with both. There is complete disagreement over whether the life of America should be regulated by the intervention of one dictatorship or another; but both agree on the necessity for such a dictatorship, and both assert a degree of infallibility almost staggering. Personally, I believe that neither a Fourth-Assistant-Vice-Commissar nor a Fourth-Assistant-Vice-President can possess such an abundance of wisdom.

That the common man might be happier, that his life might be more harmonious, that he might be free of many psychological pressures, if he were left to regulate his own manner of living, occurs to neither group any more than does the idea that a majority of individuals find idleness unspeakably boresome and would be busy without the solicitous efforts of taskmaster, Vice-Commissar of the Collective World or Vice-President of Gigantic and Titanic Combined Corporation. In none of the summers since Pharaoh's efficiency expert anticipated Bedaux have men forgotten to plant gardens or to sow the fields to wheat, any more than apples have forgotten to follow the blossoms upon the trees.

My viewpoint in this is the viewpoint of an individual who believes in individualism; and I do not mean the mockery of "rugged individualism" so dear to the heart of the spokesmen of exploitation and monopoly and special privilege. I admit to a heritage of prejudice in this respect, to a belief that the rights of all men are inseverably linked so that you can neither harm nor degrade nor torment one individual from among all the billion on this planet without in some degree wounding each of the others. Likewise, I admit to a belief that power is very dangerous to any man, rendering its possessor both hurtful to others and menacing to his own personality.

As I came to write this chapter, I turned to a book that I had not examined since I left college. In *Leviathan,* I found, Hobbes had drawn a picture of the world as the authoritarian would like to see it; and the master satirist had chosen, as the repentant author of *Voice of Destruction* points out, the symbol of the Beast from the Abyss to provide the name for his mock Utopia. Here is order and forethought and a race of supermen, and throughout there comes to the nostrils the odor of the decay you might sense in the woods when you pass the spot where some farmer has dragged away the carcass of a dead horse. It is apparent that Hobbes was describing no ideal community of his own imagining, but was presenting a searching criticism of all the ideals of a master-and-slave paradise that had been dangled before men's eyes in the past. Men want no such commonwealth, whether the devising of a Plato, a More or a Butler. The sane man has no more wish to be a superman than to be a slave, nor does he desire to escape the ordinary vicissitudes of human life by becoming one with the pigs of Circe.

Both Left and Right dangle enticements in the form of comforts before the eyes of the public, with an invitation to submit to dictatorship in one form or another and obtain in return some degree of security. It is an old theme. The followers of Catiline once sang the theme song of the Left, as those of Sulla did of the Right. Free corn, free circuses; somebody else's oil, some other man's blood.

Always these enticements are accompanied by the stern warning that in whatever might that day happen to be the modern world, whether the modern first century or the modern twentieth century, the individual is impotent in the grip of powerful circumstances, that he is being borne forward on some wave of the future to a predestined shore, and that unless he is very stupid he had best make quick terms with the clever persons who are willing to take over his affairs and administer them at the extremely reasonable price of his glad acceptance of slavery.

The elements that combine to generate the poison of fascism may be catalogued as readily as the ingredients of the Hell's brew of the witches. Instead of the relatively less noxious sting of adder, maw of shark and root of hemlock, the component elements for fascism are economic and psychological conditions. Let us list them and see how many exist in American life:

1. A centralization of industry within an imperial and favored region. This obviously is present, since the concentration of manufactures in the relatively small Eastern area is acknowledged, is advocated by many sectional and ultraconservative spokesmen as desirable, and is accompanied by a concentration of wealth in those areas.

2. An unnatural centralization of population within the industrial area, with rising tensions between various economic classes and ethnic groups. The concentration of population within the Eastern empire is a fact; the tensions are increasing; it is not necessary to look to benighted Boston for examples, for they exist in such civilized communities as Detroit and Chicago, as well.

3. The development of a system of control over the national economy by those who are neither owners nor workers within the industry affected. The increasing power of management is a great menace to American business. In years of record earnings of corporations, management retained under its control excessive surpluses that were not distributed to the owners in dividends, and an increasingly arrogant attitude toward ownership by management is evident.

4. The erection outside the *de jure* government of a private government. In the instances of the railroads, with their enormous bureaucracy dominating many aspects of America's economic life, and of the great oil corporations, that treat independently with foreign governments in defiance of legislation and national tradition, this already exists.

5. A tendency to substitute administrative law for that created

either by the custom of the country or the action of the representatives of the people. This follows, almost of necessity, from the complexity and centralization of business, since controls must follow the pattern established by the object to be controlled. It nevertheless paves the way for fundamental changes in the political order.

6. A weakening of the political subdivisions of the nation affected. In this country, through their own negligence, inadequacy of service to their citizens, and unwillingness to assume responsibility, the autonomous State governments have increasingly become mere geographical units. Efforts to solve local, State or regional problems upon those levels are less vigorous annually, owing principally to the apathy of the leadership and the growing recognition by the public that prompter, if less effective, steps will be taken by the central government.

7. The development of two parallel psychological trends: a feeling of impotence on the part of the average citizen, and the search for a scapegoat upon whom to lay the collective political, economic and ideological sins of the era. Certainly this trend has been evident, in both phases, in America since the end of the First World War. Facts are stubborn in this particular and defy twisting; they also merit examination.

It was shortly after the neurotic twenties arrived that the hate organizations made their initial appearance in America: the Klan, the Black Shirts, the Silver Shirts, and their companions. It was about this time that Boris Brasol brought to this country the infamous *Protocols of Zion,* the handiest bit of forgery ever to feed the appetite of the anti-Semitic propagandist. It was about this time that the minority groups, naturally apprehensive, began to take the inevitable, ridiculous defensive measures to protect themselves from what they regarded as ridicule; for example, driving from the stage the comic Irishman and the comic Jew, two of the best loved characters in American folklore. It was in this era that a man was defeated for President of the United States upon the ground that he shared the religious beliefs of Charles Carroll of Carrollton.

It would be naïve to deny that in the thirties some of these native hate groups became deliberately or unconsciously the effective weapons of foreign powers. The facts have been presented all too often by too many investigators. But the obvious fact, that no amount of foreign-bought propaganda could have been effective unless the tensions that prepare the way already existed in America, seems to have escaped many of these investigators. The bacteria of religious, racial and ethnic hate do not flourish except where there is economic uncertainty and psychological tension; and however reprehensible those might be who encouraged the malady's spread by emptying their test tubes of virus here and there, they could not obtain any success if the other factors were favorable.

The fundamental factor, of course, is the feeling of the average man that he is powerless to assert his individual will, to express his individual personality, or to influence his personal fate. His dignity as a man is assailed, and in anger he turns to seek an enemy. Then the hatemonger presents him with a ready-made victim, whispering in his ear, appealing to his eye with his nasty little pamphlets, telling him: "All your troubles are due to the polacks and the kikes and the niggers. They are plotting against you. They are burying guns back of the church or the synagogue or the lodge house. They are going to rise. They are going to kill you. They are going to get you unless you get them first. Kill them. Kill them."

It is an old trick. It was not new when the anger of hungry Rome was diverted from the monopolists who were stealing the Egyptian corn crop to the timorous followers of Peter and Clement, hiding in the catacombs and scrawling their professions of faith on the rocks that underlaid the Seven Hills. It was old when Philip of France directed the hate of his people toward the Templars. It was no novelty to the Tsars, who always found it convenient to substitute another pogrom for needed agrarian reforms. It was handy at Nuremberg and Berlin and Munich. It is always handy; it is always more economical to substitute the blood of men for the bread that men are seeking.

Incalculable as the cost has been to mankind in the thousands of years of history, enormous as has been the suffering of mankind in those years because of this hate, there is no cause for dejection. Always, at the last, the dictators and the oligarchs have failed; they have run headlong into the good sense and the good heart of the common man. It has been possible to delude men into transient acceptance of the inevitability of insecurity and misery, of the certainty of war, of the weakness of the individual in comparison with the tremendous power of the apparent or concealed government that has authority over him; but it has been impossible to keep man in subjection long.

Nevertheless, it is folly to invite to America the internecine strife of classes. It is possible, with a little forethought, to avert such a calamity. It is relatively simple to assure an economy of abundance, in which there will be no conflict between private initiative and public initiative and in which individual opportunity is compatible with the welfare of society.

It is possible to maintain a political system, in which government can be limited to its legitimate functions: ". . . to form a more perfect union, establish justice, insure domestic tranquility, provide for the common defense, promote the general welfare, and secure the blessings of Liberty to ourselves and our posterity."

The legitimate functions of government are the preservation of that degree of mutual protection necessary to enable men to enjoy the use of their possessions, and to permit men to carry out conveniently those enterprises that are desirable for their joint convenience, comfort or happiness. While this implies necessarily a certain amount of interference with the individual will, it obviously imposes restrictions upon only the irresponsible or the vicious. Moreover, it implies the right, within certain restrictions, of the people to engage in any form of experimentation that they may think desirable, either individually or collectively. It implies their right to assign one service today to one unit of government, and at their considered wish or their mere whim to reassign it tomorrow to some other unit of government. Governments themselves possess no rights; theirs is a trusteeship for power and not an ownership of power; and this is true whether the government is formally organized as a political entity or is as informal as that exercised by a conspiracy of producers of paper matches.

It is comparatively simple to implement such a political and economic system in America. Despite the vandalism of the exploiters, our natural resources are still enormous. Despite the curtailment of our productiveness by artificial devices, there can be jobs in the next year for sixty million Americans. Despite the existence of a dangerous colonialism that must be terminated,

America can sustain a population not of some hundred and fifty million but of three hundred million or more. Despite the warmongers' cry for bigger and better battles and larger and more magnificent cemeteries, Americans can live at peace with each other and with the rest of the world.

Men did not cross the Atlantic in fragile ships to seek security, but to find opportunity to express their individual personalities. They came in a search of one thing: freedom. It is a little old-fashioned, a little anachronistic, a trifle quaint like the Chippendale bureau of your great-grandmother, to think, today, in terms of the indivisibility of freedom. It has become something of a fashion to believe that the happiness of one man is the minute subdivision of the happiness of all men, rather than to believe that the happiness of all men is the sum total of each man's happiness and that, therefore, the happiness of each man is of special significance to all other men. It is a little old fashioned, a little out of step with a world that understands better the mathematics and physics of fissionable materials than the way of a serpent on a rock or the way of a man with a maid, but I confess to somewhat greater faith in the line of American democrats— Williams and Sam Adams, Jefferson and Franklin and Mason, Forsyth and Blair and Benton—than in many of the theories that are advocated by those who will be attending conferences and committee meetings for the betterment of something or other at the very moment when the trumpet sounds for Armageddon and the place of every man is on the barricade.

Freedom cannot be divided, as selfish men have tried to divide our common country. There are many aspects of freedom, depending upon the point of view of the watcher and upon the refraction of light from its innumerable facets; but in the end, freedom is the right of every man to do as he pleases, so long as he infringes upon the rights of no other man. And nowhere, in all the world, can some men be free until everywhere all men are free.

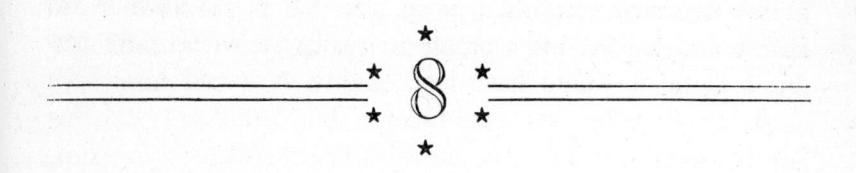

PROPHETS OF DOOM

In the twelve years that I had some contact with Franklin Delano Roosevelt, and admired the many sides of a versatile imagination, an inquiring mind, and a great heart, there are three things that I remember best about him; and none is from the infrequent conversations that I had with him from time to time, or his public acts, or his great career with its gigantic improvisations that saved a nation and a world.

One was a sentence in his last message to the American people. Somehow, I read it in the light of that last letter that Thomas Jefferson penned to the people of Philadelphia, when they invited him to attend the fiftieth celebration of Independence; the great letter that the Squire of Monticello wrote in the last week of his life with eyes too dim to see across the mountains and the valleys to the college that he had devised out of a belief that knowledge and freedom are inseverable, but with vision unobscured to see into the future of mankind; the letter that concludes: "The light of science has now made it plain for every eye that the mass of mankind has not been born with saddles on their backs, nor a favored few booted and spurred, ready to ride them."

The Roosevelt message, penned like that of Jefferson in his final hours, has for me a prophetic quality. It would have possessed truth, it would have had validity, it would have been challenging, under any circumstance; but, associated with his last moments as it was, it becomes his final heritage to America: "The only limits to our realization of tomorrow will be our doubts of today. Let us move forward with strong and active faith."

The second of these recollections was the long day in which Roosevelt's body moved toward its final resting place in the rose garden overlooking the Hudson of his childhood, and the reiteration over the radio, throughout those hours, of the most impressive marching song of our people:

> Mine eyes have seen the glory of the coming of the Lord;
> He is tramping out the vintage where the grapes of wrath are stored;
> He hath loosed the fateful lightning of His terrible swift sword ...

It moved, did the song, as inexorably as the march of men whose eyes are fixed upon a goal so high that, though sometimes their feet tread in the mire, though sometimes a rank is broken as one or another falls, there is no stopping them, today or tomorrow or forever.

My first contact with the song, as a living reality, came when I was a boy of seven, and talked with a very old cousin who had fought with Lee's men in all of the bloody engagements between Bull Run and the Wilderness. He told me about Fredericksburg, where, he said, the Yankee soldiers fought their best, and really won the war. Until then, there had been no Union army but only a rabble for Jackson to outwit. Burnside, with almost incredible folly, had attempted the impossible; Fredericksburg was one of the most crushing defeats ever sustained by the men in blue; yet, to my elderly cousin, it was the turning point in the war.

Seven times Hooker's men crossed the river and charged. Seven times they were driven back under a fire that withered their ranks. Finally, they charged no more; there were no men left. But that day, the soldiers from Connecticut and Pennsylvania and New Jersey had not turned back as they did at Manassas Junction; they had fallen forward, as becomes a man. The fifth time they charged, reforming their ranks, there was a company with a Rhode Island insignia, and the men were singing. My kinsman had heard the tune before, a score of times, but not the new words and the solemn progress of the rhythm:

> He has sounded forth the trumpet that shall never call retreat;
> He is sifting out the hearts of men before His judgment seat;
> Oh, be swift, my soul, to answer Him! be jubilant my feet! . . .

I was rather young, but I remember one snatch of what he said, that April in Newnan more than a half-century after the war had ended.

"Up until then, son, I felt like we had them licked," he said. "After that I never was sure. They hadn't learned to fight by Fredericksburg, but they had learned how to get killed, and not to run. I knew they'd come back some other time; and yet, after that I never really hated Yankees."

I had not thought of him, his story, or the charge of Hooker's men and their singing, for thirty years until that day when their song made a requiem for Franklin Roosevelt. Yet I remembered that my cousin's story was the beginning of an understanding that an American must love all of our common country, and certainly the American, for whom "The Battle Hymn of the Republic" was a dead march ending upon a note of triumph, was one of those who saw our whole country and saw our country whole.

But I remember best, I think, that December evening when the most loved and familiar voice in America came into thousands upon thousands of homes to read "Even Unto Judas." It is a sentimental Christmas piece. Heywood Broun was not too proud for tears; and Roosevelt had the massive humility that was unashamed of sentiment, too. So the story of the old minister, and of how a man's thoughts may shift with his point of view, and of how a man can change that point of view and those thoughts and the judgments that depend on those thoughts, came back to me; and I recalled an old preacher in the North Georgia hill country, and what he had to say about that to me.

He was not a learned man, and he served four small churches scattered over a radius of some thirty miles that involved mountain roads difficult to cover. He had acquired a strange mixture of unrelated erudition, the product of much reading. He had an enormous knowledge of the Bible. He had, most of all, that strange awareness of the immanence of God, that rather terrible thing of which the circuit riders were always talking and for which they were always praying: the Witness of the Spirit. It is fashionable to scoff at such things today, though less fashionable than in the more naïve twenties, when everyone knew that bootleggers, prosperity, peace and porcine contentment were here to stay and that trains soon would run on time all over the world even as they did in Italy. Now that the morning-after hangover, as the national disorder, has been replaced with the agony of a spastic colon because of worry over the probability that someone playing casually with some fissionable material may miscalculate a formula and explode the world in six seconds and thereby interrupt permanently the worries of the colon's possessor, men are less certain of such things.

The circuit rider was leaning against the well-shed while he talked with me. He had an interesting face, with many lines, a magnificently expressive mouth, enormous eyebrows and an air of serenity.

"I see where science is about to catch up with common sense," he twitted me, for I had been talking that afternoon about what science could do toward building new industries in the South. I meant applied science, for which he had a certain amount of contempt, I think; but the science he referred to was the other kind, on which true knowledge rests. "I never held with the theories of those that didn't believe the Earth was the center of the Universe. As a matter of fact, every man is the center of his own Universe. They are saying now that a man is surrounded on every side by Time and Space, as if we haven't known that from the beginning.

"You know, I have always wanted to see one of these submarines, and maybe to go down in one of them, just to know whether I have been illustrating things right to myself in my mind. I think of Space as being something in the middle of Time, like the submarine in the water; with Time on every side, before and behind and above and below; and a man right in the middle of Space."

I told him that his illustration was strikingly original, but that I did not understand enough about physics and mathematics and the theories of Whitehead and Einstein to comprehend such things. As far as I was concerned, I told him, his illustration appeared reasonable in many ways; but if it were true, then a man might look backward or forward or sideways into Time.

"And that's just the point," he said, drumming against the bucket with a long forefinger. "And that's just the point. A man can do just that. It was Easter last week, for instance.

"Suppose a man looked at the crowd gathered around Pilate's house on that Friday, and he thought what a cruel and wicked mob of people it was, and how they had all taken money or drink to stand in the street and howl for a Man's life. He'd think that men were a bad lot and going straight to Hell, if he only saw them on Friday. But suppose he could turn himself around, and look back to the Sunday morning before, and see them in the streets throwing palms underneath the donkey's feet. Then he'd think that men have some sense and appreciation of goodness when they see it. He'd not ever understand that they were the same people: but they were. They are always the same people." He ran a hand down the chain of the well. It was a strong hand, for my friend had plowed a good many acres of corn in his day. He was silent for a minute or so, as if he were engaged in looking backward and forward through Time.

"You know, either one of us could have been in either crowd. We have to be careful. You know what I think? I think that everything you do today, or I do, affects not only what is going to happen but what already has happened, years and centuries ago. Maybe you can't change what has passed, but you can change all the meaning of what has passed. You can even take all the meaning away. That is why men have to be careful all the time."

His fields were beautiful examples of contour-plowing, so that the soil might not wash away and be lost in the awful engulfment of the sea that he had never seen but the image of which he could borrow as a symbol of man's suspension in a universe of loneliness, with his own deeds for companionship.

There are those who foretell for the United States an early "maturity of the national economy." The picture that they draw of this era of maturity is a little disquieting.

It is to be accompanied by a stratification of the classes in our American society. There will be an apparently dominant aristocracy of wealth, eating its head off in luxurious pigsties, but actually dependent upon a bureaucratic hierarchy of management. This new managerial middle class, which will be to the present small-landowning, small business, and small capitalist class what the new mercantile class was to the yeoman farmer of the Middle Ages, will actually be all powerful; it is not explained precisely why these all-powerful bureaucrats will permit the aristocrats to exist and wield nominal authority, but it is presumed that they will do so out of a kind of superstitious reverence. Beneath all these will be a proletariat of unskilled workers, sharecroppers, common laborers, migratory harvest hands, and other employables too weak economically to defend themselves; these will be more or less protected for the value of the labor they shall contribute unstintedly to the enormous enterprises of the middle class.

This new middle class, which will consist entirely of chain-store managers, chain-store supervisors, branch-managers of manufacturing and distributing corporations, governmental bureaucrats in reduced numbers, foremen and highly skilled workers, will be under the direction of an upper-middle class of Vice-Presidents. Moreover, this new middle class will partly absorb and partly uproot the old propertied middle class, so that rank in the hierarchy of bureaucrats rather than home-ownership will be the index of success, since everybody will be transferred annually to another chain-store, or branch factory, or distributing point.

All this is to be accompanied by further centralization of industry in the Nation, so that controls will tighten gradually over all enterprise. Capitalism will be preserved, in the persons of the sacrosanct aristocrats, but free enterprise will be abolished, because it will be necessary in the public interest to compel all corporations to obtain Federal charters and to limit strictly the nature of their businesses. There will be regulation, but no form of competition.

The Western and Southern colonial possessions, being inhabited largely by farmers, will be retained as sources of raw material. I am glad they will be retained; but they will be supported, in those days, by various doles, since the operation of our national economy will not actually require their existence.

In foreign affairs, we shall tend toward an inevitable imperialism, dominating one portion of the world after another until we encounter some obstacle to halt the expansion. Then we shall pass into a static period; and that will be followed by one of gradual disintegration, it can be presupposed. I assume the presupposition, because very few of these peerers into the future look any farther than tomorrow; they never seem to wonder about the day after.

I have condensed somewhat this exposition of an often-expressed view, but I have not indulged in deliberate satire; I have tried to state it as accurately as I could; it is very difficult, on the next morning, to describe every feature of a nightmare, even if it had been most vivid in the hours just before dawn when little sins sit on the footrail of the bed and grimace.

The people who agree upon this future for America are not all alike. Some of them welcome such a society; most of those who belong to the extremes of Left or Right welcome it. Some do not like it, but they believe it just the same, either because they have heard it so often or because somewhere in the course of their education they pursued all the faulty analogies of the Hegelian extremists and logic-choppers and arrived at a manner of reasoning that defies accurate analysis.

Among those who believe and do not like it is Leo Cherne, one of the ablest economists of the Nation and one of the most literate. He writes in English instead of in a technological jargon, and therefore he possesses the capacity of scaring your socks off, if you happen to read *The Rest of Your Life* on a gloomy night when every noise outdoors seems the footstep of a movie monster. A brief passage from his prophecy exudes the general miasma of his discontent with the future he foresees:

> Hardest hit in the middle classes will be the small property owner engaged in production. His future will be but a shadow of the impressive past. The oft-praised sturdy character of the old property-owning middle class equipped its members to beat a path to economic success, but the evolution of the economic mechanism which once allowed success has made it harder and harder, with the passing decades, for any large number to reach the highest levels. . . .
>
> Access to opportunity was the essence of a frontier society where the basic problem was to discover and exploit a pioneer nation's resources. As long as the frontiers remained, the middle-class dream of crossing the barrier and ascending into the capitalist

level appeared realizable. But with the passing of the frontier, the progress of technology, the depletion of natural resources, the rationalization of industry, the organization of distribution and mercantile establishments on a grander scale, the dream of independent enterprise begins to grow dimmer. . . .
This inability to strike a balance will sharpen the schizophrenic conflict between middle-class ambition and the realities of its economic position, a conflict already revealed in its past. The Populist tradition, which epitomized the most vigorous middle-class action, produced its anti-trust laws, its Federal Trade Commission, its Robinson-Patman Act, and the fair-trade laws. But, like whispers against the wind, these failed to stem the inevitable agglomeration of small property into big property and the evolution of laissez faire into monopoly. The laws were the expression of political attitude; their uneven enforcement the expression of the conflicting economic ambitions. . . .*

Reading this extremely well-documented volume, the first impression is that the author has discovered somehow that the earth shortly will plunge into circumstances in which time will be reversed, and that we shall find ourselves back in the days of the second century or thereabouts. For the description, fundamentally, is that of the era in Roman imperial days when all real authority had been gathered into the hands of the freedmen, the most prosperous of whom became *equites* and major figures in the bureaucracy, while the minor ones operated smaller enterprises for the nominal owners who were their patrons. The predicted future of America is indistinguishable from the actual period between the accession of Domitian in 81 and the decentralization of the Empire by Diocletian in 305. It is documented by references to the production of industry, the complexity of

---

*From *The Rest of Your Life*, by Leo Cherne, copyright 1944, reprinted by permission of Doubleday & Company, Inc.

distribution, the difficulties of governmental control, and the lamentable tendency of men to go mad under such conditions.

The conclusion that Cherne, who does not like it, draws, and that others, who do like it, draw, is a reasonable conclusion from the available data. But it does not follow necessarily that it is the only reasonable conclusion that might be drawn from the data. It is even possible that some additional datum might be discovered, some little thing in the mechanism of the wheels that has not been taken into account; some little thing in the mechanism of the wheels such as men disinclined to submit to this apparently obvious inevitability.

Whether Right or Left or Unhappy, the Hegelian manages to reason inaccurately. One of them is never encountered who does not fall back, at some time or other, upon the analogy that seems to be the foundation of their curious metaphysic.

"If you give a scientist a bone, he can reason the exact kind and proportion and size of animal from an examination of it," they always say. "In the same way, from any given datum it is possible to predict with certainty the eventual synthesis."

The vision of the paleontologist, excavating a fossil tibia and instantly describing the precise species of Sauropoda to which the animal that once used the tibia belonged, held me in a kind of awe throughout my sophomore and junior years in college. It was obvious that all of mankind's reason from Aristotle to Russell could not have been faulty, except their own, but the analogy was so pat that it was difficult not to be impressed. The hearer is dazed into forgetting that there must have once been some Sauropoda of that kind, that other parts had been discovered, that a knowledge of the general theories of anatomy of big lizards would be useful, and that an enormous amount of information lay behind the reasoning. Although the Hegelian logicians use very large words, and have a ruthless disregard for the science of semantics, they will admit for the most part that those who indulge in analogic reasoning are not only bound by their own analogies but are forced to submit to the boredom of having other analogies forced upon them.

One day I observed a very small child playing with a set of building blocks; and ever since that time I have presented to every Hegelian a metaphorical building block and invited him to imagine the precise pattern of arrangement of the entire set. The first time I tried it was upon a fellow-student who was reading Engels and Stirner simultaneously; his cries of bafflement, rage and indignation are still heartwarming to me; they were the pride of my stay at Sewanee, though I do not think that I made any contribution to his recovery, which has resulted in his becoming a good Democrat, with a capital "D," and a man of substance in his community.

If the prophets of doom are reduced to the status of green youths indulging in an evening bull-session, it is because they have invited this pinprick that they will never feel through the impervious integument of their vanity. The prophets of doom have evoked this imaginary future either because they desire it or because, afraid of it and affected by the nervousness of the age, they feel that it menaces them. It is something to be afraid about. It is something to avoid. It is avoidable. The theory of its inevitability is based upon a deterministic fatalism, upon superstition, upon a dilution of Spengler and his cult; there is no evidence that can be utilized through inductive or deductive logic to support a conclusion that it must happen. It could happen, however, if something is not done about it.

This much is recognized by the Southern Agrarians, a group of poets and professors who advocate a return to the plantation system as a defense against industrialization. They are happy escapists who combine a sound sense that much is wrong, that something can be done and must be done, with a desire to retire into the world that Watteau designed and that existed, if at all, among the figurines of shepherds and shepherdesses who inhabited, not the Forest of Arden, but the Victorian mantelpiece in your grandmother's house. The Agrarians have been scourged by stout tongues using a verbal cat-o'-nine-tails, and rather undeservedly. For their criticism is trenchant enough.

Embodied in the foreword of that curiously uneven volume *I'll Take My Stand,* which surveys the present Heaven and Earth, finds them marred, and desires that they pass away and be replaced, is a more profound criticism of the viewpoint of the prophets of doom than has been voiced elsewhere.

> The amenities of life also suffer under the curse of a strictly business or industrial civilization. They consist in such practices as manners, conversation, hospitality, sympathy, family life, romantic love—in the social exchanges which reveal and develop sensibility in human affairs. If religion and the arts are founded on right relations of man-to-nature, these are founded on right relations of man-to-man. . . .
>
> It is strange, of course, that a majority of men anywhere could ever as with one mind become enamored of industrialism: a system that has so little regard for individual wants. There is evidently a kind of thinking that rejoices in setting up a social objective which has no relation to the individual. Men are prepared to sacrifice their private dignity and happiness to an abstract social ideal, and without asking whether the social ideal produces the welfare of any individual whatsoever. But this is

absurd. The responsibility of men is for their own welfare and that of their neighbors; not for the hypothetical welfare of some fabulous creature called society. . . .

If a community, or a section, or a race, or an age, is groaning under industrialism, and well aware that it is an evil dispensation, it must find the way to throw it off. To think that this cannot be done is pusillanimous. And if the whole community, section, race, or age thinks it cannot be done, then it has simply lost its political genius and doomed itself to impotence. . . .*

The simple life advocated by the Agrarians, which is not so simple a life after all, is not what America is seeking. Many Americans are among the potential six million seekers of new bathtubs; and they desire one built on modern lines, where you can test the temperature of the shower and then flip a switch with some certainty that you will neither freeze nor scald.

Moreover, the theories of the Agrarians eventually hinge upon the adoption of some kind of feudalism. For all that it endured longer than any other form of society in the Western world and perhaps worked better than any that was tested before the invention of the steam engine, although it possessed the virtue of harmony to balance the defect of order, feudalism is not what men are seeking today; except the unhappy poets like T. S. Eliot. Feudalism required extraordinary qualities, and there is scarcely one Bayard to a generation, and the master of Trail Lake, William Alexander Percy, sleeps with those ancestors who harried the marches of the Douglas.

The democratic system has its origins in the vivid radicalism of the Hebraic holy writings, especially Jeremiah and the minor prophets. As a practical device in the Western world, it dates

---

* From *I'll Take My Stand:* The South and the Agrarian Tradition, by Twelve Southerners. Copyright, 1930 by Harper & Brothers.

only from the seventeenth century; it is little more than two hundred years old. It appears to be the most practical plan that has been evolved to avoid the inherent evils of dictatorship, oligarchy, and chaos, because, unlike feudalism, it depends upon many men instead of upon a few and substitutes the choice of all the governed for the accident of birth. It has not passed out of the laboratory stage yet; to abandon the experiment at this point would be an admission of futility. The defects in its operation appear to be chargeable mainly to accidental miscalculations in the economic system that accompanies it. To abandon the system, without an effort to make it work, is extravagant in the extreme.

Too many men have spent too much of their lives, of their blood, of their faith in the democratic experiment for us to cast it aside improvidently. That was what my old Methodist preacher meant when he said that "everything you do today affects not only what is going to happen but what already has happened. You can change all the meaning of what has passed. You can even take all the meaning away."

It would be no less than tragedy for mankind to change the meaning of Jeremiah's defiance of the coward king; or to rob Algernon Sydney and Richard Rumbold of their proud words on the scaffold; or to let dust gather on the brave pages of the last three issues of "The Old Cordelier"; or to make pointless Roger Williams' flight through the New England winter; or to render meaningless the singing words that Tom Paine wrote with drumhead for table in the bleakness of Valley Forge. To leach from the fabric of the past all the color put there by the blood of brave men, to leave only the grayness of the gravecloth behind, that is not to be the chosen task of this generation of America. And they can choose.

The task of making democracy work is not easy. Democracy is not an easy way of life. It requires a portion of the energy of every citizen for its success.

The interrelation of economic and political power, constituting government in its true form, is so complex that many of the remedies that must be proposed operate in both these fields. On the other hand, there are instances where the correction of a political ineptitude may correct an economic misery; or, conversely, where removal of artificial restraints upon a given sphere of production may result in improvement in the field of political government.

Basically, what is proposed is that enterprise, both public and private, be permitted the maximum of freedom in America; that sectionalism and colonialism be abandoned; that the competitive system, dealt heavy blows since the transient triumph of Hamilton seven generations ago, be permitted to operate; that government concern itself with its two fundamentals, the protection of citizens in the use of their possessions and in their civil liberties, and the provision for services that can be operated most efficiently upon a collective basis; that decentralization of government, industry, and population be permitted to come about; that opportunity be provided for the expression of the individual personality of all Americans.

When I was a young lawyer in Newnan, I had a favorite client. Jack was a shrewd individual who owned—the verb is meticulously chosen—a wife and eight children, all of whom were employed. Each week he collected the nine pay envelopes. He had, but did not own, a brother named Alfred.

Jack's principal luxury was litigation, in which he was singularly successful. Periodically, he became embroiled with a neighbor, or someone bumped his battered pickup truck. Thereupon he appeared at my office, accompanied by a cloud of witnesses who had observed every minute detail of the event and who had tenacious memories and capacities for vivid description; I do not know what I should have done if he had come accompanied by a jury, also. From the skimmings of the nine pay envelopes and the proceeds of the various actions against those who had wronged him so outrageously, Jack managed a fair degree of prosperity and devoted his entire time to the management of his nine properties until Alfred's condition became a cause for alarm. Alfred prospered less each year, since he was unpossessed of wife or child, disinclined to litigate, and wholly unwilling to work. Finally Jack made an appeal to me to assist him in getting Alfred into the county almshouse. I reluctantly obliged my valued client and after a week of harassing the county commissioners, Alfred was admitted to the comfortable home that Coweta County maintained for its indigent aged at that time. All appeared well and everyone appeared satisfied, for the space of nearly three weeks; and then Jack descended upon me again.

As he approached, I foresaw nothing less than a half-million-dollar damage suit that could readily be settled for not a dime below three hundred dollars in real money. But he had fresh complaints.

"Something's just got to be done about Alfred, Colonel," he said, bestowing upon me the complimentary military title with which all Southern lawyers are invested when admitted to the bar. "Alfred ain't happy."

He must have read the astonishment, for he continued rapidly. "I went out to see Alfred on Sunday, and he was a-settin' on the front porch, just a-rockin' and a-rockin' and looking mis'able. When I tries to cheer him up and says to him: 'Now Alfred, the people fixed you up with a nice room and plenty to eat three meals a day and plenty of firewood and nothing at all to do, and even free chewing tobacco. You ought to be real happy about it 'stead of sittin' and rockin' and lookin' mis'able.' And you know, Colonel, poor Alfred just looked up at me hurtlike and said: 'I know, Jack, but there just ain't any opportunity out here.' "

Even in the exploited South and West where prosperity and opportunity alike have been curtailed by unwise political and economic policies in the past eighty years, even in those regions which the Fascists and the Communists and the prophets of doom appear to agree must be retained only as enormous almshouses, there exists among individuals a desire for opportunity.

The objective of the program, which has been outlined so far only in vague generalities, is the establishment of a social pattern in which men may develop their individualities by the exercise of the maximum of personal liberty in every field. It is a temporary program, designed for today. The institutions of man are unstable. His hold upon earth is tenuous. His place in history has been brief. Any economic system and any political system that is inflexible, or that aims at too distant an objective, or that is presented by its proponents as the ultimate solution of men's relationships with each other, is an economic or political system that will prove unacceptable to people.

Experimentalism and extemporization and improvisation are inevitable in human society. There may be a science of life, but there is an art of living as well.

9

A SIX-POINT PROGRAM

THE ABANDONED WAR plants that dot the landscape of the Pacific Coast States, the Providence Canyon in Georgia that is eating away many cubic yards of earth with each passing year, and the terrific pressure within Chicago's Black Metropolis to find living space and from without to deny it living space, are all indications of the same malady. The people of the United States have won for themselves political independence; their Bill of Rights contains the needed guarantees against interference with civil liberties; but we have failed to make the needed adjustments in our economy in many instances and we have failed to change our public policies as rapidly as economic realities demand. In consequence, we have permitted unknowingly the erection of a private government to duplicate our public government.

To maintain that an industry can exist in Georgia, Oregon, or New Mexico, only as a crude processor and a satellite of some monopoly, indicates a weakness that is not characteristic of the American people. To insist that the Negro has only the choice of living as a sharecropper in depressed areas or of crowding into the filth and clangor of an urban slum is to believe that America has no physical or economic frontier.

If you will stand, as I have stood, upon the mountain top where Tennessee and Georgia meet, and if you will look over the seven Southeastern States that are revealed to you, you will see one physical and economic frontier. If you will go, as I have gone, to the Pacific Northwest and see the almost immeasurable resources of Idaho and Oregon and Washington, you will see another frontier, both physical and economic. And there are others. There is room in America for a multitude of people and there is room in America for opportunity for each of them. It requires planning, but not a planned economy, to give each of them room and to give each an opportunity. It requires some vision, some willingness to admit and correct mistakes, some forebearance, some time, and much work. But it can be done.

There are some definite things that are required to bring about this condition:

The decentralization of industry to permit the development of sections of our country that now have sub-standard incomes, that are underdeveloped, and that are subject to the hazards of a colonial economy.

This decentralization of industry can be met, in part, by utilizing the enormous warplants built by the government in the past five years. In a few instances, it may be necessary to provide the equivalent of temporary subsidies to such industries by the Federal government; in most instances, it will not; where this is necessary, it must be remembered that these subsidies have been granted in the past to existing concerns, either through tariffs or through actual grants, such as those of much of the public domain to the transportation companies.

Decentralization of industry will be accompanied by a decentralization of population to a considerable extent, but since America can sustain a population at least double that which it now holds, this process will be so gradual and so painless as to provide no shock to the economy of any part of the Nation.

With twelve million new housing units needed, it is only intelligent to utilize the opportunity to provide homes for Americans where there is less congestion, and where there will be greater opportunity.

Abandonment of a colonial policy toward the Southern and Western States.

This is not only an economic issue, and thereby a phase of the question of decentralization; it is a political issue as well. In the distribution of Federal assistance to the aged, to highways, to dependent children, to public health, and to vocational rehabilitation, the deliberate policy, mitigated somewhat since the advent of the New Deal in 1933, has been to maintain colonialism and a low standard of living. Federal grants-in-aid have been predicated upon an "ability to match Federal funds," with a result that Southern States must levy crippling taxation or provide inadequate services; usually they split the difference and do both to some extent.

The West, in many ways, is more in chains to the transportation monopoly than the South. Transportation, as it exists in America, is secondarily an economic issue. The transportation companies are invested with many of the powers of government, including the highest one of eminent domain. In no sense are they similar to such private enterprises as a manufacturing plant, or a corner fruit stand, or a grocery store. They have been the instruments of political colonialism in the South and West, as well as agents for the exploitation of these regions.

Establishment and enforcement of a system of free enterprise in the United States.

This will entail the adoption of a policy of smashing monopolies instead of coddling them. The most dangerous single cloud on the horizon of American business, big and little, and the most ominous threat to the stockholder in American business, is the tendency of some lawmakers to sponsor measures such as the Bulwinkle Bill, exempting large segments of enterprise from the operation of the criminal and civil statutes against monopoly. This is the Hitler technique of eating the economic and political authority of a nation in the manner that one devours an artichoke, by peeling off a leaf at a time.

Where corporations are convicted of monopolistic practices, immediate cancellation of their charters and enforced liquidation to preserve the shareholders' rights is the only practical solution.

Where patents are involved in monopolistic conspiracies, the placing of the patents within the "public domain" is the obvious remedy.

Where bureaucratic managerial despotism denies the stockholders their earned dividends, the taxing authority of the Nation must be invoked to compel them to disgorge the stockholders' money.

Increasingly careful distinction must be drawn between corporations that are "free enterprise" and corporations and businesses that partake of the nature of government. This is not a matter of size. The automobile industry appears in general to be operated on a thoroughly competitive basis; it constitutes neither a natural nor a conspiratorial monopoly; it should be left alone. But, again to use transportation or electric power as a comparison, these enterprises depending altogether upon gifts of authority from the government, must be regulated more and more closely in the public interest.

The yardsticks, incidentally, for measuring rail and electric rates are wholly unsound, if these enterprises are to be regarded in any sense as private concerns. They must not be allowed to eat America's cake and keep their own.

Reëstablishment of a decentralized system of government in America.

The basis for decentralization exists in the State governments. If these will demonstrate their capacity for responsibility, the problem of decentralization will be half solved. To meet specific regional problems, such as those of the Missouri Valley and the Northwest, the creation of regional authorities on the pattern of the Tennessee Valley Authority would be indicated, until such time as State governments by experimentation and development of a sense of responsibility are equipped to proceed with such programs through compacts among themselves.

Federal agencies already are experimenting with a certain degree of decentralization. The removal of Rural Electrification Administration and of many units of the Social Security Board from Washington contributed to their efficiency and gave their executives a fresh point of view upon American problems. During the war years, emergency agencies such as War Manpower Commission were compelled to delegate much authority to administrators on the regional level, with excellent results.

It is neither impossible nor improbable that in future years increasing authority will be given regional offices of Federal agencies and that fewer decisions will be made in Washington. Such a policy might correct many delinquencies in the Federal government.

Provision for mutual job-insurance for all the American people.

There is no essential difference between an agreement by the citizens of the country to outlaw unemployment and an agreement by the citizens of a village of three hundred to provide for a community garbage collection system. The difference is in degree, not in principle.

There can be sixty million jobs for Americans now, if we want them. There can always be as many jobs as there are Americans in the normal labor force, if we want them. There can be work for all, at all times. That does not mean that incomes will not be subject to some variation, from year to year and from decade to decade; but it does mean the preservation of a minimum standard of health, comfort and productiveness.

This involves a considerable amount of planning, which should be greatly decentralized. It is not necessary to wait to act until unemployment spreads over the entire Nation and paralyzes the entire economy, as would be inevitable with the planning on a nationwide scale. Proper regional planning would permit quick application of remedies.

Adoption of a foreign policy that will permit America to live at peace.

It is impossible for America to adopt a "world policy." America is not the world. We cannot enforce our ideas, our philosophy, our way of life, upon other men in other nations. But we can adopt a foreign policy that will enable us to live with other nations.

There is a curious notion among those of Left and Right that

America must turn itself into an armed camp, convert its government into some equivalent of a military republic, abandon its traditional policy of absolute civilian control over the armed services based upon the theory that our forces are essentially civilian warriors, outline for ourselves zones of influence, and proceed to apportion to other "great powers" other zones.

It is not necessary to predicate our national foreign policy upon accords that involve the maintenance of undemocratic regimes in countries that have become satellites of other "great powers." It is not necessary for us to indulge in a "mild spree of imperialism." Nor is it necessary for the United States to retire into an isolationism that invites weakness in our dealings with other nations.

It is apparent that we have neglected to think of the possibility that close attention to our domestic problems is a needful prelude to world peace. A disorganized American economy, such as prevailed from 1924 until the New Deal's improvised remedies began to take some effect a full decade later, was one of the principal contributing factors in starting the chain of events that led from the burning of the Reichstag to the invasion of Poland.

The retreat of democratic philosophy in the years since 1900 has been one of the major causes of a disorganized world. There has been a tendency, due perhaps to the desperate effort to mislead the American people into equating the managerial dominance of our economy with our traditional economic and political systems, to disregard moral values in their application to world affairs. Charles Sumner's great speech against the barbarities of the Grant Administration in Haiti would have fallen on deaf ears in these years, as did Augustus O. Bacon's indictment of our misdeeds in the Philippines; even a Beveridge could resort, as early as the turn of the twentieth century, to the cheapest sophistry to defend the horrors of our occupation of Mindanao. Engaged in a shameful quarrel with the Republic of Mexico over the laws of that country, invading Nicaragua on a pretext, supporting a lawless dictator in Cuba, the America of the twenties was in no position to exercise any moral influence in the world.

The abandonment of "power politics" in international affairs should be the first step in the establishment of an American policy that will permit our country to retain the friendship of the people of other nations.

Admittedly, all these suggestions, for improving the economy of America, for adapting our political institutions to changed social conditions, and creating a new frontier both physical and economic, are predicated upon a philosophy of personal responsibility. Most of the tenets of democracy derive from such a philosophy. For some years, the individual has been engaged in a psychological retreat from responsibility and has sought to evade responsibility by identification with the mass. But that psychology of despair is not so pervading in America that it cannot be lifted from the minds of Americans within a decade.

Nor is it claimed for these suggestions that they will make America a Utopia. The world is not finished. There will be much left to be done. There will be many things to be made, such as bathtubs and washing machines and automobiles and children's toys, before there are enough things for every American. There will remain injustices in the economic and social order. There will remain differences in the desires of individuals.

Nor will this system necessarily be workable when, as a result of its operation for a century, the population of America shall have risen to 250,000,000, instead of rising briefly and then becoming static as the Left, Right and prophets of doom insist it must. The America of a quarter billion citizens may have other problems.

Nations can solve no problems. Governments can solve no problems. The placid assumption that a geographical or political unit is wiser than the men in charge of its administration is an error. The collective wisdom of the people, if they are informed, is greater than that of any one man.

Democracy is not a lazy man's form of government. It is easier to be a slave than a free man, if the master is indulgent and the food not too bad. But slavery is an institution that, sooner or later, must cause deterioration of the master.

It is perhaps safer to remain free than to risk the consequences of seeking out a master. Perhaps it is better to be free, even if it involves assuming each for himself a share in the guilt of the Nation. Perhaps it is worth being free, even though the penalty be to see what we have made of our lives.

10

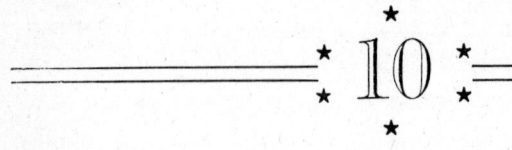

OUR COMMON COUNTRY

THE INADEQUACY OF the American industrial establishment, and the unwisdom of its concentration in a narrow, defenseless area unsupplied with raw materials, was the earliest lesson of the war. The doctrine of scarcity, which has pervaded the thought of American manufacturers since 1920, was reversed sharply. The doctrine of centralization had to be reversed even more sharply, for obvious strategic considerations. Had the Japanese chosen to sneak their carriers into Atlantic waters and attack, suicidally if necessary, the narrow industrial area that lies between Baltimore and New York, crowded without defense against the Atlantic, they could have halted our preparation for the struggle and our aid to Britain and Russia. That they determined instead upon an attack at Pearl Harbor merely demonstrates that the professional military mind all too frequently does not understand that the industrial potential of a nation is the primary consideration in war, unless the blow to be delivered against the enemy's armed forces can result in complete and immediate victory.

Colonial America, the Southern and Western States, was invited not only to assume its share of responsibility for furnishing men for defense, but was called upon unexpectedly to assume a great share of the responsibility of arming them. At the same time, they were asked to provide sixty-five per cent of the minerals needed to win the war, more than half the food for America and our allies, eighty-five per cent of the oil needed, and most of the timber that the country was devouring.

This they did, although the contributions requested were of capital assets such as coal, oil, timber and mineral wealth, to a very high extent. To claim credit for their contribution is unseemly; it was a duty that was performed adequately, courageously, unstintingly, and without ostentation.

Today the most immediate question for America to decide is whether this country is to be one nation, or whether it shall permit an empire-within-the-nation, to turn the greater part of our common country into colonial appendages and make the people of the South and West inmates of gigantic almshouses.

The consequences to the rest of America, the imperial portion with its fourth of the area and almost half of the population, deserve examination; for the great majority of these Americans are unaware of the danger to our common country and of the peril to themselves.

The United States is capable of sustaining a population of not less than 250,000,000 individuals, the fourth largest market in the world reckoned in terms of population, and the largest in the world reckoned in terms of capacity both for production and consumption. Yet there are suggestions that the population should remain static, rather than adopt a policy of decentralization.

The choice exists between the establishment of this divided Country—with the frank recognition of the Fascist implications involved and with the foreknowledge that it must eventuate in a political totalitarianism of some kind within a few generations —and the decentralization of the American economy, with the equal development of all sections of our country and the growth of an agrarian-industrial civilization. The choice exists now; it will be increasingly difficult to retrace our steps if a mistake is made. It will be impossible to recapture the great industrial installations, for the production of synthetic rubber, of light metals, of steel, and for the mass-production of consumer goods, if they are turned over to monopolists and junked. It will be difficult to readjust our economy, if we shift in the near future to the importation of raw materials to maintain the grip of the East on industry.

The soundest prosperity in America is to be found in those States where there is a proper balance between industry and agriculture, and where there is relative completeness in the manufacturing cycle: production of raw material, crude processing and fabricating.

Statistically, ten of our States possess such an economic picture. That these ten States have fifteen per cent of the total area of the Nation, sixteen per cent of the population, fourteen per cent of the manufactures, fourteen per cent of total income, twenty per cent of the national farm population and farm income is largely attributable to the nearness of an urban, industrial population that can absorb agricultural production of the higher-value crops. This permits a sound diversification in farming, although there are other factors in some of the States such as the availability of waterways upon which the products can be shipped to broader markets at low rates.

The level of employment in these States has been higher than in others. They have been exceptionally prosperous, by all applicable indices, throughout the past forty years. They maintain high levels of State services, in general. Their tax structures are well balanced, productive, and seldom regressive, although there is some reliance upon sales taxes.

While the economy of these widely separated ten states of Wisconsin, Maine, New Hampshire, Vermont, Indiana, Minnesota, Iowa, Florida, Missouri and Louisiana is not in every way completely harmonious and devoid of pressures, any comparison between this group of States and other States of the Union suggests that they are less susceptible to depression, better able to adjust themselves to ordinary ups-and-downs of business, and more prosperous in the sense that there is a generally wider level of decent living standards than is general in the country.

That the industrial areas, even including Ohio and Michigan, which are partly exempt from some of the maladies of the East, confront desperate situations when depressions occur, that their unbalanced economy accelerates the depression, and that the distribution of total income in those areas among the individuals who make up the total of citizens is frequently strikingly inequitable, is obvious to any American who has visited them.

That the underpopulated and underdeveloped West, and the underdeveloped South with a large but not increasing population, because of migration, could become new frontiers for development and could sustain many new industries and increased populations is also apparent.

The Western States, seventeen in number, have more than three fifths of the land area of the continental United States and only a little more than a fifth of the population. Though they produce half of the mineral wealth of the country, though they fare best in the Nation in the ratio of farm income to farm population, the Western States do not get quite their share, per capita, of the national income because they are permitted but half their share of manufacturing.

The Southern States, which, with the exceptions of Florida and Louisiana are underdeveloped, also are deprived of their share of manufactures, and in addition have low farm incomes. The South has thirty-nine per cent of the Nation's farmers within the territory described as "underdeveloped" in the report of the historic McCarran Committee, which investigated the centralization of American industry; but the share of the national farm income for these Southern farmers is only twenty per cent, or approximately one-half their portion.

The key to American prosperity obviously is to raise the per capita incomes of the Southern farmers and workers to the national level, and to permit the West to attract new population. Decentralization is the method by which a permanent prosperity for the country can be obtained.

But there are other aspects of the problem than that of economics.

There is currently a demand that America be made and kept strong enough to repel any armed attack. A glance at the industrial map discloses the ridiculous strategic weakness of the country. Although the greatest coal reserves of the country are located in the Western States, these are wholly undeveloped and would not be available in emergency. Except for the Michigan and Ohio areas, the industrial establishment occupies a narrow strip along the Atlantic seaboard, smaller in total area than the State of Kansas, intensely vulnerable to attack from the air. Indeed, if the realities of national defense are considered, it would seem that, under existing conditions, the principal need is for an overpowering naval and air force, since the conditions do not exist under which an army could trade distance for lives and provide any defense whatsoever for the concentrated industries of the Country. The atomic bomb intensifies this peril.

Decentralization of industry would provide the country with a defense problem of much smaller proportion.

There are sociological aspects to be considered.

The migratory workers, driven from their homes in the South, in the Dust Bowl and elsewhere by the impoverishment of the land, essentially remained agricultural workers until the phenomenal demands for manpower by the war industries. These migratory workers were the products of the bad use of land; they were the victims of single-crop agriculture, of the turning to farming of grazing land, of erosion through soil-mining.

The country now faces the creation of a new class of migratory workers, for whom we might adopt the name "industrial Okeies." Potentially, there are three million of these in the Western States, the seventeen States that are most underdeveloped and underpopulated.

In 1939, when the first expansion of Western industry was undertaken as part of the national program of preparedness and of making America the arsenal of democracy, the part of the population of these seventeen States living in the areas that were chosen for industrialization accounted for forty-one per cent of the entire population of these States. Eleven million people lived in these urban areas. Within four years this had increased by more than a fourth, to a total of 14,000,000 Americans living in the thirty-nine war production centers.

That not all of these individuals were able to transfer their families to their new places of employment is evidenced by the fact that, while three million citizens moved to these urban industrial areas, 1,436,000 of them were workers. Allowance must be made for the element of youth in the group and for other factors, including the tendency of many workers to leave larger children with relatives back home when they went to these communities. If the families were assembled as units, it is probable that slightly more than four million people were affected by the trek of these new pioneers, who are seeking to build a new industrial West.

Many of these people came from agricultural areas within the Western States. Some were migratory workers who ranged about the whole Nation, and who selected the Western industrial areas as sites of their transfer from the harsh life of moving seasonally from citrus to beans to tomatoes to cotton. Some were highly skilled workers imported for employment requiring their special abilities.

All of them, however, whatever their origin, face the same threat of dispossession and unemployment, if the industrialization of the West is thwarted. The money that they have saved will not go into new homes or into new business enterprises. Instead, they must invest them in jalopies and join the agricultural migrants in rushing from one end of America to the other in search of employment. Those who oppose the decentralization of industry and the development of the West are asking Americans to condemn three million of the citizens of our common country to this kind of life; a life in which they will move, presumably, from auto to refrigerator to steel to glass, as their agricultural counterparts move from crop to crop.

The danger to the three million Western workers is more acute and more serious than that to the one million Southern workers who entered war production areas. The Southern workers were drawn, to a larger extent, from the ranks of those employed in service employments, small manufacturing plants that closed during the war, and farm families that retained their agricultural holdings. The Southern industrial workers also were saved, to some extent, by their own knowledge that many of the industries which they were entering were duration-only in their nature and will be saved from the psychological shock that must accompany the Western worker's discovery that the steel plants, the light metal plants, and the other enterprises of the West can be closed in the interest of Eastern industrialists.

The Western states are capable of supporting a population of not less than one hundred million, with proper and gradual development. Chemurgical discovery and agricultural experiment may make it possible for this estimate to be doubled. But the figure belongs to the future, and our concern is with the people living there today. Attention should focus on the three million, upon their possible fate and their possible contribution to the West and to the Nation.

If the Western industrial establishment is maintained and expanded to provide employment for these workers, another three million people will be drawn to the West to assume the jobs in service enterprises, small businesses, distribution, and the like.

This will mean a near-by market, increased by six million

persons, for the agricultural products of the Western farmer, which, in turn, will require that the farm population be increased by a half-million at least.

The permanent increase of Western population by six and a half million citizens will mean a demand for more housing in that area, and for more consumer goods. It would mean a new prosperity for the West, and a greater prosperity for every part of America.

The case for the industrialization of the West is more insistent and more dramatic than that for the South, simply because the West has such an enormous area, greater than that of all Europe outside Russia, and such a scant population. The possibilities of trade with the Orient catch the imagination of anyone who sees the waters of the Pacific as a merchant's route instead of an avenue to war. The courage and gaiety of the people of the West, the beauty of their country, the wealth of their forests and mines and farms, these are assets that belong to all America for use and enjoyment and not for exploitation.

To any American who will spread a map of the Western hemisphere upon a table, or lean over a globe and examine our half of the world, the relationship of the Southern States to Latin America becomes even more obvious than the relationship of the Pacific States with the Orient. To by-pass the magnificent harbors of Tampa, New Orleans, Mobile, Jacksonville, Brunswick, Savannah and Wilmington and sail some thousand miles northward to discharge their cargoes and reload their ships would be folly for those engaged in South American trade.

When we examine the items that the United States will ship to South America, the folly appears greater. They will include textiles, aluminum products, steel products, and a wide variety of consumer goods based on plastics. The imports that America must absorb will include wool, lumber, copper, guano, edible oils, and rubber.

Now examine briefly the picture of Southern resources. It produces the Nation's cotton; it has a monopoly on the bauxite of the country, from which aluminum is made; it produces most of the synthetic rubber of America and most of the tire fabric; it has ample coal and iron ores to sustain a tremendous steel industry.

But the South is restrained from manufacturing fine textiles for the American market, and hence is unprepared to provide them to South America. The South does not fabricate many aluminum products. The South makes no tires. The South's steel industry is an appendage to that of the East, with which it does not compete.

For example, it would be logical for the woolen mills of the Nation to select new sites. This will be easy, because even the highest of protective tariffs will not save the industry as it now exists, with ancient and inefficient plants that cannot compete with those of Europe even on our own protected market. The entire woolen industry must be rebuilt.

In making a choice of sites, it would be intelligent to locate approximately two thirds of the new plants in the South and the rest in the West, where domestic raw materials are available. The marginal and salvageable plants of the East could provide about half the consumer requirements of that area, permitting an exchange with the South and West of manufactured goods for manufactured goods, instead of exchanging manufactures for raw materials as now is the case.

Decentralization has been the subject of periodic study in the country and of debate in Congress for many years. The most serious and sincere effort to visualize its relationship to reconversion and postwar prosperity has been that made by the McCarran Committee of the Senate, which enjoyed the somewhat difficult name of "The Special Committee to Investigate the Centralization of Heavy Industry in the United States."

The findings of this committee, backed by voluminous reports and illustrated by maps and graphic charts, can be summarized in a few paragraphs written by its Chairman:

> There are a lot of people these days who are paying loud lip-service to the cause of our free enterprise system. But our free enterprise system requires certain conditions and not loud protests to remain healthy. It creates more wealth faster than any other economic system the world has ever known. The profit incentive is the secret of our phenomenal economic system. But profits become a serious problem if they cannot be reinvested and put to the business of creating more wealth. Accumulating savings become another burden if investment opportunities are lacking. Our profit system, as any citizen can see, if it is to be healthy, must at all times maintain a margin of new enterprises for transforming profits into capital that is adequate to the rate of profit and the volume of accumulating savings.
>
> The usual distinction between small and big business is, perhaps, too sentimental. A more realistic distinction would place the emphasis not so much on small business, because it is small, but upon independent enterprises and upon new enterprises, new opportunities, new developments, and upon the encouragement and protection of all these. Profits and savings must find their way back as capital in the business of production. This is our major problem. All other problems are secondary.
>
> As can be seen, the impulse to centralization is basically anti-capitalist. It places the interests of a small group above the obvi-

ous needs of the whole economic system. In the end, as we have seen it happen in Europe, the apostles of centralization go from economic pressure, to freeze out competition in advance, to the more drastic step of controlling the apparatus of government in order to make their power more complete. The result is a system more feudal than capitalistic, with emphasis upon control rather than freedom, authoritarian rather than rational government. Sooner or later the whole order collapses, and those who forgot that they were only a part of a system find that they have in their blindness caused the collapse and ruin of the whole economy and the whole social order.

The social order that Americans dreamed of always has been an agrarian-industrial society, in which individual independence can exist.

There are some units of manufacture, perhaps, that do not lend themselves to this process. The mass production industries, to a limited extent, must be of such size as to provide the maximum of efficiency. Only an individual thoroughly conversant with the specific problems of an industry and of a given plant can say at what precise point the maximum of efficiency is reached.

However, the mass production industries already are turning toward decentralization. The automobile industry, for example, is spreading its parts production over the Nation, although confining it largely to those areas which are within the transportation zone arrogantly designated as "Official Territory" to distinguish it from the Southern and Western colonies. Only the assembling features of mass production require any considerable degree of concentration, and engineers have suggested that this may be a matter partly of superstition. Many industrialists, oddly enough largely from the ranks of those enterprises where there remains a high degree of owner-management, have advocated greater decentralization, plants of smaller size, greater autonomy for local management within the plant.

The conclusion then becomes inescapable that the objection to decentralization arises from an urge to obtain and exercise power. Obviously the industrialist whose workers are huddled together in congested urban areas is not bothered by the threat of individualism among them, such as would arise if his workers were members of urban-rural families, who might at any moment retire to the farm. Obviously the other extreme, where the circle meets, the occupant of the extreme Left position, sees that the developing tensions within the congested industrial area invite a turning to his doctrines.

A high degree of decentralization, a closer relationship between agrarian and industrial areas, would mean smaller cities and, very likely, larger small towns. It would mean the creation of a propertied middle class of skilled workers, persons employed in the service enterprises, professional men, and small businessmen.

It would mean the economy of producing many items of consumer goods much nearer the consumer, with the incident economy of avoiding transportation costs. On the other hand, oddly enough, it would mean a certain amount of specialization of industries within regions. Because of the existence of a well-trained labor force in the existing industrial areas, because of the existing facilities, much of the fabrication of finished goods, where raw materials were available within the area or where their transportation is not too costly, would continue there for many decades. But the new plastics industry, the new industries built on pulpwood, the bulk of the textile industry, would tend to move South, while the West could turn first to supplying its own growing population and then toward trade with the Orient which is hungry for American products.

Most of all, it would mean that Americans would have homes. The creation of a large homeless population, without roots in the earth, is dangerous. There seems to be, among all men, a longing for some space that is home. The faces of the uprooted may be masked with gaiety, but underneath can be discerned the lines of care and tension and uncertainty.

As the cities move toward the farm, the tendency of the rural population to desert the farm in desperation would end. For the farmer there would then exist the incentive of good profits and comfortable living on his own acreage, and of easy touch with friends in the urban areas. For his children there would exist the choice between farm or industry, without the necessity of abandoning all ties of home. For America, it would mean a national self-sufficiency that would curb any tendency toward imperialism and that would invite trade with other nations upon the rational basis of fair exchange of surpluses.

The only other course is a greater centralization, a greater crowding of populations into the already congested Eastern industrial areas, a gradual thinning out of population in the South and the leaving of the West both underpopulated and undeveloped. From this can evolve nothing but a disintegration of the American democratic system into some form of totalitarianism, both economic and political.

It is not necessary to accept this choice, nor is it necessary to retreat into the fantasy of those who would like to see an Arcadian simplicity where each man holds the handle of his own plow and each woman spins the yarn for her own frock. Development of our great remaining frontiers, the South and the West, can permit us to reshape America to the measure of our dreams.

We can preserve the dignity and the self-respect of the individual. We can unite our Nation in a spirit of justice that knows no sectional boundaries. We can clear the way for the production of $170 billion in goods and services annually, so that a high standard of living can be maintained even after the taxgatherer takes enough to provide for the retirement of our national debt. We can find ourselves engaged in friendly, profitable commerce with the other nations of the world.

There are those who sneer at the ideal of every man retiring in the twilight to the security of his own home, to the peace and the beauty of his own vine and fig tree. There are those who find that picture of America quaint and nostalgic, but too difficult to be worth the attainment. There are others who profess the belief that man is a predatory beast, without stimulus save the hunger for the flesh of his kind; and these see a world in which the only coöperation is the coöperation of the wolf pack, howling at night in the wilderness, snapping and snarling at each other, at war with all, a killer destined to be killed.

It is not true. With patience, men can build what they can envision on the dimly seen shore of their aspirations. With sweat and anguish, with heartache and toil, men can search out for themselves the truth that will make them free, and, having made them free, will keep them free.

11

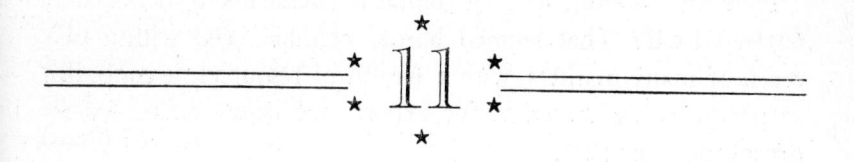

OUR COLONIAL REGIONS

SOMEHOW, LOOKING AT Ducktown and at Providence Canyon, at the washed and gully-cut hillsides, at the thin top soil, you get the feeling that the Southern States have been exporting the very earth. There is something terrifying in that thought; something even more alarming than the thought of exporting its people; something more frightening even than the hunger of a sharecropper's family. For the good earth, with its rich smells, is man's home and somehow sacred; and the thought of the bleeding hills and the red rivers is more pitiful than anything else in the picture of the South.

Only exploitation could account for the enormous waste of human and natural resources. Why were not these people engaged in more intelligent farm operations, planting crops that would not loot the earth of the stored richness that they were obligated as men to leave as a legacy to their children's children? Why were not many of them engaged in industrial employments? Why must they go to Dayton and Detroit and Danbury and Dedham to find employment for their native intelligence and their hard-acquired skills?

Had the South, with a fantastic masochism, deliberately fettered itself? That seemed hardly credible. Yet, within easy reach of many markets, with a wealth of resources, it continued to produce raw materials for export and heavy goods for reprocessing elsewhere.

The South was not alone. The States of the West have been ruthlessly robbed of their reserves of mineral wealth and remain retarded in their development from the same basic cause. The poverty of the South and the sparseness of population in the rich Mountain States and elsewhere west of the Mississippi are related and attributable to the same basic reason.

It is only a slight oversimplification to make this assertion. I am well aware that there has been an abuse of Southern farmlands by reckless owners, generations ago and today, bent upon extracting every immediate dollar from the soil. I know that there are enormous obstacles of nature to be overcome in the West. I know that distances are great in both sections. I know that natural waterways are inadequate; that the West is new, with only a century of history behind it; that the South has endured the impact of two desolating wars on its own soil. But these are excuses and not explanations.

Looking further and deeper you see that the Southern and Western regions have been kept as colonial appendages; that the tall firs of the Pacific Northwest have been cut as ruthlessly as the yellow pine of Georgia and Mississippi; that absentee control, and to a considerable extent absentee ownership, have made three fourths of America, inhabited by half our citizens, into areas in which rural and urban slums are as commonplace as stump-scarred hills.

Southern and Western industries are prohibited from marketing their products in competition with manufacturers in the industrialized East.

In no perverse spirit did the people of the South and West forge these shackles. They were fashioned outside our jurisdiction.

The shackles remained because of the failure of a timid, reactionary Interstate Commerce Commission with its maddening jargon and ox-cart methods for handling transportation problems in an age attuned to jet propulsion. Before this lethargic body the Southern Governors Conference, and others, had been parties for years to proceedings for the adjudication of freight rates. Literally, the case of the South and the West against high and discriminatory freight rates was resting before the Interstate Commerce Commission, interred but not dead.

The freight rate case of the South, stripped of the mysteries of transportation gibberish, is this: The rates on manufactured goods moving within Eastern Territory, lying roughly east of the Mississippi River and north of the Ohio and Potomac rivers but including part of Virginia, are much more favorable than rates on similar products moving by rail within Southern Territory, located south of Eastern territory and east of the Mississippi, or from Southern Territory to Eastern Territory.

The situation has been justified by a bit of economic folklore in which the South is said to have "less favorable transportation conditions," despite a number of cost studies made by the Interstate Commerce Commission's staff over a period of years which disclose that the cost of rendering rail transportation service is actually cheaper in the South than in any other region.

Propped up by such absurdly vague generalizations, the freight rate barrier has continued as a retarding influence on the location of new industries in Georgia. Relatively few manufacturers will assume the burden of paying a tariff in the form of the higher freight rates incident to locating in Georgia when locations having more favorable rates are available within Eastern Territory near its rich markets.

The story is told by the figures of the United States Department of Commerce, which disclose that Eastern Territory in peace time had over one half the population and nearly three fourths of the value of manufactures, while the South had nearly eighteen per cent of the population but less than nine per cent of the manufactures!

One excuse for failure to adjust the freight rate pattern is that long-established economic practices may be disrupted and changes, if any, must be made slowly. Interpreted, this means that the heavily industrialized East does not want additional competition from the South and West and that the Interstate Commerce Commission is not courageous enough to change the rate situation to allow such competition to arise. As a consequence, the consumers in the East, as well as those in the rest of the Nation, pay more for manufactured products because the industrial development of the South and West is stifled.

As has been pointed out by Frank Barton, economist in the Executive Office of the President, Bureau of the Budget, this concentration of industry has caused an increase in the amount of transportation service paid for by the Southern farmer.

The freight rate structure has aided concentration of manufacturing production, with its accompanying masses of population, in the Northeast. On the other hand, much of the food and other raw material production is centered in the South and West.

Long hauls by rail are necessary to move these agricultural products to the Northeast, requiring that enormous amounts of transportation service must be paid for by the farmer in lower prices for his product. The more transportation he buys, the less is his profit.

With a freight rate structure that would give equal encouragement to industry in the South (and again the West is included), industry would flourish, and a greater market for farm products could be created within these regions, nearer of course to the source of many of the raw commodities. The amount of transportation service the farmer would purchase to get his products to market could thereby be cut down and his profit increased.

The Interstate Commerce Commission missed its opportunity. The repeal of the Neutrality Act began the change in the national economy, which was greatly augmented with the entry of the United States into the war. New plants for war production sprang up in every section of the country. Under these conditions, the Interstate Commerce Commission could have introduced a rate structure which would not only have facilitated the movement of men and materials for war, but would have rendered equity to the South and West and would have set the stage for successful reconversion. Instead they sat and waited—for what I do not know. The Nation has paid heavily for this inaction in excessive rates for the transportation of war materials and equipment.

It was apparent that with the end of the war, the same discriminatory rate pattern would be in existence to stifle Georgia and the South if we awaited action by the Interstate Commerce Commission. At this point I might say that many of my Southern friends have for years wagged their heads and stated that we could depend on the Interstate Commerce Commission to give us relief. We could not wait. The prospect for return to peace with the old rate structure was imminent. Under the Constitution of the United States surely there must be a way to obtain fair treatment for Georgia other than waiting interminably for an outmoded Interstate Commerce Commission to creak to a decision.

The question naturally arose as to why competition between the various forms of transportation does not do more to give Georgia justice in freight rates. We know that regulated competition between individual railroads and between railroads and other forms of transport is a basic concept in our economic system of free enterprise. With this in mind we examined the procedure used by the carriers that supposedly conformed to the law by which railroads are directed to establish reasonable through rates with other such carriers.

What we found was amazing. Many people have the idea that the Interstate Commerce Commission fixes railroad freight rates and that there is no room for the operation of private rate-making machinery. Such is not the case. The law provides that each railroad shall initiate its own rates and shall file them with the Commission. The law further provides that, when rates are filed with the Commission, they shall become effective, without any action by the Commission, at the end of thirty days from and after their filing unless, within the thirty days, some interested party goes to the Commission and asks for and obtains a suspension of the rates so filed or unless the Commission, on its own motion, brings about a suspension.

The record shows that more than ninety per cent of rates filed with the Commission become effective without any suspension, investigation, or other action by the Commission.

It is here the railroads find room for full play and activity of their private rate-making machinery, which expends its energies in the direction of causing the railroads to agree on which rates shall be filed with the Commission and which ones shall not be so filed.

These organizations of railroads for consideration of questions as to whether railroads shall or shall not file rates with the Commission are complicated and far flung; they consider and decide many questions which Congress delegated to the Commission and to the Commission alone for decision; they appease certain shippers to the end that there will be no protest to the Commission when the rates are actually filed; and these shippers and their paid lawyers often reciprocate by defending the rate-making machinery and the rates made by it; and these appeased shippers and their lawyers often join with the railroads in belittling all efforts to break up the conspiracies.

For example we have witnessed large shippers and their commerce attorneys testifying before the Commission in favor of general increases in a "permissive" way—that is, the Commission has entered orders to the effect that the railroads might increase rates in certain amounts if they so desired.

Then we have seen the railroads, under these "permissive" orders, fail to increase rates on commodities in which those particular favorable witnesses were interested. There are other ways in which certain shippers and their practitioners are favored and appeased.

The result of such doings is that when the rate-making machinery is under attack the railroads defend it on the ground that the shippers favor it, and they produce shipper witnesses who do defend it. So, there is tremendous room for the private rate-making machinery, but it comes into head-on conflict with the antitrust laws.

As a part of the pattern of this unlawful private rate-making machinery there exists what may be termed "economic coercion." This coercion is a subtle thing. It is something apart from physical threats against a railroad which is friendly to the South. Rather it involves meetings of railroads at times and at places, where and when it is simply understood that, under the peculiar circumstances, it would not be good business for a Southern railroad to fail or refuse to conform to the wishes of those present; economic sanctions, such as diversion of business, can be applied too readily.

We want economic coercion, or any other type of coercion, lifted from the railroads of the South.

In his book, *Justice In Transportation,* Arne C. Wiprud, Special Assistant to the Attorney General, outlines in detail the organizational setup and operation of this private rate-making machinery, which he characterizes as "the grand conspiracy in the transportation industries to fix the rates charged for public transportation in this country." He adds, "In no other field of private or semi-private enterprise has such a vast scheme of price-fixing been so boldly conceived and executed. The over-all conspiracy has succeeded in eliminating virtually all competition in the making of rates within and between all forms of transportation. The ability to manipulate prices arbitrarily is the essence of monopoly power. Such manipulation of rates is being exercised by all branches of the transportation industry. The transportation industries have in effect achieved monopoly prices. . . ."*

Further he states, "Whatever the origins of these rate inequalities and discriminations may be, however determined the transportation industry may be to perpetuate them through its private rate-making machinery, however reluctant the Interstate Commerce Commission may be to revise its ancient formulas, it is now clear that these and other barriers to the full use of our national resources and the development of the balanced regional economies must be struck down. There is no other way to achieve an expanding national economy, the prerequisite to all economic improvement for the people in the postwar world."

President Truman, when Vice-President, characterized Mr. Wiprud's book as "a penetrating analysis of transportation problems. It should be read by everyone." Since his elevation to the Presidency he has let it be known that his views on the book remain unchanged.

The monopolistic setup is headed by the Association of American Railroads, with headquarters in Washington, D. C. We discovered that before a Southern railroad can change a rate, the proposal for change must be submitted to the Southern Freight Association in Atlanta for approval by other carriers, whether they actually handle the traffic involved or not.

John J. Pelley, President of the Association of American Railroads, with banking and financial power and connections behind

* From *Justice in Transportation*, by Arne C. Wiprud, published by Ziff-Davis Publishing Company, 1945.

him, ordered, or suggested to, all railroads in the United States that they make rates—not in the interest of any region or individual railroad—but in the interest of the American railroads as a whole.

This "suggestion" was carried out according to public records: (1) A. F. Cleveland, Vice-President of the Association of American Railroads, has stated in writing that the Association's recommendations have been carried out, and (2) the procedural technique of the private rate-making machinery was made to conform to this suggestion. This was a simple and innocent-looking change in procedure. Fundamentally, the conspiratorial setup is that no Southern railroad will change its rates by filing new tariffs with the Interstate Commerce Commission unless and until the matter has been considered and has been approved by rate-making bureaus and organizations composed of representatives of nearly all important Southern railroads.

The wording of the papers setting up these bureaus and associations is to the effect that the Chairman of the Southern Freight Association, who is employed by all Southern roads collectively, or any Southern railroad shall have the power to appeal all rate proposals, including emergency proposals by individual Southern roads, from one rate committee in the South to another all the way up to the Southeastern Presidents' Conference, an organization composed of the larger Southern railroads, with publication of the proposed change held in abeyance while all these appeals are going on. This procedure is obviously for the purpose of hampering and slowing down the activities of the individual railroad in order to allow subtle economic coercion to be applied.

If the proposal survives this conspiratorial and monopolistic price-fixing technique, then the Northern railroads, if they do not like the proposal, can bring the matter before the Association of American Railroads, where the Southern proponent can be asked to arbitrate under circumstances such that in most instances he will yield to the wishes of the Association.

Under such a monopolistic and conspiratorial scheme, it is reasonably clear that the railroads' pretension of deep concern about fixing a rate structure which is favorable to the South, will bear the closest scrutiny; especially in view of the fact that at least two Midwestern railroad presidents have testified before a U. S. Senate Committee that the Association is dominated by the Pennsylvania Railroad and its railroad friends. These two railroad presidents testified that this domination was injurious to Midwestern roads.

It is significant that all power in the Association of American Railroads is lodged in its Board of Directors, which is composed of six railroad presidents from the North, seven from the West and only four from the South.

This board has jurisdiction over any railroad question or controversy, subject only to the limitation that any member of the board may declare a question to be "controversial." When such a declaration is made the board does not take jurisdiction unless three fourths of the members of the board vote in favor of taking jurisdiction. It should be remembered that this board of seventeen men sits as the repository of the economic destiny of more than three hundred railroads.

Where does this leave the South in view of the testimony showing domination of the board by the Pennsylvania Railroad and its friends?

This is the conspiracy; this is the price-fixing machinery. This is the thing over which the Interstate Commerce Commission has no jurisdiction.

Let us follow a proposal through the conspiracy and machinery and see how it works.

Assume that Southern industry wants a reduction in the rates on an important commodity moving from the South to the North. Assume that some Southern railroad is friendly to the proposal and files it with a Southern rate bureau. It winds its tortuous way through these organizations until it is agreed upon by the Southern railroads acting in concert. The Southern railroads then try to get the Northern roads to join in making the through rate, but they refuse to join after considering the matter in a meeting where they also act in concert and not individually. The proposal then reaches the interterritorial rate bureau, headquartered in Atlanta, known as the Joint Conference of Contact Committees, which is a national convention of rate bureaus. In this convention there are delegates from the Northern, Western and Southern railroads who try to work out interterritorial rate questions. The Northern roads act in concert in this convention; and the Western and Southern roads do the same. Our proposal is brought before and discussed in this convention.

The proposal is one to reduce the rate on this commodity on its movement from Southern to Eastern Territory to the same level obtaining between points in the North. The Northern railroads, acting jointly, refuse to join the Southern roads in establishing the rate. In other words, the Northern roads side with the Northern businessmen, who do not want the Southern product to come into competition with theirs in the North.

One Southern railroad quits the conspiracy and announces that it is going to establish the rate independently, notwithstanding the joint action in turning it down; whereupon certain roads in the North and certain roads in the South quit the conspiracy also and signify an intention to act independently in joining with the Southern independent in establishing the rate.

The Northern railroad rate bureau or conspiracy then appeals to the Association of American Railroads, which requests all concerned to hold up publication of the reduced rate pending efforts by the Association to "compose differences" between the Northern and Southern roads. The Association, having failed to kill the proposal altogether, begins an active campaign to compromise the matter.

Finally, the Southern independent agrees to abandon its original proposal to bring about parity and to compromise, in accordance with the Association's suggestion, by fixing the rate on a basis ten per cent above the Northern level. The application of economic coercion is apparent.

The activities of the Association of American Railroads in the matter extend over a long period of time and include meetings in different parts of the United States and the building up of a file of disheartening proportions during all of which time the independent Southern road holds in abeyance its independent action in reducing the rate. Finally, the independent never does publish the rate wanted by Southern business, which was one on the same level as prevailed between points in the North, but instead a rate ten per cent higher than desired and ten per cent higher than the Northern level.

After the controversy was all over, the representative of the Association who handled this matter, boasted in writing:

> The Southern and Southwestern lines undertook to reduce their rates on paper and pulpboard into the northern markets. This

would have probably resulted in a reduction in the rates on the entire paper group and paperboard group from the north. This controversy was finally adjusted by increasing by ten percent the level of the rates which had been proposed by the Southern and Southwestern carriers.

Therefore, we see that there is a conflict between contentions of Southern railroads that they adjust rates to promote Southern industry and the actual facts presented in the day-by-day operations of these price-fixers. This is important since the Interstate Commerce Act provides that each railroad shall make its own rates.

It is not necessary for us to guess about the answer to the question as to whether the Northern railroads' private rate-making machinery, known to the people of Georgia as the "Northern Railroad Conspiracy," expends its energies in keeping Southern products out of the competitive Northern markets of the Northern businessmen.

The "Northern Railroad Conspiracy," which is known to the railroads by the significant term "Official Lines," stated in a written brief filed with the Interstate Commerce Commission in 1935, that:

> Official Lines, therefore, are in duty bound to protect the geographical or other natural advantages possessed by shippers or producers on their lines, and as a matter of justice and equity, they may not be required to join in such low bases of interterritorial rates as to nullify or neutralize these natural advantages.

The Southern railroads, despite their present protestations, recognize and know all about the barriers which the Northern railroads have placed in the northward movement of Southern products. We know this because E. R. Oliver, a Vice-President of the Southern Railway, stated in an Interstate Commerce Commission hearing, in 1931 at Birmingham, Alabama:

> The new policy of those connections is to build a rate wall at the Ohio and Potomac Rivers which will prevent or greatly curtail the movement of southern products into Official Territory.

It is against such illegal restraint of the rail lines which should, in the American tradition, compete, that the State of Georgia is asking relief. No favors are requested, only observance of the statutes and Constitution of the United States.

In addition to the paper and pulpboard rates mentioned, it is a matter of public record that the Association of American Railroads has, in its own reports, stated that it has been successful in "persuading" the rail lines of the Nation to increase freight rates, or refrain from rate reductions, on cotton, vegetable oils, rice, grain, furniture, caustic soda products, and citrus fruits, to name a few products moving from the South.

With this evidence of violation of the antitrust laws, Georgia asked the Supreme Court of the United States to take original jurisdiction over the case. In the complaint it was stated that the carriers had conspired, through their private rate-fixing machinery, to fix arbitrary and noncompetitive freight rates for transportation by railroad to and from Georgia in contravention of the antitrust laws. Georgia asked for an injunction that would dissolve the conspiracy and free the individual carrier from restraint in exercise of its managerial discretion. In short, the State asked that the railroads function as free enterprise and not as a Fascist cartel. Article III of the Constitution of the United States provides that the Supreme Court may take jurisdiction when the disagreement is between a State and citizens of another

State. The defendant railroads were citizens of States other than Georgia.

In the suit which I had brought as Attorney General of Georgia to recover damages under the antitrust laws when there had been conspiracy in the sale of road-building material to the State, the Supreme Court decided that the State of Georgia could bring such a suit, and held in our favor. Also, the Court had much earlier decided that a copper company, located in Tennessee, could be enjoined on behalf of the State of Georgia from allowing poisonous gas escaping from a plant to denude the land of Georgia of its vegetation. The State was held to have an interest "independent of and behind the titles of its citizens." Thus, I thought we were on sound ground legally in asking the Supreme Court to consider a case involving a conspiracy to fix freight rates that keeps the economy of Georgia in a state of arrested development. Later events proved this view correct.

The railroads were highly amused by what they considered no more than a petty annoyance. The Court would never sustain our action, they thought. They laughed from their musty offices, well-fortified with years of Interstate Commerce Commission understanding and coöperation. "Everyone knows," the rail executives in essence have said, "that we are the most completely regulated industry in the country. Likewise, everyone knows that the Interstate Commerce Commission has complete control over regulation of our rates." They apparently overlooked the Supreme Court holdings, and the Interstate Commerce Commission's own Pontius Pilate pronouncement that it could not consider conspiracies in rate-making.

Others in the South joined in this defeatist attitude. Apparently long years of waiting for Interstate Commerce Commission action had become a habit. The thought of seeking redress elsewhere seemed out of the question.

Too, there are legal practitioners who make a living by appearing before the Interstate Commerce Commission. Fear of the Commission's displeasure or the thought that settling problems too expeditiously might remove a source of publicity or income, influenced some. At any rate my fellow-Governors of the South allowed Georgia to pursue the case alone.

The case was set down for oral argument before the Supreme Court to allow the Court to decide whether it would hear our case; that is, take the original jurisdiction the State asked for. Strangely enough there was want of harmony among the railroad lawyers as to whether the Court could take jurisdiction. The representatives of the Eastern railroads agreed that jurisdiction could be taken; the Southern roads denied it on highly technical grounds. The main point of the railroads was that a conspiracy to fix rates, if such existed, could not harm the citizens of Georgia and that damage could result only from the rates flowing from the conspiracy. Further it was argued that Georgia had not exhausted its remedies before the Interstate Commerce Commission concerning these rates as provided by law, and that until this was done, the case should not be considered by the Supreme Court.

The railroads' strategy here is as transparent as the windows in a railroad president's private car. If the State of Georgia could be forced to go to the Interstate Commerce Commission in an effort to have the existing rates declared unlawful, our chances of getting the conspiracy among the railroads dissolved would, in view of the Commission's refusal to consider conspiracies, go down to considerably below zero.

I argued for the State of Georgia that this was not a freight rate case; that we were not asking the Supreme Court to consider rates; and that we wanted the Court to grant an injunction to make the rail lines cease conspiring against Georgia and the South. Upon the dissolution of the conspiracy, each railroad could initiate its own rates in compliance with the law, free from the restraining hands of monopoly.

The railroads had apparently been outmanœuvered. Their attorneys thought we were going to present a freight rate case to the Supreme Court on which we would receive a refusal. This may be attributed to their underestimating the opposition and to their almost fanatical belief that almost everything even remotely related to freight rates could be considered by the Interstate Commerce Commission and by that body only.

Several months passed before the Supreme Court announced its decision. At one of its Monday sessions, as customarily held, a majority of the Court gave the railroads the shock of their corporate lives by upholding the State of Georgia in stating that the Court would accept jurisdiction over our case. There was also, I understand, a little faintness in the offices of the Interstate Commerce Commission.

In its opinion, written by Mr. Justice Douglas, the Court made this extremely interesting statement:

> Discriminatory rates are but one form of trade barriers. They may cause a blight no less serious than the spread of noxious gas over the land or the deposit of sewage in the streams. They may affect the prosperity and welfare of a State as profoundly as any diversion of waters from the rivers. They may stifle, impede, or cripple old industries and prevent the establishment of new ones.

They may arrest the development of a State or put it at a decided disadvantage in competitive markets.

It seems reasonable to believe from this pronouncement that a conspiracy among railroads, made effective by economic coercion preventing the individual rail lines from instituting freight rates that would allow the full development of Georgia, will receive severe treatment when the facts are placed before the Court. The railroads asked the Court for a rehearing on the grounds that they were taken by surprise! Needless to say, the request was refused.

About this time, by strange coincidence, the Interstate Commerce Commission, like Rip Van Winkle, began to bestir itself. There was a great bustle in the Commission's offices with bureaucrats running hither and yon. A few weeks later (by further coincidence, of course), out came the Commission with a decision in the freight rate case of the South and West that had been before the deliberate body since before the beginning of the Second World War, and to which the Southern Governors' Conference was a party.

In a decision nearly three hundred pages long the Interstate Commerce Commission agreed in principle with nearly everything the advocates of equitable freight rates for the South and West have been contending. This is a far cry from the old days when the Commission with great gravity would declare "transportation conditions" in the South and West to be "less favorable" than in the East; consequently, rates on manufactured products must be higher than in the East.

The decision of the Commission is a step forward for the South. Most important of all, the decision recognizes the justice of a uniform system of freight rate charges in the basic rate structure (known as class rates) for the East, the South, the Southwest, and the Middle West—all the territory east of the Rocky Mountains. As an immediate move toward rate equality, the Interstate Commerce Commission ordered a substantial readjustment of these rates effective August 30, 1945; class rates available to the Southern, Southwestern and Middlewestern shippers were to be lowered ten per cent; those in the East were to be raised by the same amount. Parity for the territory east of the Rockies in class rates is supposed to follow as soon as the technical details can be worked out.

Of course, the railroads could be expected to take prompt action to avoid the effect of the decision. Frantic plea after frantic plea went to the Interstate Commerce Commission to grant delay; it took so long, the railroads urged, to print many volumes of rates; it took so long to inform their widespread staffs of the changes. But temporary delay was insufficient. Into court they rushed, the same rail executives who had wept that the State of Georgia sought judicial relief instead of relying upon the Commission. Temporarily, at least, they prevented the ruling from going into effect, through an injunction obtained against the Interstate Commerce Commission.

And, most humorous of all, the verbal pop bottles began to fall on the Interstate Commerce Commission's members. From sources that once praised it as a great, impartial deliberative body came shouts of discontent. The umpire was seeing straight at last, and those who had liked his favorable decisions when his sight was not so good were howling their disappointment.

It is well to remember that the action of the Interstate Commerce Commission does not give absolute rate equality to either the South or West, because less than five per cent of the Nation's carload traffic moves on these class rates. Undoubtedly the railroads will stall and ask for more time, just as they have done before the Supreme Court—in line with their usual allergy to progress. The South does not count on too great a reduction immediately in the freight rate bill of the South and West. The fact that the Interstate Commerce Commission has ruled that uniformity is to come in the basic class rate structure on which manufactured goods move, is of prime importance.

The railroads are unusually aggressive in their efforts to influence Congress. While declaring loudly from the platform and through the press that they are not violating the antitrust laws as charged in the Georgia case, and in the suit of the Federal government against the Western railroads, the railroads are trying to jam through the Congress a measure that would exempt their private rate-fixing machinery from the antitrust laws. Known as the Bulwinkle Bill, the proposed legislation is named after the Congressman from North Carolina who introduced it. This legislation would fasten a transportation monopoly upon the American people and permanently establish the principal means by which freight rate discrimination against the South and the West has been made possible. Similar measures to gain exemption from antitrust statutes for railroad operations have failed in the past.

Congress, in the past, has regarded the railroads as free enterprises. It seems unlikely that the members will change their minds and agree that one kind of business in America is free to engage in conspiracy. But the railroad lobby is energetic; it is hopeful, too, that Congress and the people will nod some morning.

12

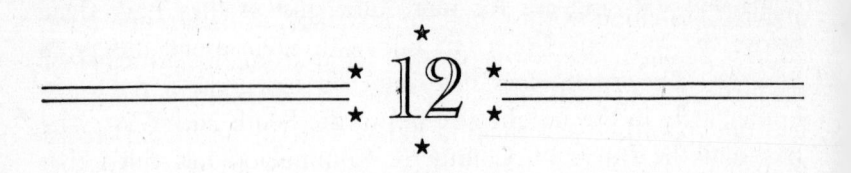

THE MONOPOLIST'S NIGHTMARE

ONE OF THE duties of a politician is the making of speeches. It is a duty not lightly to be set aside, merely because public affairs are pressing. By making speeches, the politician gets his picture in the paper, usually surrounded by other politicians and pretty girls; sometimes a citizen and taxpayer is in the picture too. School exercises of all kinds, but especially graduations, offer a fine opportunity. One afternoon early in June, Thad Buchanan and I dashed from the Capitol for me to deliver a commencement address in Glascock County. Thad was a little uncertain about his road, but presently we discovered a country schoolhouse surrounded by automobiles that gave evidence of such a gathering. We went indoors.

I thought that the principal and the chairman of the trustees seemed a little surprised at the visit, but they were extremely cordial and escorted me to the platform, and introduced me to the crowd. When I sat down from making my speech twenty minutes later, the principal whispered that I was at the wrong school and that we were expected eight miles away. As unostentatiously as possible, I made my way from the stage and we arrived in a cloud of dust, half an hour late, to deliver the same address again. I received a pleasant letter from the principal of the first school, thanking me for the unannounced visit; and I had the opportunity of shaking hands with an additional crowd of parents and voters. The Governor of any Southern State is so much a fixture at school events, and always so glad of an opportunity to make a speech, that the secret of my mistake has been unshared heretofore, except with Thad Buchanan and the principal.

In 1945, Mark Ethridge, who combines being a Southern gentleman with publishing a liberal Southern newspaper, invited me to speak to the Democrats of Louisville. It was a splendid opportunity, because Kentucky Democrats are properly appreciative of oratory devoted to a castigation of Republican misdeeds.

I was scheduled to speak about the three great Democrats, whose leadership of America in time of crisis has made Monticello, the Hermitage and Hyde Park hallowed spots for all lovers of freedom. My early reading of Jefferson's inimitable letters, my schoolboy admiration for General Jackson and my affection for and devotion to Franklin D. Roosevelt made that phase of the speech a rather simple one. But it can never hurt, in a public address, to make some reference to the community that you are visiting—parenthetically, erroneous references may prove costly as they were to Ogden Mills when he juggled football scores in a campaign against Al Smith.

Louisville has been a growing center of manufacturing, with an exceptional diversification of industry not typical of the South. I knew that its citizens had pioneered in local, coöperative financing of new industries and that the Louisville Industrial Foundation was a remarkable success among ventures of its kind. It seemed to me to be a good point of departure for an optimistic speech about the economic growth of the South, which would be an agreeable rhetorical compliment furthering praise of party heroes.

Examining the industrial products of Louisville, it was astonishing to find that the Industrial Foundation had helped to establish forty-four industries, several of which had grown into very important establishments. Louisville plants produced cigarette foil, automobile parts and bodies, magnesium products, water heaters, radio cabinets, shoestrings, office equipment, synthetic building materials, garments, stamped material products, clothing and cotton rope. It is an impressive example of diversification and has resulted in a remarkably well-balanced economy in the community.

But I examined a little further. Of the thirteen types of industry enumerated, eight were threatened directly by monopolistic practices; of the forty-four industrial enterprises assisted financially by the Louisville Industrial Foundation, nineteen faced hazards from monopolistic practices in their fields. The note of optimism that I had planned for my speech to the Democrats of Kentucky had to be tempered with a warning of danger.

There are many in America who deny that economic freedom is essential to individual liberty. Even more emphatically, they deny that there is an American tradition that includes freedom from monopoly among the basic civil liberties. Whether they are humbugging themselves or trying to deceive their fellow-citizens is inconsequential; they demonstrate a complete ignorance of American history.

For when Jefferson was demanding the guarantee of a Bill of Rights as the price for conceding the adoption of an admittedly imperfect Federal Constitution, he listed freedom from monopoly as one of the fundamental civil liberties. In the historic letter to Donald, evoking the debate between Madison and Henry in 1788, the foremost spokesman for human freedom wrote from the American embassy in France: "By a declaration of rights, I mean one which will stipulate freedom of religion, freedom of the press, freedom of commerce against monopolies.... These are fetters against doing evil which no honest government should decline."

Mme Guillotine had not then acquired her voracious appetite for noble heads. The Bastille still stood as a reminder that, although the current Louis might be an incompetent clockmaker, former kings had been of less equable disposition and of considerable firmness. The well-meaning young Hapsburg princess who was his consort had yet to make her historic suggestion of a dietetic change for the sharecroppers of France, but the monopolists had so gutted the economy of France that the discerning eye of the master of Monticello found cause for warning to America.

England broke the fetters of private monopoly in two successful revolutions. Any examinaton of the Cromwellian period must consider the transition from a wholly mercantile economy that was taking place, and must regard the intolerable burden of monopolies as providing as great a part of the anger of the middle classes as arose from either interference with religious practices or inequitable taxation. The Whig Revolution against the last Stuart eliminated most of the remaining traces of private monopoly in Great Britain. In France, however, it was as great a corrupter of officialdom as the public sale of offices and infinitely more injurious to the national economy. Colbert opposed it in the earlier years of his ministry before he ceased to be a politician and became a courtier, but in the long and fantastic reign of Louis XV it came to dominate the sale of all luxuries and many necessities.

Salt, linen, silk, tobacco, spices, many items of ironware, much of the pottery industry and a great portion of the imported foodstuffs of France were in the hands of the monopolists. The export of some items constituted limited monopolies. The trade with certain sections of the world were monopolies. Even gambling, the last recourse of the destitute, fell into the hands of monopolists, not all of whom were more scrupulous than the operators of a midway wheel-of-fortune.

Adventurers from all nations, John Law with his plans for trade with the Orient, and Cagliostro and his charming lady with even more dazzling plans, descended upon France in those days. Whether they offer any parallel to the manipulators of holding-company stocks or the builders of imaginary inventories of drugs is a question that might be considered; perhaps the comparison is too simple; perhaps this is a wiser and better day, which has learned much from the experience of the past and can be deceived by no such simplicities as the hocus-pocus of Law or Cagliostro. Our monopolists are serious men, who do not boil noxious brews in kettles and decorate themselves with mythical orders bestowed by suppositious Arabian monarchs; our monopolists may deal with dictators and monarchs as equals, but they indulge in no flummery, nor do they flee ultimately from the police. Not often, at least, though the trip of one magnate to Greece is again a neat parallel to Cagliostro's sudden departure from Paris to Italy.

For example, a serious man was Ivar Kreuger. Whether he died by his own hand in one of his innumerable town houses in France and was properly and decently buried, or whether he shot a not-wholly-imaginary double and had him decently and quietly buried before he fled to a hideaway in the South Seas, or whether that which was decently buried was a bag of cement, I do not know; the Sunday supplements have not decided the question. But he made the price of matches a little higher for everybody in the whole world, and remains the classic example of the monopolist and the swindler in combination.

Kreuger's arm reached far. In Georgia, we remember one of the reaches. During the First World War, when the import of safety matches was cut off, an immense plant for their manufacture was erected in Savannah. In 1920, when the American match monopoly, Diamond Match Company, entered into a treaty with Kreuger's Swedish Match Company, one of the terms of the accord was the razing of the Savannah plant.

The South saw the length of Kreuger's arm once more, not so long before he vanished from the salons of Europe and the clubs of his fellow-monopolists into the impenetrable mist of his legend. In 1931, his engineers and architects and plant experts descended upon Natchez, Mississippi. The depression already had arrived in America, but lethargic Natchez had been in a depression since the sixties and had not noticed the new one. But they could not help noticing the industrious visitors, who created a mild boom from one end of the city to the other, including the cluster of houses with closed shutters that have been historic in Natchez since long before "Pike County Ballads" were published. Then suddenly the visitors departed; another crew came, a demolition crew. The match plant was scrapped, as a result of the second peace treaty between Diamond and Kreuger. The price of matches advanced in several civilized countries; and among the tribes of Africa as well, or so they say.

Kreuger was such a fascinating individual that the story of the match monopoly sometimes gets lost in the recounting of his forgeries of entire bond issues of various governments; his fantastic bribes to the mistresses and near-mistresses of masters and near-masters of countries as widely separated as Italy and Venezuela; his yachts and planes and yet uncounted villas, chateaux, country places, shooting boxes and legendary mystery islands. His story only serves to link together the eras of two amazing scalawags, who had a pleasant time at the expense of the public, and who stole, respectively, a few cents a year from each of six hundred million people and a diamond necklace from a Queen who soon would need no necklace for want of a neck to adorn. But the price of matches is a little higher, from Cairo, Egypt, to Cairo, Georgia, and neither Natchez nor Savannah has factories for the making of matches.

Kreuger is interesting as an individual and as a monopolist. His possession of a magic reputation that inspired fear in his much stronger American rival enabled him to dominate the match business of the world. For in most of Europe, Asia and South America, matches are a national monopoly; one petty dictator bestowed the monopoly on a personal favorite a few years ago, and a sugar-cane worker now must pay a penny more to light a candle at a voodoo altar because of this. But Swedish Match is smaller than Diamond Match, except in its ramifications, as American investors in the Kreuger empire discovered when their claims were liquidated in 1945.

Diamond Match Company has been the object of a recent most interesting action by the United States Department of Justice. The government charges that Diamond and its affiliates, Universal Match Corporation, Ohio Match Company, Lion Match Company, Ltd., and Berst-Forster-Dixfield Company produce eighty-three per cent of all American matches. Until the war, Diamond, as agent for the German potash trust, controlled American distribution of chlorate of potash. Just as the match plant in Savannah was junked and the match plant in Natchez was never finished, American plants for making chlorate of potash were junked or never completed. So when war came there was no chlorate of potash to make ammunition and flares.

In America, before Pearl Harbor, one company controlled the production of all the virgin aluminum; two companies made ninety-five per cent of the plate glass; three companies made eighty-six per cent of the autos; three companies controlled ninety per cent of the tin can production. In one of these instances, there is a possibility that the three could be reduced to two, since the dominance of General Motors in the auto-parts field places all competition except Ford at its mercy.

Both Thurman Arnold and Wendell Berge have treated at length the mystery of why optical glass was so scarce in America on the eve of war; the mystery was no mystery at all; an American monopoly had agreed to partition the world market with a German ally, and their "trade agreement" gave control over the basic raw material for lenses to the Hitler-dominated firm.

The Southern sharecropper, fingering the fertilizer tickets that represent his indebtedness to the supplyman, is not aware that he is the victim of oppression; Southern Bourbons tell him that he is not. And if he should still feel that he is oppressed, and is disinclined to attribute his oppression to his mother's unwisdom in taking for husband one as poor as herself, he feels that the landlord is the oppressor. He is unquestionably oppressed; and his oppressors are the cartel-makers who dominate the sale of nitrate of soda, and who removed competition from their worldwide industry. Since the Southern cotton and tobacco farmer is the world's greatest customer for commercial fertilizer, the price that the South has paid for the existence of this cartel has been large enough to have provided a college education for every high school graduate of the Southeastern States.

The monopolist has been investigated exhaustively by the economist, and, according to his own story, is constantly persecuted by twin devils: the Antitrust Division of the Department of Justice and the Federal Trade Commission. In the case of the transportation monopolist, the State of Georgia has become the third devil to haunt the monopolist's nightmare. But the monopolist is not properly the subject material for the economist; he should be turned over to the explorers of morbid psychology for study; his is a case for the couch of the psychoanalyst and not for the courtroom, for the padded, rather than the prison, cell.

For the huge monopolistic units are not profitable; their profits of inflation, of rising prices, of books, are the result of scarcity and not of efficiency. This becomes apparent as soon as a period of deflation, of declining prices, of depression, comes to the country. The inefficiency of their enormous bureaucracies, wasteful and encumbered by red tape, becomes discernible.

In 1934, the ten great steel companies, each with a capital of more than $90,000,000 and with aggregate capital of $3,800,-000,000, lost nearly $20,000,000. One hundred and twenty-nine small steel companies, none with a capital of more than $15,000,000 and with total capitalization of about one tenth of that of the majors, made a little more than $6,000,000. The aggregate losses to creditors and investors through the failures of all types of "big business" exceeds that of similar losses through "little business" since the start of this century.

It is the inefficiency of monopoly that renders it objectionable from the standpoint of the modern economist, and that leads him to agreement with the "classical economists" in asserting that freedom of competition is essential to the well being of any society not operated wholly upon a collectivist model. But the same conclusion as to the undesirability of monopoly can be reached through simpler avenues of logic and ethics.

The earliest Pharaoh to desire to gain possession of the entire supply of barley in the Nile Valley, the padrone who controls the wells where New Mexican shepherds must water their flocks, the French ruler who gained ownership of all his country's salt, and the modern monopolist who seeks dominance of an industry or a utility—these were not and are not moved by considerations of personal wealth. Their desire was not for money; their ambition was not for gain. They sought power.

Power is an attribute not safely to be entrusted to any man. It is dangerous to his mental equilibrium, as any psychiatrist will tell you; it is dangerous to his soul's salvation, as any priest will vouchsafe; it is dangerous to the society of which he is a part, as the evidence proves.

For the centralization of industry, whether regionally as through the economic restrictions imposed upon the Southern and Western States within our own Nation, or whether industry-wide as in the instances of matches, aluminum, shoes and fertilizer, brings nearer and nearer a corresponding centralization of governmental control. At first this centralized control may be honest and in the interest of the public which will require defense; but inevitably it will become corrupt through its possession of power and will become master of industry, of all business, and of the Nation. If monopoly is not uprooted speedily, we shall have the choice of government by an industrial bureaucracy or government by a political bureaucracy. As for which of these is worse, it is a matter of preference; either is bitter to the taste of free men.

It is for this reason that I am deeply distrustful of two apparently parallel trends in dealing with monopoly in America. One is through permissive legislation, such as the Webb Act to permit American firms to conspire against foreign competitors in world trade but, nominally, compelling them to compete within domestic limits; another flagrant example of this trend is, of course, the Bulwinkle Bill, specifically exempting the railroads from the civil and criminal statutes against conspiracy in restraint of trade. The second trend is toward the administrative regulation of businesses that might tend toward monopoly; governmental supervision of all enterprise is an unwholesome one.

An examination of these proposals will disclose the fallacy of each.

The Webb Act was designed by its authors to permit American firms to compete with European cartels. It was designed to promote exports by permitting groups of businesses in the same field to combine or to form agreements, heretofore deemed illegal, for the purpose of getting world business away from the monopolists of other nations, whether those monopolists were party-dominated as in Germany, capitalistic as in France and Britain, or collectivist State-sponsored as in Russia. As an act of aggressive political immorality it is almost without precedent in this Nation. Its basic assumption was that, although capitalism, free enterprise and democratic processes linger anomalously in this country, they had disappeared elsewhere in the world forever because they were antiquated, outmoded, worthless and proven unsound.

It is to be remembered that the Webb Act was, in part, the product of the First World War, although it purports to be based upon a report of the Federal Trade Commission delivered two years earlier. It was a fitting introduction to an era in American life that was marked by bitter cynicism on the part of youth, by disappointment of the people in the conduct of public affairs, by disgust with government.

It is a fitting curtain raiser for a play that included in the first act Teapot Dome, the theft of the bedsheets from the veterans' hospitals, the fabulous Democratic convention of 1924, the promises of multiple chickens in ever larger pots, the smash of 1929 and the loss of billions of dollars in genuine values and tens of billions in paper profits. The second act went on with the same clichés: the phrase "now let's be realistic" was on the lips of all the central characters. Fantastic characters these were; men who carried umbrellas and men who destroyed the economy of their nation because their mistresses did not speak to each other; men who plucked the blossom peace from off the nettle war; men who shuffled papers and pretended that they were saving the world; men who asserted that a gift for compromise with armed bandits was the highest wisdom of civilization.

In the vicious ideology of the Webb Act is embalmed the thinking of a period that would have provided the greatest comedy in world history if many millions of lives had not been paid for the lack of courage, decency and common sense of the snivelling mountebanks that performed on the world stage. It was part of a theory that, perhaps, after all, maybe, it would be wise to dump the products of American farms on the world market at any price and pay some kind of subsidy, rather than plan intelligently for American and world needs and avert the mining of American soil and the consequential waste. It was a part of a way of thinking that found loans to Italy and Germany better investments than the development of the South and West. It was part of an age that could lavish praise upon the posturing, turncoat clown whose claim to a place in history rests on the myth that once he made a single train run on time.

In theory, the Webb Act was supposed to offer such inducement to American firms that there would be little temptation to conspire against their fellow-citizens, since conspiracy against the rest of the world was legalized. The record of antitrust cases filed since its enactment does not bear out the theory. The partitioning of the world market on alkali products, involving British and German as well as American firms, suggests that the Webb Act was the occasion upon which American free enterprise went to Munich.

Measures of the type of the Bulwinkle Bill are more adroit but not less dangerous. The theory upon which this type of legislation is based is this: "There are large fields of activity that probably should be monopolistic. A quick recognition that free enterprise has failed in America is desirable, but, because of the obvious prejudice of the citizens, the admission must not be made too openly. Let us therefore remove from the operations of the Sherman Act, the Clayton Act and the ancient common law against conspiracy those fields of endeavor, one by one. First we will nip off transportation, thus assuring the monopolists of a colonial empire from which to drain raw materials; next week or next year or in the next decade, we can undertake to exempt light metals, or oil, or some other basic essential."

This theory is identical with that which flourished in Tudor England and Bourbon France, when favorites were rewarded with monopolies in tobacco, Rhenish wine, Flemish lace, or Arabian horses; or, more frankly, given a charter expressly permitting the holder and none other to practice slave-raiding or piracy upon some specific sea.

The theory of legislative exemptions from offenses that have been crimes ever since capitalism overwhelmed the mercantile and feudal systems, and that have been moral crimes ever since the taskmaster of Pharaoh introduced the original speedup system in Goshen, is essentially the theory of the extreme Right, of the incipient Fascist, who believe that if the transportation moguls could make one Southern or Western train run on time all problems would be solved in America. But the theory of the Left, while perhaps less ill-intentioned, professing as it does a deep concern for the masses, is no less inherently destructive to American practices. The Left advocates withdrawing the control over monopoly, actual or potential, entirely from the judicial sphere and in part from the legislative sphere, and creating administrative techniques to control and to civilize these enemies of free enterprise.

Public ownership, or ownership through quasi-public corporations with diffused investors, of certain types of monopolies, frankly admitting their character as monopolies, might be a potential solution. It has been tried with some success both in America and other democracies, and demonstrates that public enterprise and private enterprise do not need to conflict.

Administrative control, however, is a different thing. If it is effective, it sets up strangling governmental controls, tends toward a dangerous centralization of power, and vests the direction of vast economic empires in individuals who are neither the choice of the investors in those enterprises nor of the general public. If it is ineffective, as the Interstate Commerce Commission has become, it lulls the public into a false sense of security; the sheep trust the watchdog long after he has lost his teeth and even when he fraternizes with the wolves.

The remedy obviously is one for legislative policy-making and for vigorous enforcement through the orderly judicial processes. Perhaps the laws need some attention, to provide for mandatory awards of damages in all civil actions, and to eliminate in part the practice of seeking injunctive relief without coupling with it actions for damages. Undoubtedly the criminal statutes require some reconsideration. Assuredly a second conviction of a corporation for violation of the antitrust laws should be penalized by cancellation of its charter and enforced liquidation.

If that penalty appears severe, it is only on the surface. Where corporations continue to evade the laws, it is evidence that they have fallen from the hands of their stockholders and into the control of a power-crazed managerial bureaucracy. The unfortunate stockholders, facing the loss of their entire investment through the payment of triple-damages under the law and with their properties in the hands of acknowledged lawbreakers, would be much better off if their investments were liquidated in an orderly manner and they were permitted to reinvest their savings in some business that could compete in an America of free enterprise. The present penalties under the antitrust laws are ridiculous. The fines in the fertilizer case, an instance involving a commodity essential to the economy of thirty million Americans, reached the staggering total of $35,000. The fine in the chemical and petroleum case, involving the stripping of America of its defense through a cartel in synthetic rubber, was much stiffer; it totalled $50,000. Since the amounts involved in these conspiracies were millions and billions, the fines neither punished nor impressed.

When a corporation, through its management, violates the Sherman or Clayton Acts, the penalty prescribed is negligible, on the criminal side. In practice, the amounts recoverable by those wronged in damages is inadequate. The answer is the liquidation of such corporations, with distribution of their assets to their stockholders. Certainly that is preferable to public operation, or to their continuing in charge of such conspirators as a management that has demonstrated its irresponsibility.

It would be difficult, tedious, and expensive to liquidate such of those enterprises as are actually thoroughly integrated; but the inescapable fact is that very few monopolistic enterprises are integrated in that sense; they are financial structures, with many noncompetitive plants each of which could become autonomous and which, no doubt, could operate more efficiently, economically, and productively if they were liberated from the weight of bureaucratic control. The classic example again is National Cordage, which sought a monopoly by the purchase of all individual units in one field. With the collapse of the "holding company," the plants returned to other ownership and continued to make twine, rope and string without difficulty.

The safeguarding of free enterprise is consequential to all of our people. Political liberty cannot exist in a nation where industry is half free and half slave; economic freedom is the corollary of political freedom, today as in the day when Jefferson saw the clouds upon the horizon of France and warned the people of the thirteen little States that huddled despairingly along the Atlantic coast that to execute their experiment in self-government required something more than phrases.

Today many of the natural resources of America are threatened with destruction by the monopolist, whose grip on copper, the light metals, the basic chemicals and oil seems to grow tighter with every decade.

An examination of the suits filed in the past ten years by the Antitrust unit of the Department of Justice is illuminating. Wendell Berge, with Thurman Arnold, one of the major champions of American free enterprise, has given a summation of these suits and reveals how almost every field of manufacture and distribution is under attack. Among those monopolies that he lists are cartels involving basic industries or products including aircraft accessories, alkali, aluminum, chemicals, dyestuffs, fertilizer, fluorescent lamps, fuel injection equipment, glass bulbs, gyroscopic instruments, hormones, incandescent lamps, magnesite brick, magnesium, matches, molybdenum, newsprint, pharmaceutical products, photographic materials, plastics, titanium and tungsten. These actions do not include the numerous conspiracy and antitrust actions filed by individuals; nor the two suits, already discussed, instituted by the State of Georgia, the one involving asphalt already determined in the State's favor, and the other involving the transportation conspiracy that has manipulated the economic life of the Southern and Western States.

Some of the evidence in Georgia's action against the rail lines, and much of the evidence in other actions brought under the Sherman Act, illustrate a significant fact; not only stockholders of the corporations involved, but many of the directors of the corporations were kept as ignorant of the nature and extent of the conspiracies as were the general public and the direct victims.

In some instances subordinate officials, and in many instances major officials in corporations, took action, entered into trade alliances not only against their fellow-citizens economically but against their very Country when it was on the brink of war, without consultation with ownership. The Georgia railroad suit is not alone in revealing to the public a maze of business bureaucracies that are more powerful than the investing public, more complicated than any governmental agency, more secret than any mysterious society devised by the imaginings of writers of thrillers, and capable of dealing with governments of other countries in defiance of a prohibition that has been on the American statute books since 1799.

It is true that some monopolies have been broken up by governmental action and that some have exploded into nothingness because of technological progress in related fields or because of stresses within themselves; but the operation of these latter processes is relatively unusual and exceedingly slow, and always accompanied by acute distress within the industry and the consumer-group affected.

The classic example, in American economic history, of the

spontaneous explosion of an industry-wide monopoly is the case of General Film Company, which once dominated the production and distribution of motion pictures in the United States. Because its management felt that films were nothing more than marketable physical objects, and believed the public wished to attend picture shows that presented nothing but short subjects of a single reel, and because the management could not resist a small shakedown of the operators of picture palaces, their monopoly blew up in their faces.

But a contributing factor was the moving picture trust's failure to acquire all the necessary patent rights in the field of photography and projection. This oversight proved costly, although the other factors were more important. Today the "patent pool" is one of the accepted techniques of monopolists, who never again will repeat the mistake of General Film in not acquiring the rights to the Bianchi camera, which made Southern California, and not New York, the capital of the film industry.

Technological change may come to the rescue of the nineteen Louisville industries threatened by monopoly. It did not come to the rescue of the match factory at Savannah that was demolished nor the match factory at Natchez that was never completed; for the "repeating match" is controlled by patents locked up in the vaults of the monopolists and those patents may never see the light of day.

The change to a rigid enforcement of the laws against conspiracies and combinations in restraint of trade undoubtedly will be accompanied by inconvenience to those profiting by their present arrangements. That has been so in the past. Those who have enjoyed the unearned profits of monopoly have a tendency to think that the grant of power, which always rests upon governmental license, connivance or apathy, has become a form of property.

That was true long ago as well as today. In Elizabethan England, the dashing and handsome and tastefully clothed Earl of Essex discovered to his alarm that his monopoly in the import of wine and other articles was about to expire. Upon the income derived from it, he had been able to maintain a private army, a claque of poets, and some very attractive castles and country houses. To these last, as is the custom of lobbyists and courtiers and others involved in informal government of the people, he had invited from time to time many guests of distinction. They had sipped his wine, eaten his ham, looked at his first editions, admired his etchings and approved him as a first-class fellow and a smart operator.

Now threatened with the curtailment of his income, he began to address more and more emphatic pleas to the Queen. He pointed out to her that he would be as poor as a sharecropper unless this injustice was averted, and that a renewal of his monopoly and, perhaps, its expansion to include blackbirding and piracy, would be appreciated. When she did not reply promptly and satisfactorily, he was compelled to the drastic action of trying to seize the government.

That was a little too much, even for a Tudor princess who might ordinarily appreciate the compliment of an intended kidnapping. They cut off his head. For Robert Devereaux, second Earl of Essex, that was the end of monopoly. But it was not the end of the type of plea that he devised but did not copyright.

There is one standard argument against the destruction of monopolies and cartels. The monopolist will never earn enough by all his chicanery to repay the public relations counsel who invented the widow and orphans, that amazing family consisting of a bent, fragile, work-worn and silver-haired woman of sixty and her three little tots aged three, nine and eleven. This little family group, so heart-touchingly pathetic, is the third of a nation that lives in perpetual depression; or so says their creator. They live on the fifth floor of a crowded walkup tenement somewhere in the rural Mid-West, without a neighbor in twenty miles; they subsist upon raw turnips and an occasional loaf of bread, purchased when a dividend check occasionally comes to their door from the benevolent monopoly in which they have invested their all; they salt their bread with their tears. The wind is kept from their hovel by papering the walls with shares of stock, beautifully engraved, and bearing the corporate superscriptions of "New York, New Haven and Hartford," of "Insull," of "National Cordage." In a steamer trunk, they keep the entire issues of the securities of American monopolies, toward the purchase of which went the pennies earned by the lads as papercarriers and of the little girl as a match vendor, the proceeds of the sale of grandmother's antiques, and the settlement of father's insurance. The hunger of this family is a great tragedy of America, reviewed almost every week. The hunger could be abated, of course, if it were not patently true, on the face of the story told, that managerial bureaucrats who violate the Sherman Act are not above retaining the earnings of their crimes and sending no dividend checks to those faithful and trusting four.

That the story is wholly true, I have my doubts; but I have recorded it precisely as it has been told, over and over again. It is a classic of American folklore, believed by the guileless with the utter abandon of a child hearing Red Riding Hood for the first time. I have come to believe a part of it myself.

It is time that someone went to the rescue of this family, which has become the symbol of the country's investors. Their mistreatment is not at the hands of those who wish to break monopoly, however. They have not identified the Wolf correctly; for the Wolf has learned the trick of crying "Wolf, Wolf" to divert attention from himself.

13

MAKING FREE ENTERPRISE WORK

NEWNAN WAS A good town, even in the bad days that came after the War Between the States. Although it was but forty miles from Atlanta, General Sherman was not successful in interrupting its affairs on his march to the sea. It cared for a fair number of refugees from Atlanta, after the Union Army's carelessness with fire reduced that rail center to cinders. It suffered under Reconstruction, but not so severely as some other communities. It was one of the first in Georgia, at any rate, to become enthusiastic over the possibility of manufacturing things in the New South.

Grandfather Henry Arnall was on hand to help get industrialism started in the town. As a boy he had made money selling gingerbread to Federal soldiers. He arrived from the small country village of Senoia soon after the war and went into business on something less than a shoestring with a general farm-supply store. He was thrifty, industrious, imaginative, and a little lucky.

His thrift is still legendary in Newnan. He watched every purchase for every enterprise with which he was connected, and he believed implicitly that wilful waste meant woeful want. On one occasion, the broom used for sweeping the office, the store and the sidewalk in front wore out; only the stick and a few tenacious but ineffectual straws were left. The handy man, who doubled as delivery boy and porter, sought vainly to get permission for a replacement. Unable to get a requisition, he determined upon a little propaganda and cut himself a pine top to sweep with. Grandfather Arnall observed and was impressed. There were many pine tops available within a stone's throw; they represented a local product that was better than inexpensive, since it cost nothing at all. Calling the handy man to him, Grandfather Arnall solemnly reached into his pocket and extracted a long change purse, meditated briefly, and handed him the first bonus for employee-suggested efficiency in the history of Newnan. The bonus was one nickel.

Grandfather Arnall decided that the South could never regain its prosperity unless it made things as well as grew them. He bought an old, dilapidated, water-power mill abandoned by its New England builder and went into the manufacture of cotton cord. He branched into textiles, doing very well indeed.

He left the mercantile business to my father, and the textile and other enterprises to others of the family. He left to Newnan the tradition of closing the stores for baseball games.

One afternoon, when he was well past middle life, he inquired the whereabouts of his sons. Joe Arnall, who is my father, had gone to the baseball game. Henry Arnall and Frank Arnall also had gone to the baseball game. My grandfather had never seen a professional baseball game. Upon the door he placed a hastily scrawled notice: "Closed to go to the baseball game." Accompanied by the store's remaining staff he went. He departed from the store in fury, but he stayed at the park in delight. Thereafter, the store closed at least once each week for him to attend.

My grandfather's belief in private enterprise seems a little primitive in these days, although by the standards of his time he maintained rather exceptional relations with his employees. While I do not share all of his views, I am inclined to many of them. For Grandfather Arnall was an individualist. He did not believe that a business should be run by absentee ownership through some managerial bureaucracy. Given a choice between turning his plant over to his employees to run as they chose, or turning it over to somebody to run in his own interest, I suspect that he would have gulped, stormed and done the former.

He was not swallowed up by National Cordage, in the gala days of that earliest of monopolistic monsters. He had a considerable impatience with men too lazy or too incompetent to manage their own affairs. He managed his own. Probably he managed those of his family, his friends, and his neighbors; my father and my uncles speak of him with awe to this day.

America is somewhat more complex now. There are some types of enterprise that require the accumulation of immense resources for capital outlay. Even my grandfather would have been hard pushed to operate American Telephone and Telegraph, or United States Steel, or General Motors upon the same basis that he operated his farm-supply store, his textile mill, and his farms.

There is opportunity in America for individual enterprise; there is room in America for democracy in private enterprise;

there is a need in America for control by ownership over the policies of private enterprise, accompanied by assumption of responsibility.

The first requirement toward realizing these goals is a little plain thinking about words.

Advertising has been appearing for some time containing a new phrase, not seen before in print in America's journals of mass reading. The phrase is alarming; it is "private management." It is being introduced, obviously, as the chosen successor for "private enterprise," with some suggestion in the adroitly written copy that the two expressions are synonymous.

Whether it was chance, cynicism, or carelessness that caused this phrase first to appear in the advertising of a railroad company notoriously dependent upon public assistance in one form or another, there is no very close relationship between private enterprise and private management.

All enterprise, of course, is either public or private. Private enterprise in America has been directed toward farming, manufacturing and distribution. Public enterprise, until the war called for a rapid expansion of manufacturing facilities, has been directed toward transportation chiefly, among those activities that are not commonly thought of as public services. The distinctions are somewhat arbitrary, since farmers receive direct grants from government in the form of subsidies, and since manufacturers receive indirect grants from government in the form of tax refunds and tariffs, and since a considerable part of the investment in transportation has been made by individuals. Private enterprise, in a general sense, is enterprise that is financed by individuals without public assistance. Public enterprise is enterprise that is financed by some unit of government. The country store is the classic example of private enterprise; the small-town waterworks is the easiest example of the latter.

Private management and public management, perhaps, are even less easy to define; the possibilities of disagreement over a definition are greater. Obviously, the railroads represent public enterprise, mixed ownership, and private management. Obviously the warplants built with public funds and turned over to corporations or individuals with managerial experience to operate also represent public enterprise and private management. In a limited sense, a business in receivership illustrates partly private ownership and partly public management. Some of the proposals made by Socialist economists, both here and in Britain, for the acquisition of certain basic industries or services, retaining private investors but operating the enterprise under public control, illustrate a phase of private enterprise coupled with public management.

Public management of a private enterprise is justified in such cases as liquidation, receivership, the operation of an essential utility under emergency conditions. Private management of public enterprise justified itself as a wartime measure. But the extraordinary conditions that bring about either of these transient remedies should not induce Americans to believe that private management of the public business, or public management of private business, can be adopted safely as the norm for enterprise in this country.

If we are to have prosperity and an economy of abundance, there must be in America in the coming years, the greatest imaginable freedom for enterprise, both public and private. For free enterprise is neither public nor private; the theory of free enterprise contemplates that, while each shall remain within respective spheres, the individual shall be free to experiment, to risk, to explore, to enter into any business that does not have antisocial implications, and that the people collectively shall be free to do the same. Free enterprise also calls for freedom of competition in those spheres where competition is possible, for public control or public ownership in those spheres where competition is impossible.

The basic soundness of the free enterprise theory has not been challenged successfully. The expansion of industrialism in America, a nation that was not highly industrialized until 1915, has created certain problems and perplexities that have led some economists to doubt that free enterprise, either private or public, can survive. Upon the hypotheses of these economists, the extremists have built imaginary American civilizations of the future to delight themselves and frighten the public; actually, however, the percentage of Fascists among management and the percentage of Communists among workers is equally small, equally vocative, and equally ambitious.

What is required to make free enterprise work is a modification of our popular interpretation of what constitutes private enterprise, an enforcement of our existing laws against monopolistic practices and conspiracies, adoption of measures for the protection of stockholders in mass-production corporations, and very great firmness in the regulation of quasi-public enterprises.

Both those who wish to turn many types of business over to the government for operation and those who wish to turn the powers of government over to the management of certain types of business are assuming, as their first premise, that American enterprise is stagnant and static, that American population cannot rise, and that all American frontiers have been exhausted. This myth, I think, has been thoroughly deflated and discredited. The development of the Southern and Western economy will leave ample room for new competitive industries. The problem facing the people, through their political government, is that of insuring themselves against cartels, conspiracies, monopolies and unfair competition that can prevent this expansion.

Perhaps I share Grandfather Arnall's prejudices, which served him well in the days when National Cordage was gulping up small plants over the Nation and preparing for a collapse that left its stockholders with less than a ball of twine; but it seems to me that enforcement of the existing laws against monopoly is both easy and necessary. No new, extra-legal administrative techniques are required.

What is required is the application of our new viewpoint on penal questions, as previously suggested, to the penalties assessed against corporate entities engaging in such conspiracies.

A reform of the patent laws is indicated, likewise, to prevent the withholding from the public of new inventions. Possibly this should take the form of an automatic licensing at a fixed royalty scale of all patents, where actual production is not undertaken within a reasonable time.

In most kinds of business, the gradual processes of decentralization will suffice to protect the public interest. Minimum supervision by government is all that is necessary to prevent conspiracies, to break down wholly artificial financial combinations within industries, and to assure free competition, under which individual opportunity can flourish. Since mere bigness is no guarantee of efficiency, since many small enterprises have competed successfully against enormous rivals even under the adverse conditions of today, relative harmony in most lines of endeavor may be expected.

One additional general safeguard, however, must be erected. The divorcement of ownership from management in many industries has been unnecessary and hurtful, and their reunion is indicated. This becomes increasingly difficult as the corporate structure becomes more intricately involved and as the unit grows larger, but it is essential that the stockholder in American business enterprises assume responsibility for the conduct of those enterprises and cease to be a pawn in the hands of management.

The retreat of the New Deal on the question of undistributed profits was a mistake. Although the law was unreasonable in some ways, and an approach other than through the taxing authority of the Federal government very probably is necessary, use of the taxing power may also be required.

Excepting quasi-public enterprises from the general rule, corporations should not be permitted to create large surpluses. That does not mean that there should be a limitation upon the capitalization of such corporations. If the stockholders desire to reinvest their dividends, there should be no obstacle, once the dividends have been paid to them and they have paid their taxes upon them. But the plight of the widows and orphans, so touchingly described by the spokesman for management, must be alleviated. They must not be deprived of their share of earnings; they need their dividends to purchase food and clothing, to find shelter from the oppressive heat of summer and the cold sleet of winter; their lot, crouching in the unheated squalor of a tenement, hungry and forlorn, must appeal to Americans and to American lawmakers. They must not be deprived of the earnings of the investment that the husband and father thriftily made on their behalf. The dividends must be paid. Management that withholds these dividends is irresponsible.

This will involve an incident change in tax policies, which will have to be gradual. It will involve a change in attitude toward quasi-public enterprises, which should be partly exempt from this regulation. The change in general policy should be undertaken now, while risk capital can be easily obtained and while the Federal government is guaranteeing a profit to almost every corporation affected by the proposal.

That corporation income taxes, as such, probably will cease to be a large source of Federal and State revenue will be inevitable when the change is made. That will be salutary. Broadening the base of tax collections is desirable, if the people at the base can pay the taxes.

Greater democracy within these corporate structures also is necessary. The limitations upon stockholder-participation in management, of which the withholding of books of account and record from the scrutiny of stockholders is an example, must cease. Provision must be made for choosing directors of some of these corporations other than by the antiquated method of annual stockholders' meetings. It is strange that critics of the union, and their obsolescent convention systems, who advocate the splendid primary system now used by the Typographical Union, should not have thought of its simple and almost obvious application to industrial corporations. The people who take the risks of furnishing the capital for such enterprises should have and must have a much stronger voice in their management than they have today. No greater contribution could be made toward industrial good-will than through assumption of responsibility by the people who own the enterprises of our country.

The quasi-public corporation, however, presents an exception to the rule. True private enterprise requires only very moderate adaptation in regulation to meet every challenge of today; responsible management need have no fear of stockholders, and has none; government should not intrude upon their affairs abnormally.

The quasi-public enterprise is a questionable development in America. Its rise and growth in this country has been traced adequately by no historian. It has no precise parallel in any other country, and the techniques of dealing with similar economic organisms elsewhere are extremely different from our own. Most of the suggested solutions presented seem inadequate. Quasi-public enterprises are those that exist within noncompetitive fields and that owe their existence to grants of public power, of which the greatest is the supreme grant of sovereignty, the right of eminent domain, the power to condemn the individual's property for public purposes.

Such enterprises exist chiefly in the fields of transportation, electric power, and similar utilities.

It is within these enterprises and the corporations that dominate them that the menacing managerial bureaucracy of America is to be found. It is there that the most muddled thinking about the national economy is to be uncovered.

Examining the premises laid down by the spokesmen for the transportation and utility managements, and following them to their logical conclusions is a worthwhile occupation.

Their first contention is that their enterprises represent "private enterprise," although they are endeavoring to substitute the trickier "private management" as an equivalent today. If these corporations represent private enterprise, then it follows that they are not entitled to any grant of public powers except upon such conditions as the public, through government, is willing to permit and has the power to revoke at any time. They are then governed, presumably, by the general laws permitting competition in every field of business, although it is rather difficult to envisage these stalwart defenders of private enterprise solving the problem of how three or four companies could operate street-car lines over the same streets of a city. In the absence of any method of performing this miracle, a substitute can be found only in regulation fixing their rates at the level that would compete with the lowest possible rate for the most efficient imaginable substitute; indeed, that is the "yardstick theory." There could be no concern about the welfare of the enterprise or of its stockholders. If it could not earn enough to pay interest and retirement on all its securities, it could be sold successively at reduced prices each time until it became profitable to someone.

That line of reasoning does not appeal to the management of such enterprises.

Their second contention is that they are "public utilities." In that event, it is essential to supervise them closely in the interest of the public, converting them candidly into public corporations, limiting their earnings strictly but permitting the accumulation of surpluses to stabilize limited dividends.

That line of reasoning appeals even less enthusiastically to a certain type of management, but it seems the sounder to many who have studied the American economic scene.

Experiment with public corporations of this type has been more satisfactory elsewhere than in America. Our country's only experiment was with the two successive institutions of the same name, the Bank of the United States. It was an unhappy experiment for the Nation, ending in an agrarian panic, the menace of treason, considerable loss to stockholders, and the discrediting of the Whig party. It also led to a libel upon the character of one of America's greatest public servants, Roger Brooke Taney, that has been kept alive for a century in the textbooks of the country and which the researches of even such an initially hostile, judicial historian as Beveridge could not reverse. The myth of Taney as an enemy of human freedom, like the myth of Jackson as a political spoilsman, probably will be alive for another century, for the propagandists of the Bank of the United States could teach the columnists of the McCormick press many agile tricks.

Neither of the proposals outlined above offers a true solution. The unscrambling of omelets presents difficulties, and the quasi-public enterprise is America's most thoroughly scrambled of all.

The first solution disregards the fact that there are large numbers of people who have invested their savings in such enterprises; for it is justifiable to use the term "investor" rather than "stockholder" in this case. The psychology of the country is that the dividends of this group must be maintained. Some technique must be evolved to preserve both their interests and the public's. Congress, taking that into consideration, in 1945 granted an additional subsidy to the railroads approximating the annual cost of the WPA after recovery began to take effect, by granting them abrogation of the contracts for reduced rates entered into when the Nation gave some billions of dollars' worth of land to the rail lines as a bonus.

The second solution overlooks the existence of actual or potential competition in many of these fields. You can travel by air, rail, bus, or water to many destinations. You can cook with gas, oil, coal, wood, or electricity. During the depression, the "jitney-bus" provided enthusiastic competition for traction lines.

Additional complications are presented by the chaotic picture of rail and utility finance. There are many railroads in pawn, directly or otherwise, to the Reconstruction Finance Corporation. The Securities Exchange Commission is still endeavoring to bring some realism into the power field, but the process of disentangling holding companies, operating companies, engineering companies, superholding companies, and investment companies is slow and difficult.

That there can be an immediate answer to all the questions involved does not seem too probable. To return to the era of the rapacity of the railroad barons or to the recklessness of the Insull period is incredible. To nationalize the railroads offers extraordinary difficulties and, if it were done, it might result in the choking off of competitive means of transportation or the rapid disintegration of rail transport in favor of other media, depending on technological and psychological factors that cannot be predicted.

Extemporization seems the only course. The problems of the "utilities," meaning the electric, gas, and local transportation fields, seem to be working out slowly but surely. Regulation there can be effective, and competitive sources of power on the one hand and application of the "yardstick" through such necessarily public operations as the Tennessee Valley Authority on the other can protect the public interest.

Transportation presents the greatest difficulty. The railroads undoubtedly lag behind every other enterprise in the country in efficiency. They are reluctant to make changes, to adopt new methods, or to clarify even in the minds of their management their own status; they do not know whether they are public or private business, and they are not enterprising enough, except in lobbying, to merit the name of enterprise. Possibly with careful regulation, with an absolute divorcement of the rails from any competitive form of transportation, and with some application of the "yardstick" principle in fixing certain rates, they may be restored to health. Where competitive lines exist, competition must be enforced and, in addition, the transportation companies must be restrained from discrimination against certain sections of America.

The economic pattern of America is additionally complicated by two other factors, the government corporation and the nationally owned wartime industrial establishment. The use of the latter to facilitate the development of the South and especially the West, and its potential value as a weapon against monopoly, can be visualized readily. Resolute refusal to lease any facilities to any corporation or individual ever convicted of violation of the antitrust statutes, encouragement of competitors in many industries where underproduction exists, and gradual liquidation of the governmental holdings over a period of not less than thirty years can do much to give America an economy of abundance.

The government corporation was a device of the waning days of the twenties, when the gilt had worn rather thoroughly off the bizarre ornamentation of America's economy. It came as a ready-made device for the New Deal in some of its experiments. The experiments, most of them, were good ones; even the ones that did not work too well. But the technique of the government corporation was not a good technique.

The concentration of power in the hands of the Reconstruction Finance Corporation and its numberless subsidiaries is dangerous. It has not been badly used, thus far. There were a few extremely unwise loans made in its earlier days, when it was somewhat dominated by Republican partisans; but even then it was conducted at least as prudently as the best private banking corporations.

However, the fact remains that the Reconstruction Finance Corporation and its subsidiaries now completely dominate finance in this country. Conceivably it might call all of its loans to the rail lines, foreclose, and dominate transportation. With a slight frown it might frighten industry into the weeping-willies some morning, if it fell into the wrong hands. The elements of public control are too scant for national safety.

Most government corporations operating within specific fields, however, are well safeguarded. This is true of such institutions as the Federal Deposit Insurance Corporation, which is hardly more than a Federal-guarantee mutual insurance company for banks. It is also true of the Federal Land Banks, and the Banks for Coöperatives.

The corporate form of Tennessee Valley Authority and Rural Electrification Authority, of course, is fictional. They are public corporations in the actual sense, owned by the people through their government, and under the constant scrutiny of Congress.

Accounting supervision of all these corporate bodies should be brought under the Comptroller's office for the convenience of Congress, which should exercise greater supervision in some particulars. Supervision of policies, incidentally, does not mean interference with operations and should not affect the continuity of the activities of these entities.

These suggestions represent very slight changes in the American economic system. They propose reforms, not revolutionary reorganization. They are based upon the assumption that American industry has not become static and will not become static for a good many generations.

There is a difference between planning for a dynamic social and economic system and planning for a static system. In the one instance, any planning must partake of the nature of improvisation; it must be gradually experimental; it must conserve all the possible good in existing institutions and systems, and seek to repair as often as possible rather than to rebuild. In the other instance of a static national economy, planning of a different type might be justified.

There are difficulties in making the decision about the completion of any cycle within a nation. The inevitable question arises: Who shall make the decision? Those who assert that any nation has become absolutely static, so that experimentalism and improvisation are inadequate to solve its problems, should be infallible. They should possess a degree of clairvoyance that can be attributed to no group of men in past history; they would need to know the whole future of science, of industrial and agricultural technology; they would have to discern today the dreams and desires of men who will be born a full millennium hence.

Such wisdom is asserted to be the possession of those who embrace the ideologies of any form of authoritarianism. It descends upon prospective Fourth-Vice-Presidents and incipient Fourth-Assistant-Commissars when they read Dennis or Foster; immediately they become acquainted with the breadth of the earth, with the way of a serpent upon a rock, with the treasuries of the snow; instantly they are equipped to tame the unicorn, to bind Behemoth, or to draw up Leviathan with a hook; or so they claim.

America is not yet mature enough for their services. There is the South to rebuild and the West to build before even our geographical frontiers shall be exhausted; and the new frontiers of science await exploration. The future challenges our common country to cast out its fears, and, performing each day its daily tasks and eating each day its daily bread, to use its strength, its imagination, and its courage to meet current problems and solve them.

14

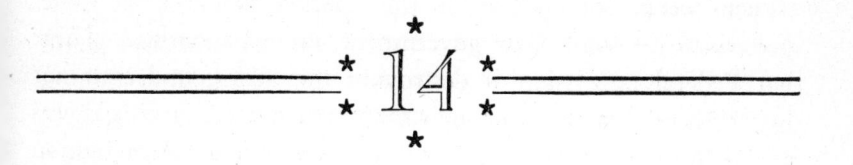

THE ROLE OF THE STATES

THE GOVERNMENTAL SYSTEM established for the United States is one of the most complicated and intricate known to any nation. In theory, it is an indissoluble union of indestructible States, forty-eight of them at this time. The Federal Constitution and most of the State Constitutions embody elaborate provisions for establishing systems of checks and balances, to prevent executive, legislative, or judicial branches of the government from becoming relatively too powerful.

Not all of the relationships between governmental units have been resolved. The debate over whether "the Constitution follows the flag" has not been settled; there were echoes of Senator Augustus O. Bacon's powerful denunciations of imperialism in a recent dissent by Mr. Justice Frank Murphy and Mr. Justice Wiley Rutledge in the case of the Japanese war criminals. The relationship between the States and the Federal government remains undetermined in many particulars; a more conservative Supreme Court than the present could discover a broad territory exempt from any government, because it lay outside State control and not within that of the national government.

Each week, somewhere in the country, some responsible spokesman for some State government utters a mournful plaint that Federal aggression is destroying the States, undermining their authority, taking over their spheres of service, turning them into nothing more than geographical subdivisions. Although a person grown politically cynical might detect that these cries about Federal intervention in local affairs come most often from Democrats when they are the party out of power, and have originated from Republican sources more often since the election of 1932, there is, no doubt, a widespread feeling that the States are being deprived of much of their power and that centralization of government in Washington is something of a menace.

Very seldom is there heard a resounding demand that States' rights be maintained by the States' assumption of responsibilities. Yet if county and municipal government on the one hand, and the Federal government on the other, displayed such a tendency to shirk responsibility as do State governments in general, there would be governmental chaos in America; and, moreover, it is extremely unlikely that the citizens' garbage would be moved next week.

When I was Attorney General of Georgia, a member of the Legislature descended upon my office to discuss the plight of the Georgia farmer.

His discussion turned very largely upon a denunciation of Washington, of the Triple-A, of interference with production and wages and prices and distribution, of subsidies for soil-building crops, and of the New Deal in general.

"They are just trying to destroy States' rights," he said. "What we need is a State law that will make our own agriculture prosperous. I am going to introduce such a bill in the Assembly tomorrow, and I want you to help draw it."

It is not uncommon for the Law Department to assist members in the preparation of bills, so I expressed my willingness to help in putting his measure into shape.

"Now what are you going to put in the bill?" I asked him.

"You just draw a bill that will make agriculture in Georgia prosperous. You ought to know about drawing up laws. You fix it and send it up to me and I'll introduce it," he said and stalked out.

I called my secretary and dictated the only farm relief measure that seemed suitable under the circumstances. In full, it read as follows:

> A Bill to be entitled An Act to Make Agriculture Prosperous in Georgia; and for other purposes.
> Be it enacted by the General Assembly of Georgia and it is hereby enacted by authority of the same:
> Section 1. On and after the passage of this act, agriculture in the State of Georgia be, and the same is hereby declared to be, prosperous.
> Section 2. All laws and parts of laws in conflict with this Act be and the same are hereby repealed.

I forwarded it to the member the next morning, but he did not see fit to introduce it at that session of the Assembly, and the prosperity of Georgia agriculture continued to be dependent upon such factors as the labor of the farmer, the condition of the weather, the state of the world market for cotton and peanuts, and the interference of Washington and its Triple-A subsidies.

But the member of the Georgia Legislature was exceptional

among the more fervently vocative defenders of States' Rights in that he was anxious to do something about the matter. The great majority of those who wail loudest about Federal interference are those most unwilling to see the States assume responsibility.

This was disclosed rather thoroughly in the fight over the Federal ballot for those in the armed services. The measure seemed to me then, and still seems to me, to be of doubtful wisdom; in addition, it did invade the sovereignty of the States to some extent. But three other things were evident; that the soldiers wanted to vote; that they had a right to vote; that the State governments were doing nothing about defending the right of their citizens.

Georgia took prompt action in the matter. A special session of the Legislature was called, and, in five days, the shortest time possible under the State Constitution, a Soldiers' Voting Act was passed. It was simple in the extreme. Men and women in service could register by mail in their home county; in addition, any relative or friend could obtain the necessary registration card and send it to them to be filled out. Ballots were mailed to all those in service who registered, and the ballots could be attested by any officer.

Democratic processes are slow and ponderous. It might have been impossible for the State governments to prepare for service voting in the Congressional elections and State elections of 1942; but, certainly, in the interval before the Presidential election of 1944, it should have been possible for even the most dilatory State government's leadership to find out that there was a war, that a substantial number of young men had been drafted and that a large number of girls had enlisted in the Wac, Wave or Spar. Only when it was discovered that the Roosevelt

Administration was suggesting that Congress find some way for those in service to cast their ballots was the reaction immediate and intense; Congress must not invade the sacred premises of the States; the Federal government must not provide a ballot for State officials, including Presidential electors. The suggestions that the State governments get busy and do something themselves were either unanswered, in general, or were given the reply that the States did not have the money to provide such services.

There is a gulf, of almost the exact dimensions that separated Dives and Lazarus, between States' rights as set out in the Kentucky Resolutions and States' rights as described by the tired political hacks who seek an excuse for doing nothing. The States have power enough to solve a great many problems; they are equipped to defend their citizens against any menacing wrongs. But they are not busy righting wrongs or solving problems; they are busy complaining and applying to Washington for assistance, simultaneously. They refuse to get their forty-eight houses in order.

The Georgia ballot measure was ready for the primary and the general election of 1944. In the Democratic primary, the percentage of service votes approximated that of the whole population; but in the November general election, more men and women in the service voted proportionately than any other group. That is acceptable as evidence that those in the service did want to vote and that a State system of voting could be devised that would make is unnecessary for the Federal government to interfere.

Georgia was the first State to pass a Soldiers' Voting Law. A number of others followed. Some **were** effective; others, including that of New York, seemed designed to prevent service men and women from obtaining a ballot. The percentage of votes cast by those in the Army and Navy was higher in Georgia than in any other State, an indication that the promptness of our action and the effectiveness of the law made it easy to get ballots, even when the Pacific had to be crossed twice by the slip of paper that represents the highest privilege of a citizen.

One excuse for State inadequacy is the condition of State finance. It is the nearest approach to a valid explanation that is ever offered; it has some merit. For the States have been inadequately financed for many years; most of them had large debts when the war started; many of them had and still have debts that have been on the books for generations.

When I took office as Governor of Georgia, I found that, some years before, the Navy had turned back to the State a magnificent silver service presented by the State to the battleship *Georgia,* which has been decommissioned. That silver service brought me into direct and personal collision with the State debt. For Mrs. Arnall found out that it had never been paid for, and expressed somewhat forthrightly a demand that the forty-year-old bill be paid or the silver removed from the Executive Mansion and stored somewhere else.

Eventually the State Auditor tracked down the heirs of the silversmith who had provided the service, and who had lost his business in consequence; the debt was settled and the ornate punchbowl and the candelabra and the cups made their reappearance at the Mansion. It took considerable searching to uncover the details of the transaction, for the bill for the silver did not appear on the official list of Georgia's debts, which, when I became governor, totalled $35,961,630.35 more.

In proportion to the annual tax revenues of the State of Georgia at that time this was a debt larger than that of the Federal government before the war and after the New Deal expenditures for national recovery.

A nation can afford deficit spending for a considerable period. Sometimes such deficit spending is unavoidable, as in the case of war. Sometimes it is desirable for social or economic reasons. But a nation possesses absolute sovereignty; it can issue fiat currency, as did Lincoln to finance the War Between the States; it can devalue the currency, as Roosevelt did to reëstablish a relationship with other currencies and to prevent ruinous deflation in 1933; it can borrow limitlessly, because it has limitless tax resources. A State government possesses none of these rights. It cannot wisely owe money, except for self-liquidating public improvements. Without jeopardy to its citizens and its own solvency, it must have a balanced budget.

Georgia obtained a balanced budget. Georgia became debt free, officially, on July 1, 1946, with the calling of its remaining outstanding bonds and the establishment of reserves in the State Treasury to retire fully a few certificates that had not matured and could not be called before maturity.

To obtain that result, within a three-year period, it was necessary to reorganize State spending methods and to practice an economy that was onerous and sometimes unpopular.

The Legislature of 1943 passed a realistic appropriations act that left some margin for debt payment. It also increased the controls of the Budget Bureau over spending. But its greatest improvement came from giving the State Auditor genuine independence. That officer, who is Assistant Director of the Budget, the Governor serving as Director, had been appointed by the

Governor since the post was created. The Legislature followed my recommendation of having him elected by the Assembly.

Georgia, like most of the other Southern States, relies heavily upon excises to meet the cost of government. In a period of reduced gasoline sales, reduced sales of cigarettes and alcoholic beverages, and with the State income tax system affected by the increased Federal taxes which were deductible in computing net income in Georgia, we set to work to increase spending for education by more than one hundred twenty-five per cent and to eliminate the State debt. The Legislature had given me a remarkably efficient State Auditor, in the person of Edmund Thrasher, a career man in government with an intimate knowledge of departmental spending and a capacity for saying "no" in every dialect, including the sign language.

Avoiding unnecessary expenditures is difficult for any government, and economy is never too popular. There were occasional eruptions of signs in the Capitol washrooms, saying: "Do not use but one paper towel! Georgia is in debt." While there was never any actual shortage of carbon paper, pencils, and stenographic notebooks, there was a certain irritation felt about the economy program among State employees; and there is a possibility that in our zeal to dramatize the need for economy we occasionally annoyed people.

Georgia's debt was not altogether a new debt. Part of it dated back to 1838, when Georgia began construction of its Western and Atlantic Railroad, linking Chattanooga and Atlanta and the West to Georgia's Atlantic ports. For over a century the bonds had been refinanced periodically, but the thought of actually redeeming them seemed never to have occurred to anyone. There were other odds and ends, including a mass of transactions involving the State Highway Department, which had been in a state of insolvency, technically at least even in its best days, since its creation in 1921. The rentals of the Western and Atlantic Railroad had been discounted for many years to come, through rental-anticipation warrants. There were various smaller items of floating debt.

The State debt had figured in many political campaigns. There always had been much dispute as to its amount, its creators, and the purposes for which the money had been used. There had been a great many charges of breach of faith with the voters, of waste, of criminal extravagance. One State officer had been convicted of using Highway funds to build a home for himself. The ugly scandal that had developed over the asphalt monopoly, led to my introduction into the maze of antitrust law enforcement. The very existence of a State debt, behind which mysterious financing projects could hide, was an invitation to bad government and dishonest government. A balanced budget, the gradual development of reserves sufficient to stabilize income in times of economic fluctuation, and a planned program for public works are essentials to good government at the State level.

There are certain other aspects of State financing that present differences from the Federal pattern. There are some public services to which the State, operating through corporate Authorities, can lend assistance and credit in building self-liquidating facilities. Had the Western and Atlantic Railroad been built under this kind of system, the debt would have been retired before the War Between the States. Georgia is experimenting slowly in this direction, and contemplates the use of this device to erect facilities, docks and warehouses, at the ports of Brunswick and Savannah, which need development. These obligations, however, will be direct obligations of the Port Authority, redeemable from its earnings; they will not be on the State's debit ledger in 2064.

In the future, unless some Governor is called upon in an emergency to use the public credit to "repel invasion by the common enemy" as permitted in the Constitution, Georgia can create no public debt except by the consent of a majority of citizens voting in a referendum. No floating debt can be created under any circumstance; every item on the budget, when it is approved each quarter, is covered by an immediate transfer of money from the State Treasury to the department account.

In July 1946, the State Treasurer stamped "paid in full" upon the Georgia bonds that had been redeemed. Some of my friends, who regarded some of the evidence of indebtedness as nothing more than evidence of a considerable fraud practised on the State, suggested that a bond-burning ceremony be staged in Louisville, the old capital of Georgia, where General James Jackson burned with fire from heaven the infamous Yazoo Fraud papers, representing another great waste of Georgia's wealth. They suggested a duplication of the Jackson staging. A pilgrimage to Jackson's shrine seemed a little ostentatious to me; the debts, at their worst, did not represent the marauding of historic financial buccaneers as did the theft of the Yazoo lands; where fraud was involved, and waste was far more common than fraud, the debts redeemed in my Administration represented the accumulated pilferings of petty rogues who stole stamps and dabbled in asphalt deals. So we burned the bonds at the State Capitol in Atlanta, and used an ordinary match instead of a sun-glass to ignite them. They burned readily enough; they were old, and dry and brittle.

State Auditor Thrasher, however, indulged himself in a tremendous luxury in celebration of the event. In an orgy of spending, the first in his official life, he published in every county-seat paper in Georgia a financial statement, disclosing the anticipated expenditures, the cash on hand, the reserves in full, and the fact that there was no State debt. It cost $8,000; but it gave Georgians for the first time in their lives a chance to see precisely where their State government stood.

The picture of Georgia and of Georgia's State finances does not differ too much from that common to most States in America. It seemed worse, because of the intolerable affront to education through the discrediting of the University, and because of the widespread publicity given Georgia's evil chain-gang penal system. But in more than half of the States, the pattern is basically the same financially. In most of them, State government is indolent and unwilling to meet the challenge of today. There are no States that are well run, by the standards of the best and most wisely operated municipalities, such as, for example, Cleveland, where the ghost of Tom Johnson still watches over his City on a Hill and forbids that its light be concealed.

There must be some readjustment of the general tax situation in the Nation, so that State finances may be better ordered. The Federal government must share some of the most lucrative fields of taxation with the States, rather than preempt them for itself, and force the States to regressive forms of taxation. The solution of this difficulty is not impossible, if the State governments show inclinations to assume responsibility and to demand a share in the yield of productive taxation. Until they do so, the Federal agencies will continue to expand and will continue to need increasing grants from Congress, and Congress will be reluctant to share taxation with the States when the States have no plans for spending money except in their conventionally wasteful and disorganized way.

Nothing would give good government in America greater impetus than a gradual decentralization. Many in the Federal establishment concur, and are attempting to bring Federal agencies closer to the people by apportioning greater authority to regional offices and by removing many agencies from Washington. The States, however, present the best medium for decentralization; they already are here; they already have powers; they already have functioning organizations; they have almost everything but a sense of responsibility.

The need for governmental reform at the State level is acute. In emphasizing the shortcomings in Georgia, where I am most familiar with government, I do not mean to suggest that its State government was much worse than average. Indeed, its basic organization of agencies and its distribution of authority among the three branches was better than in many other States. The appellate jurisdiction of its court of last resort was more adequate than in Massachusetts. The Governor's authority was not so dangerously hedged as in Connecticut. The tax system was not in the chaos that seems chronic in New Jersey, nor was it as regressive as that adopted in Ohio in recent years.

Nevertheless, Georgia's government was filled with anachronisms. There was the penal system, for example.

Georgia's chain gangs were anachronisms. They had outlived their usefulness. It may surprise many to learn that once, a half century ago, they marked a very genuine advance in penology in America. That was the day of the "silent system" in the East, and of the "convict lease system" in the South. The horrors of those days were rather thoroughly forgotten; the men who suffered under them are dead; the misdeeds of the wardens and the lease owners are recorded only in mildewing newspaper files and dust-covered books in the reference stacks of libraries. Georgia was one of the first States to break the "lease system," and substitute work on the public highways for the prisoners.

The chain-gang system was a bad system. I do not know of a good system of dealing with men who have committed crimes. No government has found a good system. The chain gang was not good, but it was less evil than the lease system, and it was not marked by unusual brutality until the automobile came.

The prisoners on the Georgia chain gangs were not the only victims of technological progress in history; the weavers had their story to tell generations before; and at the turn of the century child labor was so common that it was assumed by most Americans to be an institution sanctified by Divine ordinance. That there were parallels to their mishaps, doubtless, was small solace to those on the chain gangs, who found that, with the coming of the auto, the monotony of their lives was exhilarated by a speedup and stretchout system that was brutally enforced by the lash, by staking out in the sun, by coffinlike sweat boxes.

The penal establishment suffered from duality of control. There were county chain gangs, where misdemeanor prisoners and felony convicts assigned by the State worked side by side. There were State chain gangs, called by the euphemistic title of public works camps, that were worst of all. There was the State prison, a new medium-security unit with an adjacent farm, that had been established with excellent equipment for manufactures, but that had been stripped of machinery and was a hotbed for idleness and vice.

The county camps had become bad immediately after the auto's arrival made roadbuilding imperative; but they were soon relatively cleaned up. My own acquaintance, before I became Governor, had been with camps of this kind, devoted mainly to routine maintenance on rural roads. The prisoners were well fed in most of the counties, seldom overworked, and not treated with cruelty except in the inevitable incidence of a few sadistic guards.

One of the aggravating features of the Georgia penal system was the extraordinary system controlling clemency, the granting of paroles and pardons. It had become an open scandal. The frequent charges that pardons were bought and sold by political racketeers made discipline difficult in the prison system and affronted the public. The same commission that administered the prisons had the power to recommend clemency, but the personal approval of the Governor was required in each case. The day that I took office, enough files of clemency requests, bearing commission approval, came to my desk to require three months' work, if no time were devoted to any other work out of an eight-hour day.

Cleaning up the clemency problem was one early and easy accomplishment. A nonpartisan board, protected by constitutional status, was created and given full authority over all pardons and paroles. A modern parole system was inaugurated for prisoners. The results were immediate and striking, and so much was accomplished so rapidly that many of us assumed that the other ills of the prison system would disappear rapidly.

They did not. The State-operated work camps came to public attention. Conditions at the State Prison were revealed. I requested the committees of the Assembly assigned to consider penal legislation, to make an investigation of conditions. What they uncovered was shocking.

After the State Senate's committee had visited one State camp, it rendered this report:

> We find acts of cruelty at this camp in the whipping and beating of prisoners. As for example, the assistant warden admitted that an ignorant white boy was sent a pair of pajamas by his poverty-stricken relatives and on the night after receiving them he put these pajamas on to sleep in them, when it was a rule that they should sleep in prison night gowns. The assistant warden learning that the prisoner was wearing the simple article sent him by his family took him out of bed and gave him a whipping. This exemplifies the kind of reasons and excuses found by some of the officials for whipping prisoners in Georgia.

The House committee investigated another State camp. Its report was not more optimistic:

> We found much evidence of cruel and inhuman treatment of prisoners on the part of certain wardens and guards such as the use of picks or leg irons, the use of sweat-boxes, together with mistreatment of prisoners by so-called walking bosses who resort to the use of clubs, sticks and other brutal means of punishment. We found in many instances that such treatment of prisoners had definitely proven injurious to the prisoner's health and was certainly not conducive to the purpose of rehabilitation.

The presiding officers of the two branches of the Assembly, at my request, also made rapid surveys of Georgia's prisons and of those in some other Southern States that had cleaned house earlier. A brief portion of their report disclosed:

> In no other state did we find leg irons. In no other state did the prisoners complain of floggings and beatings. In no other state

did we find the prisoners generally sullen, bad tempered and talking of revolt. In Georgia alone we found no intelligent effort being made to rehabilitate the prisoners and fit them to return to civil life. If the State does not make an intelligent effort to rehabilitate these men and women they will be criminals when they return to civil life and will finally wind up in the penitentiary again.

The factual reports of the members of the Assembly produced in Georgia the condition of public sentiment that I anticipated, a condition that no amount of other criticism could have produced. The public was aroused over prison conditions. There was a brief counter-attack by the political opposition, which suggested that the Administration was interested in coddling prisoners.

Their eventual argument was that the prisoners would not work without harsh treatment and that the State would lose financially by reform of the penal establishment. Of course, it is obvious that the use of man power to perform laboriously operations that a machine can do much more efficiently is not economical. Moreover, the economic aspect was unimportant; it is not the function of a penal system to make money, but to reform the inmates. The Georgia chain gang, and the marble-plated State Prison at Reidsville with its grumbling and idle inmates, reformed no one; they functioned to destroy lives, to check the future of men and women.

As the facts permeated Georgia, the State became more aroused. I called the Legislature into extraordinary session and laid the problem before them. In my message to that body, I told them:

When I was driving about Georgia in the summer of 1942, a

friend pointed out to me a large tract of land. If ever land had been blighted and destroyed in value, robbed of its richness, that land had been. It was stripped of topsoil, so that the red clay was disclosed. It was gullied and washed, so that the few saplings growing upon it were twisted and warped. It grew no crops. It could hardly grow the hardiest and most persistent weed. That land was a relic, my friend told me, of the convict lease system. The man who had owned it died long ago. His estate vanished in litigation. Even the land was cursed by his misdeeds.

That picture has been in my mind ever since.

It is inescapable that if we destroy men, we destroy everything. These men in prison have committed wrongs against society. They have killed, and stolen, and cheated. They have wrought upon themselves the disapproval of their fellow citizens. They have been taken into custody and tried in our courts and judged guilty for their misdeeds and sent away to be taught that they must live in decent harmony with their fellow men. It is the intent of our people, as it is the letter and spirit of our State law, that when they have reformed, they shall be set free, that they shall walk abroad like other men, breathing the air of freedom as do other men.

In the past we have denied them the treatment that any man must have. We have caged them like wild animals. We have let them thirst and hunger. We have beaten them. We have chained them. We have forged iron bands about their legs. We have denied them the very solace of the Christian religion, for when I took office as Governor of Georgia there was no full-time chaplain at the prison where more than a thousand Georgia men were expiating their crimes and seeking to be rebuilt into useful citizens.

I know that we live in a practical day. We hear a great deal of talk about being practical, being efficient, doing what is wise and prudent. I think it is high time that we talked some once again about doing what is right.

It is not right to shut a man like a mad dog in a cage and whip him with a rubber hose and work him as a brutal drayman might work a sick horse. And when I think of boys huddled with professional criminals obtaining no education and no religious instruction, I am disgusted and I know that you are; but when I think of men—men made in the image of the most high God—dying in prison without the consolation of a man of God at their side, I am heart-sick. These things must not continue in our State.

I do not believe that these shameful conditions can be corrected by less than a complete reorganization of the penal system. There has been no true reform of that system since, almost a half century ago, Georgia ended the iniquitous sale of human beings under the guise of the lease system. It is the responsibility of the General Assembly to consider the needs of the correctional institutions and to formulate the kind of system that Georgia needs and that Georgians desire; a humane system of rehabilitation for these social misfits that will enable them to be restored to society as men and women, not wild beasts.

The extraordinary session on penal reform lasted five days, the minimum time in which a measure could be enacted under the State Constitution. A new Department of Corrections was established. Prohibitions against brutal disciplinary methods were written into the law. Provisions for segregation of first offenders and juveniles were established.

Reorganizing the prison system proved a difficult administrative task. An outstanding Georgia businessman, Wiley L. Moore, agreed to accept temporarily the thankless job as Director of the agency. The Federal Bureau of Prisons permitted several experts on their staff to assist with the planning.

They removed the shackles from prisoners. They gave them ordinary work clothing instead of stripes. They improved the food supply in the prison and in the camps. They sifted out personnel, and employed better, and better-paid, wardens and guards. They used gallons of disinfectants. They removed the criminal insane from the State Prison to a new building attached to the State Hospital. They inaugurated a system of classification of prisoners. They began to work harmoniously with our Board of Pardons and Paroles for rehabilitation.

The Georgia penal system is not the best in the Nation. It will require several years to school personnel, to equip the State prison properly, to provide all the facilities needed for complete segregation of first-offenders of different age groups. The pattern has been established, however, and the work is well under way.

If State governments are slow to correct abuses, they are also too frequently unwilling to conduct experiments for the benefit of their citizens.

Georgia's economy is based upon agriculture. There has been a gradual shifting from a cotton economy to diversification. Livestock topped cotton as a cash producer for farmers of the State in 1945, and tobacco and peanuts are important sources of revenue, with the poultrymen and the dairy farmers becoming more important annually.

Dairying and poultry raising became more profitable when new industries developed in Georgia during the war. This was confirmation of the belief that diversification depended upon a balanced agrarian-industrial economy.

One experiment was with the problem of industry. The war plants had trained and developed a pool of skilled workers, who would be unemployed when the plants closed. Many could return to their former occupations, without the serious loss of earning capacity. Many others, however, would face employment at lower skills and lower wages than they had acquired as a result of their training. The Georgia Agricultural and Industrial Development Board recommended a program of small industries, identified with the agricultural and other resources of the State. Their findings had a great deal to do with the establishment of more than three hundred new industries in Georgia in 1945.

The board also undertook some valuable experiments in agriculture. Diversification of farm production is unquestionably desirable in the South. It can result in a much higher average farm income. It is easy to determine the basic relationship between diversification and the existence of an industrial population, able to consume the products of the farm. But practical testing of production costs of specific crops, actual demonstrations of the possibilities of speedily rebuilding marginal land to productivity, were needed in Georgia.

Cason Callaway, chairman of the board's agricultural panel, had conducted some remarkable experiments in West Georgia. His suggestion of a number of experimental farms over Georgia, owned by local businessmen and operated by skilled farmers, was adopted. A hundred corporations, with seven members investing $1,000 each in the local enterprise, have been formed in Georgia to test out under local conditions the possibilities of diversification. The experiments will be of unique value to the State; they will disclose what problems the average small farmer must solve, and what difficulties he must overcome, in adapting himself and his land to diversified planting instead of cotton raising.

Each small local unit has engaged a practical and experienced farmer, most often a man with training in an agricultural college, to operate the farm. The new crops include blueberries, strawberries, celery, onions, many kinds of truck seldom planted in Georgia before, as well as the more usual crops. Several farms are experimenting with small grains, which Georgia produced in large volume before the War Between the States. Most of the farms engage in some dairying, and a majority will have fish ponds. After a five-year experimental period, the farmer in charge of each hundred-acre tract will have the right to purchase the farm on liberal terms.

No portion of this program was expensive to the State. As in the case of Georgia's pioneering in the field of vocational rehabilitation, the eventful profits from even a modest success will far outrun all the costs and leave the gains to the individual and to the community as profit, economically and socially.

State governments generally seem opposed to making any experiments for which they may be called upon to bear a part of the expense. They are inclined to limit experimentation to fields in which the cost is borne by the Federal government.

During the campaign of 1942, when I was travelling about Georgia with all the conventional equipment of a candidate, including sound trucks and an advance car to pass out handbills, our party made a practice of establishing field headquarters in some conveniently located town and then working from that base. To finance the day-by-day operations, I passed over various sums to one or another of the staff.

One week end, the whole force moved into Albany, using it as a base to visit the Southwest Georgia area. Albany boasted, just outside the city, a wide-open community that tolerated, perhaps even encouraged, games of chance in which the chance was assumed wholly by the player. One night, after two speeches during the afternoon, I went to bed; but Cookie Phillips, the leader of the caravan and the individual to whom the funds currently were entrusted, went on a tour of the high spots and discovered a roulette game.

Ten-dollar bill after ten-dollar bill of my campaign money found its way to the table in exchange for chips that reverted quickly to the man at the wheel. Finally, Cookie pulled out a solitary five, played and lost, and prepared to leave.

"You quitting for the night, Cookie?" one of the onlookers asked him.

"Sure, I'm quitting," he answered. "Done lost five dollars of my own money on that thing."

The attitude of State government is not too different from that of Cookie Phillips. Experimentation at their own expense seems to be very painful indeed.

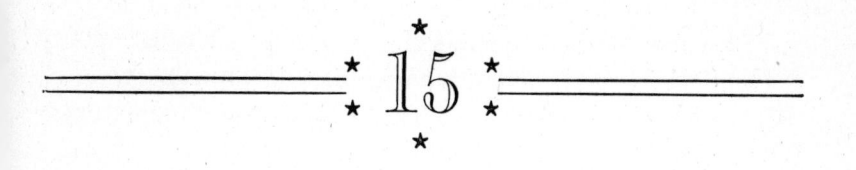

A MODERN STATE CONSTITUTION

MANY OF THE proposals that I submitted to Georgia in the campaign platform of 1942 required constitutional amendments to be carried into effect. They made an imposing list of reforms for the Legislature to consider: constitutional boards for the common schools and the colleges, restrictions upon the Governor's authority to dismiss employees of departments, independent agencies to deal with clemency and with fish and game resources, the "teen-age amendment" reducing the voting age to eighteen, and reorganization of the budget system.

The Assembly acted promptly, and unanimously, on these measures. With the exception of the "teen-age amendment," every one of the Administration measures passed unanimously. In late summer of 1943, the voters ratified the amendments.

In submitting to the people the twenty-eight measures adopted in 1943, the Legislature brought to 301 the number of amendments to Georgia's Constitution that had been submitted since the document was adopted in 1877. At least that was the number finally agreed upon as correct; so frequently had the Constitution been amended that five amendments had vanished in some way, and the records disclosed only 296 that had been either adopted or rejected, although unquestionably 301 had been submitted.

The 1943 Assembly agreed with me that the Georgia Constitution needed thorough revision. The seventh Constitution in the State's history, it had been written immediately after President Hayes ended bayonet-and-carpetbag rule in the State. Its framers had seen the reckless abuse of the authority of the Governor, so they shackled that office. They had seen the wanton waste of public money by the General Assembly, so they limited the purposes for which appropriations could be made to the barest minimum. They had seen the public credit, not only of the State but of its towns and counties, loaned to dishonest promoters, so they placed drastic restrictions on the authority of local governments. General Robert Toombs, who dominated many of the sessions of the Constitutional Convention, was dissatisfied only in his failure to outlaw tax exemptions for favored railroad corporations; their lobby was too strong; but the general result pleased him and he declared that the Convention had "locked the door of the Treasury and thrown away the key."

A new Constitution for Georgia was not a novelty in 1877. Georgians are willing to experiment in government. The State was one of the few in this Nation to attempt a government without a written constitution, operating on the British theory of parliamentary government. Constitutions were adopted in 1777, in 1789, in 1798, in 1861, in 1865 and in 1868. The Constitution of 1868 was a Reconstruction document, and among the worst of those instruments inflicted upon the South.

The Constitution of 1798 was the handiwork of General James

Jackson, the revolutionary hero and friend of Thomas Jefferson. Among the earlier State constitutions in America, it probably was the best, except for that of Maryland. It was a model of simplicity, and except for a change in the method of election of the Governor, originally chosen by the General Assembly, it was amended only in minor particulars until the War Between the States.

The Constitution of 1877 proved too rigid. Demands for public services increased, and each demand required one or more amendments to the Constitution to satisfy. The local communities found themselves in a strait jacket; as local public improvements became necessary they sought local amendments to the Constitution. Of the twenty-eight amendments submitted in 1943, twelve were local in character, and this was the smallest number of local amendments in several sessions of the Assembly.

One of the obstacles to decentralization of government in the United States is the inadequacy of State government; and one of the major causes of this inadequacy is the antiquated character of most State Constitutions. Georgia's Constitution of 1877 had become a hodge-podge of amendments, some of which were in conflict, of exceptions to general rules, of emergency legislation that should have been dealt with by statute, and would have been, if the Constitution had been more flexible. Georgia's constitution was no exception to the general rule in the Nation. There are a few modern instruments that harmonize with the day, and a few old ones that possess sufficient flexibility to meet modern conditions; but most State Constitutions need thorough revision.

Most State Constitutions, for example, were written before the days of modern public services, such as electric light, gas, and motor transportation. Utilities of those days were limited almost entirely to railroads and streetcars, and the streetcars were horse-drawn; people used kerosene for lights and often drew their own water from their own wells. Naturally, few State Constitutions contain provisions by which a local self-government unit might finance the erection of a waterworks or an electric distribution system through the issuance of self-liquidating revenue certificates. There were no self-liquidating projects in the days the instruments were written, except, perhaps, turnpikes and tollbridges.

Theoretically, it is possible to write a State Constitution so simply, placing so much authority in the Legislature, the Governor and the Judiciary, that statutory measures can deal with every problem and frequent amending of the basic law will not be required. Modeling a State Constitution on the Federal Constitution in these particulars is thoroughly possible.

If this were done, of course, it would necessitate the establishment of a cabinet system in the States, permitting the Governor the same general authority given the President. It would require placing almost all State agencies under the Governor's power. It would require more frequent and longer sessions of the Legislatures of the States. It would very likely result in smaller legislative bodies, less representative of the people since long sessions would not attract men not making a career of politics and government. It might result in more efficient government, in the most limited sense of the word "efficient."

For efficiency in government is not precisely the same thing as efficiency in an electric motor. An electric motor is employed to move the wheels-and-cogs of a machine, or to pump water, or to cause a ceiling fan to rotate; its efficiency can be measured readily.

The efficiency of government is measurable first by a basic standard: Does it carry out the will of the people? The other aspects of efficiency are secondary. If it is not capable of being responsive to the public will, it is inefficient absolutely; as a motor would be inefficient if it were designed for a well-pump and would serve no other use when you wished a motor that would turn a lathe.

Many of the relationships between subdivisions of a State have to be set out in a State Constitution, unless complete authority is vested in the Legislature; and there is a well-established opposition in most sections of the country to giving the Legislature such broad authority, without a popular check upon the result, just as there is objection to giving the Governor complete authority over the executive field.

It is almost unavoidable then that a State Constitution should be rather long and rather detailed, and that it should have to be amended rather frequently. It is also necessary that it be completely revised at intervals.

The Georgia Legislature took this view of the matter. Instead of summoning a Constitutional Convention, a Revision Commission was appointed. The twenty-three members of this Commission spent more than a year in studying the existing Constitution, debating changes, collating the amendments and reconciling them, making improvements in text, and adding provisions needed to modernize the instrument. The result was submitted to the 1945 General Assembly, which spent much of the session in reviewing the work of the Commission and discussing the recommended provisions. The new Constitution was approved by the Assembly and submitted to the people for ratification. They approved it overwhelmingly.

All the reforms of 1943 and 1945 were written into the instrument. The poll tax, a statutory tax that was a prerequisite for voting, had been eliminated by legislation, but the new Constitution specifically forbade the Legislatures of the future from making tax payment of any kind a prerequisite for the franchise. The voting requirements were modernized, so that literacy would be required of all voters and so that no person could qualify as a voter through property qualifications or under the "grandfather clause," by which a citizen otherwise disqualified could become a voter if one of his ancestors had served in the army of his country.

New financial provisions were adopted, to guarantee that Georgia would not create another floating debt. The educational establishment was placed on a more modern basis, with the county as the administrative local unit. A merit system for State employees was set up. The judicial system was simplified, and the State Supreme Court was increased from six to seven members, to avoid deadlocked decisions.

Some of the new provisions of the Georgia Constitution merit consideration as promising innovations in State government. These deal with State finances, with the increased independence accorded the local self-government units, and with the elimination of special favoritism in the tax structure.

The new Georgia Constitution eliminates one of the most complicating devices in State Finance, the allocation of taxes for specific purposes. Not every State in the Union is afflicted with a virulent case of this allocation-of-receipts, but most of them are. The device probably was hit upon by some farsighted legislator, whose vision was on political advancement. It apportions the income of the State among agencies without appropriation by the simple device of giving each agency the proceeds of a tax. In Georgia, with some reasonable relationship to reality, the gasoline tax was allocated to highways, in part; the other part went to the public schools. The schools also received the proceeds of the taxes on whiskey, beer and wine. The Confederate veterans, who numbered less than a score and who, with the widows of Confederate veterans, actually received about a hundred thousand dollars annually from the State, were allocated the proceeds from the tax on cigars, cigarettes and tobacco.

The system was a result of attaching a tax to a necessary function of government or to a widely demanded public service, so that the people would accept it without complaint. It had the slight drawback that on many occasions one agency would be rolling in wealth, while some equally essential service was curtailed for lack of funds. Since the allocations continued for the life of the tax, the people had no control over public spending through their legislative representatives.

The control over taxation and appropriations by the legislative branch of government is the life of democratic institutions. Legislative bodies frequently make unwise and extravagant grants of money; even more frequently they refuse adequate appropriations for essential services until popular pressure becomes insistent; but there is no other prudent way to handle public affairs. Moreover, if those in the executive branch of government present the statement of the needs of agencies in an intelligent manner to the Legislature, the members are usually prepared to apportion the income of the State prudently.

I believe the Georgia system of appropriations with relation to need, made by the Assembly each biennium from the State Treasury into which all State income flows, is the best system for State governments to adopt. Perpetual appropriations are a menace to good government.

Many States have granted tax exemptions to favored corporations. In Georgia, the tax exemptions granted to certain railroad lines had continued for more than a hundred years. Continuation of such subsidies by the State seemed unreasonable. There was a greater volume of debate over the section ending such tax exemptions than over any other, but, eventually, the Assembly agreed with the Revision Commission and passed the measure terminating these favors and abrogating the tax exemption contract. By coincidence, the Georgia vote upon this matter came almost at the same time that Congress abrogated a contract with certain railroads for fifty per cent reduction upon government freight, which had been entered into in consideration of grants of money and lands variously estimated as between a billion dollars and twenty billion dollars. In the case of Georgia's action, the railroads seemed unhappy, and entered into litigation that promises to be prolonged; they argued that a contract of that nature could not be broken by legislative action. In the case of doubling the Federal freight bill, there has come no complaint and no comment upon the sacredness of contracts; on the contrary, the rail lines issued a communiqué stating that, after all, they had spent the money grants and sold the lands, and that those were good reasons for ending the agreement.

One of the amusing aspects of the oratory of the more vehement States' rights advocates is their inconsistency upon the subject of decentralization within a State. In general, of those who seek to defend a do-nothing policy by urging that any innovation reduces State authority, the most vocative oppose any home rule for towns and counties.

There are a few instances in which the Federal government has increased its power at the expense of the States more or less deliberately; there are a good many instances where the Federal government has assumed responsibilities that might as well have been assumed by the States; there are very many instances in which State governments have kept their local self-government units in leading-strings.

The historical background of various States has played a considerable role in determining the status of the local units. Generally speaking, the local units have more autonomy in New England than elsewhere in America, although the best managed among larger cities seem to be found in the Middle West. The New England colonies lacked a central government in their formative period; it was a long time before Massachusetts Bay exercised hegemony within the borders of what has become Massachusetts, and the men of Plymouth still had charity and courage to withstand Boston in defense of honest pastors and men of good will for many years. Connecticut's township system has much to commend it. Local government in Vermont has a rugged independence.

New York retains traces of its position as conquered territory, as well as the effects of an upstate fear of dominance by the sprawling and teeming metropolis. The Southern States, which represented unusual methods of colonization in some instances, have veered from one extreme to another; in the period after Reconstruction most of them, including Georgia, stripped local government of almost all its power.

Georgia is now pioneering in an experiment in self-government, believing that decentralization can be carried to the local level in many particulars.

It required not less than thirteen changes in the Constitution of Georgia to attempt this experiment. The major measure provides that the Assembly shall provide various optional forms of government for counties and municipalities, so that citizens may adjust their government to their taste without having to appeal to the Legislature.

A mere listing of the other twelve provisions discloses the unwieldiness of the previous system of government in the State, a condition paralleled elsewhere. These included:

1. A requirement that notice shall be given of any local legislation to be introduced in the State Legislature. No bill may become law unless to it is attached a certificate of publication from the newspaper that is the official organ of the unit of government affected.

2. No special or local bill can lengthen or shorten the term of any elected local official, without a local referendum. Previously, political rivals of legislators had often found themselves dismissed as town mayors or as county commissioners.

3. Cities and counties were permitted to make zoning laws without submitting them to the State legislature.

4. Counties were permitted to spend revenues for many new purposes, including airports, parks, libraries, workmen's compensation for injuries, retirement funds for employees, and to create reserves for public works.

5. Political subdivisions were permitted to contract with each other for exchanges of services. Previous to this measure, two counties could not agree to permit children to attend the school nearest to them but in the county in which they did not live.

6. Bonds may be issued by a majority of registered voters voting in an election. Previously, counties and municipalities

could issue bonds only by obtaining a two-thirds majority of the registration; since Georgia had a permanent registration system, this resulted in great handicapping of public improvements.

7. A three per cent additional bonded indebtedness to meet emergency needs was permitted, with the proviso that these bonds should be repaid within five years.

8. Political subdivisions were permitted to borrow money in anticipation of revenues instead of issuing warrants, in order to stay on a cash basis.

9. Counties and municipalities were permitted to issue revenue bonds to build or acquire gas or electric utilities.

10. The Assembly was authorized to provide methods by which county and city governments could be merged.

11. County officers may be compensated on both a fee and salary basis, with local approval. Previously, the county had to choose between the two systems arbitrarily.

12. No future "local amendment" to the State Constitution can become effective unless it is approved by the people of the local unit involved.

The extent of decentralization of government in Georgia may be determined from a scrutiny of these reforms. Local government could not deal effectively with local problems; eventual determination of all local questions had to be made by the State Legislature. The condition was not unique; more than half the States of the Union lack adequate provision for self-government upon the county and municipal levels.

Governmental units must be large enough to deal economically and effectively with the problems of their citizens. They should not be larger than is necessary. It is equally irrational to assume that State government can provide for the national defense as for the removal of garbage. Local governments lack the taxing authority necessary to provide adequately for education, public highways, public health, and many other services; they are too small in area to deal with many of these services. In many instances, the Federal government is too large a unit to perform services effectively, or Federal administration may involve a degree of standardization discouraging to experimentation or distasteful to a large majority of the citizens in some relatively large area.

To look upon any government as anything more than a convenient unit for carrying out the wishes of the people and for permitting them to perform collective tasks conveniently and inexpensively is a grave mistake. Governments are useful servants; when they become masters, when they lay any claim to special loyalty from their citizens and seek to divert to themselves the emotion of patriotism that properly should be expended by the citizen upon the community of which he is a part and not upon the government that is set up to serve that community, there is danger. The danger is to the rights of the people.

16

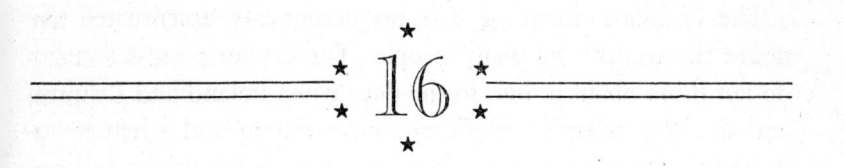

JOBS AND GOVERNMENT

When I was Attorney General of Georgia, I continued to live in Newnan, which is forty miles from Atlanta. Commuting that distance is commonplace in the East, but presents some difficulties in the South, and the Arnall household owned only one car. Within the first month of my term in the Law Department, I had been reduced three or four times to catching a ride to Atlanta as best I could. Thereafter I became a systematic hitchhiker, and I never failed to catch a ride that put me in the State Capitol at the opening hour.

I enjoyed the business of catching a ride to the city. Naturally enough, there were drivers for whom I became a fairly regular customer; but there was ample variety among those who generously stopped for the traditional jerk of the thumb, and most of them had other passengers.

During that period, America was preparing an army and an industrial establishment for war, and out of the conversations with Georgians who were riding to new war plants or to induction centers, I obtained some view of the pattern of American thinking.

The ominous threat of war unquestionably accentuated the desire for security in many people. Those who possess security do not think about it, but, in the days when Poland and Belgium and the Netherlands and France were falling and when it appeared that the foundations of earth's way of life might collapse and engulf all who lived, there was much thought of security everywhere. However, not all of the desire for security stemmed from that source; much dated back to the years when prosperity sought a corner to turn and found none, when hunger followed poverty as a fellow-lodger in too many American homes.

The people I met on these daily rides from Newnan to Atlanta came from two age-groups that knew intimately the Great Depression. They were men a little past their prime who had seen the savings of their lives either disappear in a flash, as a soap-bubble might explode, or wear away through the bitter four years of desperation that marked the climax of a decade of irresponsible political and economic leadership. And there were youths, some fresh from school, on their way to defend America from outside enemies; these had known the teeth of poverty in childhood, and the scars showed.

The concern of both groups was for employment after the war, a war which most of them saw as inevitable.

Employment is still the main concern of the people of America. It is possible to select a number of more or less adequate synonyms for what the people wish, and to call it a desire for full employment, or full production, or national employment security, or jobs for sixty million. It is, perhaps, more elusively simple than any of those terms; it is a simple desire to provide for themselves and to provide for their families by working.

This simple duality of desire is difficult to convey in words. For the men who were on the highway from Newnan to Atlanta and who told me these things were perfectly clear in expressing their wishes. They did not want jobs solely to provide a living, nor did they want jobs solely to keep them busy. They wanted jobs that would do both things for them. They wanted productive work; they wanted to see and feel the things that they made with their hands; and they wanted to eat, every day and not just some days.

Perhaps that explains it badly. Simple things are difficult to explain; that is why the simple things often are concealed by clouds of verbal and ideological obfuscation. It is probable that the myth of man as an economic animal was the outgrowth of several men saying: "We want to work so we can eat and so our families can eat." Of course, if man were wholly an economic animal, the phrase about families would not occur in the sentence.

There are sixty million Americans who want jobs so they can eat and so their families can eat. That is one expression of a socio-economic equation. America requires a production of $170 billion in goods and service, at 1944 prices, to provide employment, maintain public services and debt retirement schedules by all units of government, and supply the consumer goods that mean comfort and a decent and healthful standard of living for all the citizens.

For those who believe that almost everything, including the aspirations of men, can be set down arithmetically, here is the statement in full:

60 million jobs = $170 billion national income = a prosperous America.

The attainment of this goal must be accompanied by adequate wages and good working conditions for employees throughout America. Part of the philosophy of the system of free enterprise and competition revolves about the assumption that submarginal plants will be withdrawn from operation when their productiveness lags to such an extent that they can not meet the prices of more efficient organizations. The subsidization of such enterprises, by a tariff, or by decreasing the pay or lengthening the hours of workers, or by cartel arrangements restricting the production by more efficient units, is obnoxious to the American philosophy of free enterprise.

To obtain satisfactory wages and satisfactory working conditions, the industrial worker looks toward unionization, just as the farm worker looks toward becoming an independent landowner. Through the union, the individual worker expects to protect his investment in acquired technological skill, to safeguard his interest in a fair distribution of national income, to provide for himself and his family a standard of living that is adequate and an opportunity for advancement that provides the psychological urge for accomplishment.

Although, historically, the unionization of American workers is more than a century old and its inception identifiable with the Jackson era's upsurge of nationalism, industrialism and popular government, modern unions represent but fifty years of advancement of the industrial worker's cause. Since democratic government antedated it by many generations, beginning historically in the seventeenth century, since capitalism was already established, and since industrialism was a century old when labor attained its first influence, the union movement in America is in its youth.

Youth is both criticised and critical. The view adopted by some critics of the American Federation of Labor, of the Congress of Industrial Organizations, of the Railway Brotherhoods, and of the great independent unions parallels their views on anything or anyone else that is young. They seize upon the obvious mistakes of union leadership, with the avidity that a town snob seizes upon the gaucheries of a high school girl uncertain about the use of a salad fork at her first formal dinner.

Why a greater maturity, a broader social consciousness, a more precise scrupulousness and more self-restraint should be expected to pervade the ranks of the workers than the ranks of those engaged in management is not readily understandable. There is a very considerable brashness about some of the labor leaders. There are demagogues among them, although few who compare with some of the demagogues who embarrass the leaders of business by their ridiculous antics. There are dishonest men among them, though few who have demonstrated the skill of some of the great Robber Barons of the nineteenth century. There are men among the labor leaders who are avid for power, but the irresponsible quest for power has beset every movement in history. In these faults, the labor movement has no monopoly.

Without the existence of strong unions, the worker would have been hopeless of obtaining good wages and good working conditions. He would have been compelled to turn exclusively to political organizations to make his voice effective, and that would have invited some form of totalitarian regime. Collective bargaining is the device that can produce the greatest democracy in the American industrial system.

The South is turning toward unionization, and the benefits are apparent. Without the unions, the wage differential would forever hang over the head of the Southern worker. The wage differential is the device, paralleling the freight differential, by which Southern workers are paid a lower wage than workers in the industrial areas for equivalent work. Its elimination is a necessary step in the organization of a Southern agrarian-industrial economy.

There is an increasing degree of genuine statesmanship in the labor organizations. The membership, much of which was recruited in the years since 1933, is becoming more familiar each year with responsibility, and will be entirely capable of coping with the internal problems of their unions within a few years. As effective elements in the country's socio-economic system they are entering a period of wider usefulness to every citizen. The faults in union organization are easy for critics to discover; they are less important to the members, at the present time, than the problem of making a living. But unions in their struggle for the freedom and liberty of the workers must not arrogantly deprive other men of liberty and freedom.

Usually, when a critic of the unions begins his diatribe, he prefaces it with a description of a "responsible union," and if pressed to identify such a union admits with some reservations, that the Typographical Union is satisfactory. Then he contrasts the rather direct democracy of the printers with the representative democracy that is practiced in other organizations.

The comparison deserves examination. The Typographical Union is a great institution in America, and its membership must weary of being held up as a standard of democracy, responsibility, and intelligence; and of the misuse of the comparison to attack other organizations of workers.

In the first place, the relationship between the Typographical Union's members and their employers is extraordinary. Many of the employers were once printers; almost all of them have a direct and personal knowledge of the craft; almost all have close personal associations with the men on the production line. In the second place, the literacy and intelligence of the members of the Typographical Union perhaps is only about that of the average college faculty, but it is adequately high to insure the operation of a very intricate system of selecting national officers. Finally, the members of this extremely skilled and highly paid craft are employees of enterprises that, with few exceptions, are owner-managed; very few publishers are representative of the new managerial bureaucracy, and even if they are not identified with ownership they are necessarily autonomous and independent in their day-by-day operations and compelled to assume a great degree of responsibility.

To compare such a union, dealing with some hundreds of individual employers in hundreds of cities, with unions dealing with not more than a dozen employers, each with more employees than there are Typographical members, is an absurdity. The unions in the mass production industries obviously present such problems of organization as can be met only through representative, democratic techniques.

In representing their members in dealing with ownership, the unions generally do an excellent job. In inducing their members to assume many responsibilities of citizenship, including that of voting, the unions are increasingly useful to America. But there are many things that the unions, as such, cannot do for the workers of the country.

Providing employment for sixty million Americans is one of these things.

That end can be attained only by a general coöperation of all citizens, by the correction of defects in the economic system, by governmental coöperation on every level, and by careful planning.

While it has the appearance of a play upon words, the truth is that more planning is necessary under a free economy than under a planned economy. The paradox resolves itself instantly on examination, because under a planned economy the consumption of any item produced is predetermined, perhaps without much consultation with the consumer. Under a free economy, where there exists no inflexible caste system economically, planning must be upon the basis of preparing for a large number of possibilities.

The planning that must be done by the workers, by management, and by ownership is more consequential than that by political units. However, it is impossible to blueprint that type of planning; it is impossible even to catalog it; it continues day by day in every enterprise in America, on every farm in America, and in every shop.

Society upon the national scale can plan only through its government; or, more accurately, the organization through which planning on such a scale is developed is government. If such planning is conducted by two different organizations, as, let us assume, a council of all labor unions or a council of all industrialists, as well as by the formally organized political government, then duality of government exists; and duality of government leads to inevitable chaos.

Government, whether the legal political government or some extra-legal form, can plan for all the people only within a limited sphere, unless the doctrines of totalitarianism are embraced. Society acting through its legal political government can plan only to mitigate the results of ineffective private planning or of accident or, as the quaint legal phrase has it, in its curious joining of opposites, of "acts of God or of the public enemy."

Government cannot plan too widely to prevent disruptions in the economy of the Nation, without interfering with individual freedom. But all of the people can join in a mutual insurance against many hazards.

The first consideration of planning by all the people through their government must be for the welfare of the individual.

The greatest single hazard to the individual, economically, is unemployment through economic disturbance. The second greatest is unemployment through illness.

Into the controversy over the manner in which Americans should insure themselves against the cost of medical care, I have no desire to enter; if I did so, I would display the foolhardiness of one who enters such a battle unarmed with facts. But that unemployment compensation should be extended to those who are ill, for the benefit of their families, seems self-evident without too much debate. It is the simplest and most immediate palliative that can be applied to the illness in many instances.

Unemployment compensation, by whatever euphemism called, has only the usefulness of bridging the interval between employment. It is helpful to the individual and to the morale of the individual. It conserves savings for greater emergencies. It prevents the sacrifice of assets under a form of duress. But it solves no problem; it contributes nothing to keeping sixty million Americans upon jobs.

Government can influence employment, however, in two definite ways:

1. By encouraging production through an enlightened tax system, through adequate enforcement of the statutes against conspiracies in restraint of trade, and by adopting a policy of equal rights for all sections of America.

2. By a planned system of public works of genuine utility, whose construction can be used to cushion periods of temporary unemployment.

With proper decentralization of American industry, with an end of the policy of treating the Southern and West regions as colonies, and with tax laws flexible enough to withdraw surpluses for the reduction of the national debt during periods of rising incomes and to withdraw less in periods of falling incomes, the political government can assist greatly in avoiding depressions. With none of these three policies is there any disagreement anywhere in America among serious students of our economy, whether they be liberals or conservatives. There may be disagreement, on occasions, about the methods of applying these policies, but the basic principles seem so widely accepted that they require no additional explanation.

The extremes of Right and Left in America declaim vigorously against the laws against monopoly, but it is improbable that American opinion will follow them.

But disagreement upon government spending as a preventative of depressions is widespread.

Examination of the views of critics of this policy, usually conservative economists, reveals that their criticism is of specific techniques; and very many of their criticisms are sound.

Government cannot plan upon a national level for public spending to prevent depressions. The expenditures should be for permanent improvements. These two sentences summarize the justified criticisms of observers and the remedies.

Only the national government, however, possesses the resources to spend for such public works. Only a well-paid, permanent, carefully selected staff of engineers, statisticians, and administrators can carry out such a policy, and the assembly of such a staff by any unit of government except that of the Nation is hard to imagine.

This does not mean that there is a dilemma. On the contrary, the entire system of planning can be decentralized and regionalized. It can be set up, ready to go on very short notice in any part of America. And the improvements planned can be of a permanent and long-range type.

Had such a system existed, it would have been easy to determine as early as 1924 that the American economy was sick in several spots. Under the suggestions already outlined, the withdrawal of money from consumer expenditures into capital investments and speculations would have been discouraged by use of the taxing authority of the Nation, and something would have been done about the agrarian discontent in the Corn Belt and in the South.

The "something" would have taken the form of considerable public works spending in those areas of depression, that would have resulted automatically in a resumption of employment and a restoration of buying power.

While it is obvious oversimplification to assume that the

existence of a regionalized public works program would have prevented the depression of 1929 from eventually overtaking America, unless other correctives were applied at the same time, even this single thing would have abbreviated its duration and alleviated its intensity.

An enormous portion of the suggested Federal spending would be in the nature of investment in self-liquidating projects. The Tennessee Valley Authority has been one of the most profitable investments in the history of Federal finance, in addition to its accomplishments for a depressed, exploited and temporarily submarginal area. There is no reason to doubt that the Missouri Valley Authority, if its creation is not blocked by the shortsighted and the selfish, will be an equally profitable investment. Investments in schools, hospitals, and other needed public buildings return no such profit in dollars-and-cents, of course; but it is cheaper for the Nation to keep such needed items of capital outlay in good condition, to expand such facilities wherever needed, by expenditures made in times when the spending will produce definite social gains.

Such a policy will not eliminate altogether some of the discomforts of our economic system. It is not a policy that will provide full employment, in the sense that totalitarians understand that word; but it will make it possible for all those productively occupied to earn a living under all circumstances, and it will preserve our fundamental political and economic forms in this country.

In a sense, these suggestions represent an apparent compromise between the desire for security and the desire for opportunity. Actually, they only represent provision for that degree of security which is necessary if there is to be opportunity for all in the Nation.

There is no inspiration to man in hunger and fear. The acquisition of national wealth, wealth for all the people, must be encouraged. Nor should the acquisition of wealth by the individual be discouraged. Personally, I want an America in which my son can become President or a millionaire, if he wishes to become President and the people agree, or if he wishes to be a millionaire and will work for the money; I want an America in which the son of any citizen can become President or a millionaire; but I want an America in which possession of wealth equates no possession of power, and in which hunger and fear have been eliminated.

Provision for security for all our people, upon some mutual basis undertaken through their government, is one of the essentials in providing opportunity for everyone. The opening of new frontiers, geographical in the instances of the South and the West, technological in the instances of new industries based on plastics, the light metals, and other natural resources and scientific discoveries, can provide the opportunities for Americans.

17

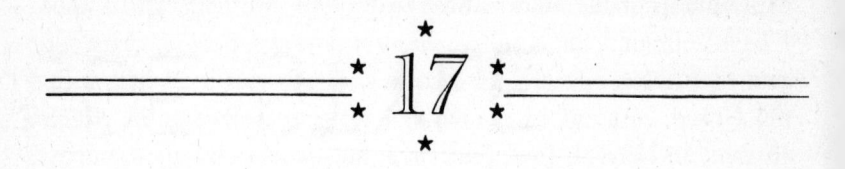

PEACE AND PUBLIC OPINION

ONE DAY AMONG our luncheon guests in Atlanta was Madame Chiang Kai-shek, one of the most interesting and complex personalities of our times. Distinguished and engaging in her own right, she is the wife of the Generalissimo of China; and she was the sister-in-law of Dr. Sun Yat-sen, who visioned a free China in a free world and whom I have admired with intensity since boyhood.

I know very little about the world. Iran and Iraq, Inner Mongolia and Burma, Annam and the Cameroons, all of these are names that spell mysteries as deep for me as the mystery of Prester John's shadowy kingdom. Of China geographically I know almost nothing: it was a great yellow daub upon the world-map when I was a schoolboy, and, later, a considerable portion was cut off and given a Japanese-sounding name and a new color. Of the great past of China, I am hopelessly uninformed; of the ideas, or some of the ideas, of Lao-tse and of the Reverend Master and of Sun Yat-sen I have some conception. And China is representative of my knowledge of the great world that lies outside the United States. In books I have followed the social experiments of the Danes and Swedes and Norwegians. In books I have followed the disintegration and restoration of the Gallic soul of France. From the histories and newspapers, I know that the Grand Duke of Muscovy became ultimately Tsar of All the Russias, and that various Tsars were assassinated by their courtiers or were blown into small bits by direct-actionists who disliked their autocratic rule; and that eventually a new government representing a merger of ancient customs with new bookish ideas was established in that vast region, with its multiplicity of tongues and peoples, that we call Russia.

But Madame Chiang, either through graciousness or because she was glad to be in a section where she spent a part of a happy girlhood, did not talk of world affairs. She took time off, for a little while, from being a great person of the world and remembered the days when she was Mei-Ling and a student at Wesleyan in Macon, and when her feet tapped as gayly as those of any Southern girl when the band played "Dixie."

She talked of the little campus that had been Wesleyan in those days, and of the contrast with the new fine buildings that had been erected since. She talked of people that she had known at college, and of what had become of them afterwards. Some of them were known to us, and, to that extent, the conversation developed into pleasant gossip.

From the history books, it can be ascertained that a dreadful new device of war, the spears of the Macedonian phalanx, rendered inevitable and permanent the domination of the world by the barbarian masters of Greece; even the warriors of the Theban Sacred Band could not stand before their charge. From the history books, it can be ascertained that the longbow, with its terrific fire power, established for all time English hegemony on the continent. From the history books, it can be ascertained that the dreadful hand cannon of the Great Captain, established forever the ascendency of the combined arms of Castile and Aragon throughout the world. Philip of Macedon, however, is as dead as his son's horse, Bucephelus. The Maid of Orleans did not find the arrows of Bedford's men invincible. The Great Captain sleeps as sound as either the gallant Gaston de Foix or the miserly Ferdinand.

From the newspapers, it can be ascertained that the atom bomb will render war so horrible that there can be no more war; that nations must agree, or all men must perish; that a bomb in the disguise of a fountain pen may at any moment lay waste New York or Leningrad or Rotterdam or Buenos Aires.

The weapons of war have grown more horrible with each generation, and more costly to use; but it is most unlikely that war will end because of its horrors. It can end only when some of the underlying causes of war are eradicated; and even the elimination of the economic roots of war will not prevent the waging of war as a sport or for ideological reasons, unless the sound sense of men asserts itself.

But if war will not be ended simply because war is horrible, because the bodies of men and women and children burned by atom bombs are as distasteful objects as the bodies of men and women and children smashed by the rocks of catapults or seamed with wounds of swords, spears, maces, halberts, and tomahawks, war also will not end simply by preparation for its coming.

The turning of America, and of other countries at the same time, into armed camps will not preserve peace. In this country there has been a growing tendency to permit decisions of the utmost consequence to be made by high-ranking members of the general staffs of the various services. This departure from the norm of American thinking also represents a very real departure from the constitutional theories upon which the political establishment rests. The majority of American States embody in their State Constitutions specific provisions for the supremacy of the civil government over the military at all times. The Second Amendment to the Federal Constitution not only attests the dread that Americans have felt at the possible ascendency in public affairs of the professional military, but the extent of the precautions they took to protect their institutions against such interference. The man-on-horseback has never been popular in the United States as a political leader. That there is a clear intention of certain of the extreme Right, backed by the muddled thinking of some utterly honest but utterly stupid professional soldiers, to convert the United States into a "military republic" hardly requires more than assertion.

The economic waste incident to the maintenance of huge armaments is enormous. The waste of time involved in maintaining huge bodies of men in military establishments is even greater. Considering that wars are not won on the battlefield until they have been won on the industrial front, and that America's capacity for production has twice been the margin for victory, the expenditure of suitable sums for experimentation, for training of technological personnel under civilian authority, for organizing civilian-constituted and civilian-controlled militia, would be far better justified.

An independent, intelligent foreign policy for the Nation, however, is its best safeguard against war. Some criticisms of our foreign policy are implicit in the very organization of the agency through which they are conducted. The tendency to substitute for men in the policy-making level of government so-called "career diplomats" has been one of the most damaging influences in our conduct of international affairs. The names great in American diplomatic history are not the names of men who rose gradually through the hierarchy of a State Department bureaucracy.

The great ambassadors in our country's history, from Franklin and Jefferson through John Forsyth and Charles Francis Adams to Joseph Davies and Josephus Daniels, have been men identified with popular government. They have been policy-makers rather than technical experts. They have been exponents of the American point of view, as that point of view existed at that time. While occasional professional diplomats have been successful, the number of these who have risen to the first rank is far below their proportionate number in the diplomatic service, and these exceptional men probably would have been more effective had they been in closer contact with America.

On the other hand, the grave mistakes of American policy can be laid in the laps of the "career diplomats" in all too many cases. The unhappy embroilment with the Republic of Mexico, possibly the most disgraceful episode in our entire conduct of foreign affairs, was largely their handicraft, although the part played by certain special interests must not be overlooked. The superb skill of the North Carolina editor-politician, Josephus Daniels, in restoring good relations between the United States and its southern neighbor has received less recognition than is deserved; his brilliant achievement in Mexico City was the harbinger of the "good-neighbor policy," and was as able an example of representation of the Nation as was Franklin's at Paris or Adams's at London in 1863.

The United States does not need spheres of influence nor satellite nations; the United States does need good will throughout the world.

My family name is a little unusual in the South, and I had always considered it a variant or corruption of Arnold, until I became Governor of Georgia and letters began to come to me from other Arnalls scattered over the world. The first was from a man of my own age in England, but others followed fast: from a merchant in Australia, from a rancher in New Zealand, from a colonist in Kenya which was a land so unfamiliar to me that I had to seek a map to identify it, from several of the provinces of Canada, and from the Union of South Africa. There were several score of these letters, and I discovered that all over the world there were Arnalls engaged in almost every occupation or trade or profession by which men seek to make a living for themselves and their families.

I do not know these cousins of mine. By the chance of our births in different lands, I never played games with them in the backyards of Newnan homes as I did with those Arnalls and Coles and Farmers, who are my cousins in Georgia. I never shared with them the huge family gatherings of my youth, when all the uncles and aunts and distant cousins were assembled to eat fried chicken in commemoration of some anniversary, nor snickered with them as youngsters over the remains of an enormous churn of ice cream.

The man in Devonshire grows roses in a garden that is very old; and the boy from Capetown was going into the air force within a week, and I do not know whether he has returned to

Capetown or whether he found his grave somewhere in the Pacific, for he has not written again. The man in Kenya did not describe his occupation, though I gather somehow that it has to do with a plantation of some sort; the Australian merchant has a line of ladies' clothes.

It is improbable that I shall ever see the rose garden in Devonshire, or the ranch in New Zealand. It is unlikely that I shall meet any of these Arnalls face to face, or any of my other cousins wide sown about this planet; for I have many: there is a strain of Salzburger somewhere in my family, so more cousins must exist in the Netherlands and in Germany; and others yet are in the hills of Scotland and in Ulster.

I wish them well, these cousins that I shall not see and with whom I have not traded biscuits in my boyhood over the back-fence in quiet Newnan. I wish them well, and I have no wish that hell shall rain from the sky upon any of them, or upon any who are dear to them, or upon the places that they call home in Devonshire or Toronto or Capetown.

Or upon any man, anywhere.

That is why I feel that the conduct of our relations with other countries is a matter for the individuals who make up America to determine; that is why I do not feel that it is a matter for experts to decide for us. Even if the heads of the experts were wiser than the heads of all the people combined, I am not sure that it is entirely a matter for heads to determine. There is such a thing as good will, and while it may not be measured as precisely as a scientist might measure the discharge of energy from a milligram of plutonium, it can and does have measurable effect upon the conduct of world affairs.

The relationships of nations are not essentially too different from the relationships of human beings. Madame Chiang and I were able to talk, pleasantly, of experiences and friends we had in common, and that my knowledge of her vast complex China was much smaller than her knowledge of my vast, complex America, was no bar to conversation about those things we did share. My distant cousins, from Glasgow to Capetown, share with me a relationship that provides a unity of interest not dispelled by the great distances that separate us or the differences in our upbringing in our youth.

The victories that America has won in its relations to foreign nations were victories won by popular opinion. Public sentiment, disgusted with the systematic looting of China after the Boxer Rebellion, demanded that America's share in the indemnity be used to improve the relationship between the two countries; today upon that slender basis of sentiment rests the very considerable influence that our Nation has in the Orient. Public sentiment, undeceived by the adroit sophistries of Beveridge and unaffected by the franker imperialism of those who talked about "Manifest Destiny," demanded and secured independence for the people of the Philippine Republic; and America's relations with the people of the Pacific islands rests on a sound basis.

The defeats that America has sustained in foreign relationships have occurred when the popular conscience either remained unaroused or was disregarded by those in power. When the Grant Administration, disregardful of the prophetic warnings of Sumner, violated the independence of Haiti, a small power, a pattern was set that was followed in the instances of Cuba, Nicaragua and Mexico, to the injury of our relationships with Latin America. We have not overcome that loss of prestige; years of patience, of the practice of good will, of dealing directly with the people of those nations and convincing them of the honesty of our intentions which they have such excellent reason to doubt, will be required to undo the folly of listening to experts who understood all of the facts except those that were important.

That the traditional American policy of support to all nations maintaining a libertarian government is the wisest basis for the conduct of international affairs would appear obvious. It is the only basis upon which the United States can maintain continuity in its foreign policy.

Between 1921 and 1933, this was not the American policy. The attitude of the American government, in those years, was frankly to engage itself to the support of the new totalitarianism in Western Europe. American career diplomats favored Mussolini in Italy; one notable representative of our diplomatic service of that day wrote lush articles for the popular magazines in praise of the train that once ran on time. Efforts to maintain a democratic regime in Germany were systematically thwarted, although in that instance the American policy was less consciously one of supporting the Brownshirt counterrevolution than of tagging along with other powers that believed a democratic Germany undesirable.

To eyes trained to political realism, as were those of Jefferson or Forsyth, the March on Rome would have been discernible as the prelude to the March on Warsaw; Dollfuss' massacre in the streets of the workingmen's section of Vienna would have been recognized as the opening gun of a war against democratic forces everywhere in the world; the Japanese aggression against China would have been identified as a rehearsal for the attack upon Malaya. As a matter of fact, the man in the street knew those things; they were indiscernible only to the experts, who knew everything about international affairs except the facts and who drew every conclusion from the evidence except the correct one.

Only the force of public opinion can prevent a recurrence of a world war; but the force of public opinion can be very great. In America, it was great enough to correct the error of our conquest of the Philippines; in Great Britain it was adequate to drive into a deserved political obscurity those who had supported the rape of South Africa and who had applauded the original Chamberlain, father of the umbrella-to-Munich demagogue, in taking those firm measures that included setting up the original and prototype of the concentration camps.

There has been more editing of the facts than substantial research into the economic and political causes of the Second World War. It is possible to ascertain that the collapse of the world economy, due chiefly to the collapse of the American economy and the consequent end of both American loans to, and American importation from, Europe, was a major factor. This illustrates the importance of those questions, dismissed as "wholly domestic," in relation to world peace. The encouragement of speculation to the exclusion of constructive investment in the late twenties, the uncertainty of the American tariff policy, and the growing agricultural depression in the South and West that continued in the midst of a stock market boom, all contributed to the economic chaos of the world.

British and American stupidity in international affairs, as in the crisis in Manchuria, contributed to the confusion of world politics, and helped to produce a condition where, by the close of 1932, war was almost inevitable.

The psychological and moral factors that were underlying the economic and political causes of war have received inadequate attention.

Most important of these was the wave of cynicism that engulfed the world in this period. It reached its height in America in the passage of the Webb Act and in the violation of the sovereignty of Nicaragua under the most irresponsible national Administration, excepting Grant's, that America has sustained. In international affairs, it was marked by the seizure, as possessions of the Great Powers, of the various mandates awarded by the League of Nations, by open assistance to Mussolini, and by covert assistance by extra-governmental powers-that-be to the Brownshirts in Germany.

The aftermath, as it concerned not all, but some people, is pictured by Mr. Justice Jackson in his statement to the War Crimes Court at Nuremberg:

> I shall not take time to detail the ghastly proceedings in these concentration camps. Beatings, starvings, tortures, and killings were routine—so routine that the tormentors became blase and careless. We will show you a report of discovery that in Plotzensee one night, one hundred and eighty-six persons were executed while there were orders for only one hundred and eighty. Another report describes how the family of one victim received two urns of ashes by mistake. Inmates were compelled to execute each other. In 1942, they were paid five Reichsmarks per execution, but on June 27, 1942, SS General Gluecks ordered commandants of all concentration camps to reduce this honorarium to three cigarettes.

Cynicism produces moral disintegration in any individual; perhaps not so rapidly as does the acquisition of power, but rapidly and surely enough. Moral disintegration is expressed in any society that finds the value of human life equated to three cigarettes, and those made of ersatz tobacco. Moral disintegration, like the mental disintegration characterized by the schizoid traits in current society, seeks its release from reality in flight from individual responsibility. The individual, instead of assuming for himself his share of the herd guilt of all mankind, seeks to transfer his own guilt to the mass and thereby escape it.

Parenthetically, I must express a distaste for the Nuremberg trials. The very statement of the case that I have cited, by Mr. Justice Robert H. Jackson, discloses that very many of the accusations rest upon evidence of crimes that are so recognized in every nation. It would have been more salutary had the Nazi war criminals been indicted under the laws of the nation where a specific offense had been committed and tried for those offenses that were recognized as crimes in those jurisdictions. The process might have been tedious, but the picture of fat Hermann Göring facing a police magistrate in Lille for the theft of a statue; or of Wilhelm Keitel facing a court-martial for the murder of a specific prisoner of war, along with the Colonel, Oberlieutenant, Sergeant and four privates of the SS who conspired with him in the murder, would have had a profound effect upon the moral sensibilities of all men. Placing I. G. Farben in receivership, for the purpose of completely liquidating it in the interest of those whose property was stolen by it through the racial laws of Hitler, would have been an act of justice easy to comprehend. Sending Hjalmar Schacht, one of the most vicious of the war criminals along with the sadist Julius Streicher, to the gallows for a crime against humanity—

which quite likely will not occur after all—will be less impressive than sending him to prison for twenty years for complicity in the burglary of the safety deposit boxes in Amsterdam.

The parade of horrors at Nuremberg is too overpowering for the minds of men. The picture of fat-bellied Hermann Göring or weasel-eyed Hjalmar Schacht or monocled, beribboned, Prussian Wilhelm Keitel tried by common juries of tradesmen and grocers and mechanics in the towns where they committed their outrages would have been inspiring. It would not have been practical, but merely realistic; and the makers of protocol are too practical to be realistic. The common courtroom, where common scoundrels are sentenced, is too insignificant, they feel, for such titans of infamy. So they concur in the gangsters' estimate of themselves as supermen and accord them the trappings of Götterdämmerung.

The world missed the greatest opportunity of teaching the blind believers in authoritarianism a lesson by establishing this special tribunal of all the nations to try a motley crowd of military murderers, corporate swindlers, fraudulent bankers, common bandits, and ordinary thieves.

The Nuremberg trials inevitably will be the beginning of a new cynicism. This will not be dispelled by the failure of the United Nations to recall all the mandates awarded by the recently liquidated League of Nations. Within five years, the process by which the League was dissolved, and its liabilities transferred to the United Nations while its assets were absorbed by those who had acquired them as trustees under a solemn obligation to administer them for the benefit of others, will be pictured by a new generation of isolationists as an act of fraudulent bankruptcy. Nor can cynicism fail to feed upon the practical decision to place all power within the United Nations in the hands of a "Big Three," a decision as wanting in realism in the age of the atomic bomb as any that can be imagined. Our almost deliberate courting of disfavor in France and our uncertain Latin American policy, both of which are products of the bureaucratic minds of career diplomats whose permanence within the State Department enables them to affect policies without assuming responsibility, are invitations to difficulty in the future.

The United States cannot enforce peace throughout the world, nor impose its will for long upon any great number of nations, nor avoid the consequences of mistakes in the field of international power politics. Our country can contribute tremendously to a peaceful world, if the citizens of our country will remember that the consequences of war are not visited upon nations but upon individuals.

Without a digression into semantics, there is an enormous contribution to international ill will by those who speak of American intentions or Russian aspirations or British policies with such great glibness. When war comes, it is not America nor Russia nor Britain that suffers, but the individual citizen. It is human blood and not the contribution of a geographical or political entity that colors the soil around Stalingrad, and that flecks the cobblestones of Coventry, and that reddens the beachheads in the South Pacific. It will be human blood next time that is shed, and human bodies that whimper with wounds, and human widows who wait for dead men as Andromache waited upon the walls of hapless Troy for the broken corpse of her husband; and it will be men and not geographical units that kill them; the responsibility cannot be shifted from men's shoulders to some mysterious entity that exists on a map.

America's contribution toward a peaceful world must come partly through a well-defined foreign policy and partly through the establishment within our own country of a harmonious economic and social system that will not collapse as did the papier-mâché economy of the twenties. Without too much elaboration upon each item, let me set out an outline of a few of the requisites for such a policy.

A firm rejection of any policy of American imperialism.

Adoption of the same policies in dealing with foreign nationals as with American nationals, including immediate repeal of the Webb Act, and drastic enforcement of existing statutes prohibiting American citizens, individual or corporate, from entering into any engagements of any kind with foreign governments.

Adoption of a policy, in making American loans to foreign powers, that any loans made by the borrowers to other nations shall be upon the precise terms granted by the United States.

Insistence upon the return of all mandates granted by the League of Nations to the United Nations, and the administration of such mandates in the future by joint agencies in which the smaller powers shall have a stronger representation.

Advocacy of repeal of the veto power of the "Big Three" over subject matter in the agenda of the United Nations. The right of the smaller powers to be heard on any subject at any time must be recognized.

Selection of our diplomatic representatives abroad from men who are among the policy-makers of the political party currently in power.

Open support of democratic regimes throughout the world, when they are confronted with danger from authoritarian interruption.

Coöperation in the liquidation of colonialism everywhere. The colonial system is the father of wars; in addition, in peacetime it requires such a subsidy from the world as to be unendurable economically. At the present time, it is possible that American action in this field must be limited to representations to the United Nations and to the adoption of economic policies that will penalize the production of colonial exploiters. This is less affirmative than the action of President Monroe in the case of the revolting South American colonies of Spain, but it is in the tradition of the American policy of self-determination for the inhabitants of all sections of the world.

Give increasing attention to the people of other nations. In the end, foreign policies like domestic policies must rest on the will of the people. The aims of American foreign policy must be made known to the individuals who make up the other nations of the world.

International coöperation can become a reality; but only when it is coöperation between men and not between the governments of men, often acting without the knowledge or consent of their principals.

If some such policies are not adopted, America faces a dangerous future in its relationships with other nations. Another wave of cynicism, accompanied by the retreat of many idealists into one form of isolationism and of another group less idealistic into a violent form of nationalism, can engulf the world in a calamitous war.

I should not like to see this happen, either to myself or to my cousins in Capetown and Rotterdam and Glasgow. But it is possible, unless there is a resumption of thinking in terms of individual responsibility instead of the continuance of seeking escape by placing all responsibility on that collective conscience that does not really exist.

18

"OUR REALIZATION OF TOMORROW"

His expressive hands which seemed always in motion, emphasizing a phrase or fingering the innumerable small objects that littered his desk, indicated with a gesture that he was a tired man. The tiredness, the weight of thousands of decisions, was written on his face and dulled the vibrant laughter that always had seemed a part of him. Franklin D. Roosevelt had given me an appointment, to talk politics; but he had not permitted the conversation to reach that subject.

"Mr. President, you helped me a great deal in my campaign in 1942, with advice and by talking with some of your friends in my behalf," I had begun. "This is a national election year, and I would like to do what I can for you. Are you planning to make the race for a fourth term for President?"

He did not reply, directly. Instead, he spoke of Hyde Park and of his occupation as a grower of Christmas trees. It was a somewhat unusual crop, but a profitable one, and did not impoverish the land, he observed.

"Mr. President, the first time you invited me to visit you at Warm Springs, you told me about the Christmas trees at Hyde Park," I said, when he gave me an opening. "It is a very interesting story, but the fourth term is more interesting."

He remembered my visit to Warm Springs. He remembered his own numerous visits to Georgia, to the Little White House; he inquired about the health of Dr. Neal Kitchens, and Cason Callaway, and Judge Henry Revill, and half-a-dozen more Georgians who live in Meriwether and Harris counties, and whom he knew in the days when he was fighting his way back to health. He remembered several anecdotes about them, and about his farm adjoining the Foundation. Finally, he ended and sat silent for a few minutes.

"I am very tired," he said. "My health isn't as good as in 1932, you know, and I am twelve years older."

He continued his explanation. The office was an expensive one to hold, and he wished to return to Hyde Park and rest. What did the people think?

"They would like for you to stay in office, Mr. President," I told him.

"We are in a war, Ellis," he replied. "I will not ask for the office, but if the Democratic Party nominates me, I will be a candidate. It would be as much a matter of duty as a soldier obeying orders from his commanding officer."

"Can I tell the correspondents that when I leave? They will ask me about it. I want to tell them that you are willing to continue to serve, that you feel that if the people want to keep you as Commander-in-Chief you have the same duty to stay in the fight as any other soldier. Can I tell them that?"

"You can tell them." His voice was a little flat, as if the recollections of Hyde Park and Warm Springs had gone out of it, and only the tiredness remained.

I asked him if he had a choice of his running-mate on the ticket. He told me that he wished for and hoped for the renomination of Henry Wallace.

"They tell me that Henry would cost the ticket a million votes. What do you think?"

I replied that, while I did not know the Vice-President, while I knew that he had many political enemies and was unpopular with some groups, Henry Wallace would gain more votes than he would lose for the ticket.

The President continued to discuss other possibilities for the office, discarding them one by one.

"There is Jimmy Byrnes, who is a good man and a good friend," he said, "but I have talked with some of the outstanding Catholics of the country about Jimmy, because he was reared in the Catholic Church and became a Protestant. They have no prejudices themselves, but they believe that his nomination would not only mean a loss of many votes, but that it would arouse some bitter antagonisms over the Nation. When they told me that"—his eyes strayed about the room and finally found the window—"then Jimmy's chances went out the window."

He returned to Vice-President Wallace.

"Henry is a great man, though some people don't understand him. He has courage and loyalty. Nobody has been more loyal."

I told him that, after I had talked with the correspondents, I planned to go home and line up the Georgia delegation to the National Democratic Convention for Henry Wallace for Vice-President, and to do all that I could to help renominate the man he said he preferred.

When I left Mr. Roosevelt, I told the White House newsmen that he would permit his name to go before the Democratic Convention, that he would be renominated, and that he would be reëlected. It was the first definite statement of his willingness to run that had been made.

Returning to Georgia, I prepared to carry out my pledge about Vice-President Wallace, who was then in China upon a highly important mission requiring the prestige of the second-ranking figure in the government.

The former Secretary of Agriculture was almost wholly a stranger to me at that time. What I knew of Henry Wallace, beyond the obvious facts of his public career, came from reading what he had written. In the written word, he is exceptional among public men in America for possessing the finest style and the greatest clarity of expression; the language of Henry Wallace is as fresh and lucid and direct as that of the giants of the Revolutionary period.

That he has remarkable courage, independence of thought, a disciplined mind, a shy sense of humor, much patience, and the rare virtue of humility, can be doubted by no one who has talked with him face to face.

In the convention of 1944, the Georgia delegation was among those that voted unanimously for Henry A. Wallace upon both roll calls. It was the only Southern delegation solidly supporting him. Assuredly, had his name been presented to the Chicago gathering on the same night that President Roosevelt was renominated, Henry Wallace would have obtained a majority.

With his usual loyalty, Mr. Wallace plunged into the 1944 campaign on behalf of the Roosevelt-Truman ticket, and spoke often and effectively. When the campaign had ended, I was invited to the White House for another political chat with Mr. Roosevelt. It was the last occasion upon which I had any lengthy conversation with him. On this occasion, although illness was obvious in his appearance, he looked less tired than before and talked with something of his old animation.

"Those were fine speeches you made for the party in Oklahoma and Missouri and Minnesota," he began, characteristically putting a visitor at ease by referring to the little campaign jaunt the National Committee arranged for me just before the election, "I appreciate it more, because I know you must have been disappointed about Henry."

I replied that I had supported Mr. Wallace because of his own request, and that I was not disappointed and that I did not think Mr. Wallace was disappointed.

"However, Mr. President, I think Henry Wallace ought to have any place in the government that he is willing to accept," I concluded.

"He can have any place that he would like in the Cabinet, except the place of Cordell Hull as Secretary of State," the President replied. "Henry is a great friend, the most loyal man I know." The President told me that Harry Truman would grow in stature. Were he here today, Roosevelt would know that his appraisal of Truman was correct.

The President turned from politics to say briefly that, in his opinion, the war could not last more than a year. His concern was for America in the postwar period.

"The next ten years can mean everything," he said, just before telling me goodbye.

Upon Mr. Roosevelt's suggestion, my friend Robert Hannegan, chairman of the Democratic National Committee, invited me to make the Jefferson Day Dinner address in Washington. The President's own talk to the Party and the Nation was to have been broadcast from Warm Springs. Neither speech was delivered, for the President was stricken on the eve of the occasion and the dinners were cancelled.

His final message to America, from that undelivered speech, was a summation of his own faith in the Country and its future: "The only limits to our realization of tomorrow will be our doubts of today. Let us move forward with strong and active faith."

It is impossible to evaluate Franklin Delano Roosevelt during this generation. The imprint of his personality upon America has been striking. The verdict on him as a leader of the people, as the master-strategist of our greatest military endeavor, as a statesman, will have to be written by those to come, who will be farther away from his eloquent voice, his expressive gestures, his remarkable charm of personality. It is possible, however, to examine him in relationship to American politics and, especially, in relationship to the Party that he led to four victories in national elections. President Roosevelt understood the peculiar status of the Democratic Party, its actual and potential usefulness in the country, and he outlined definitely the course that it must follow if it is to be the vehicle of adapting political institutions to social developments.

In campaign years, when speeches are delivered about the glories of Party history and the knavery of the opposition, I have contributed my share. Indeed, it is a pleasure to speak of the ruinous record of Republican recklessness and to call Republican sinners to repentance and conversion: and it is a greater pleasure to speak of the demonstrated dependability of the Democrats, whose Party for more than one hundred and forty years has been the vehicle of good government, prosperity, progress, and purity. I am still pleased with the memories of some of those speeches, which were the more thoroughly impregnated with vitriol because I know so very few Republicans personally. They are rarer than twenty-dollar gold pieces in Georgia and worth, politically, precisely $19.70 less, collectively, to a Georgia candidate. Nevertheless, I had some sympathy once with a Republican; that occurred when Wendell Willkie was taken to task for revealing what every politician knows: that some of his campaign oratory was, as he phrased it, "campaign oratory."

Nevertheless, there are three wholly objective facts about American politics and American political parties that must be examined in considering the question of how to find a party to sponsor the governmental policies necessary to carry out a program for a prosperous country with opportunity for each citizen. These facts are indisputable. First, the Democratic Party contains a greater leaven of liberalism than its major opponent. Second, it is the only existing nationwide Party. Third, it has historical continuity and a tradition of liberalism that is valuable in presenting its case to the people.

The liberals within the Republican Party are unhappy, always engaged in apology or explanation, and frequently openly at odds with their leadership. Factors of geography, early political affiliation, and personal associations acquired over the years have led such men as Aiken, Morse and LaFollette into the Republican ranks: if they remain there, they will be branded as the "Sons of the Wild Jackass" if ever their party attains control over the government. While there is a conservative element in the Democratic Party, and a fringe of bizarre reactionaries notable for a vulgar loudmouthedness, these are not dominant; indeed, they are not even allies, representing divergent trends of thought as well as very divergent tastes of constituencies.

If this were a political tract, it would be appropriate to remind the voter that the only three Republican Presidents tainted with any trace of liberalism had most unusual relationships with that party. Lincoln did not seek reëlection as a Republican, and the regular party organization unquestionably was involved in the Fremont Convention. Hayes, an honest man disgusted with being the beneficiary of fraud, refused a second nomination explicitly. Theodore Roosevelt bolted to form a new party and challenged the standpatters to don their best armor and confront him at Armageddon, where, he told America, the Bull Moose legions would "battle for the Lord."

The Democratic Party, for all its recusant elements defiant of any discipline, contains most of the organized liberals of America today. It is useless to call the roll; for any roll call of the House or Senate will substantiate the claim.

But more consequential, the Democratic Party is the only national party. Indeed, except for the efforts of the Socialists among the numerous minor parties, the Democratic Party is the only party in American history that has been a national party. It is the only party that, at one time or another, has carried each State in the Union, and that has an actual political organization in every State.

The United States sadly needs the services of an honest and effective and nationwide conservative party, if for no other reason than to provide legitimate opposition for the liberals.

It might even be profitable to trust such a party with the conduct of affairs for brief intervals, while the liberal group recovered its breath.

Finally, the Democratic Party has a continuous history of more than a century and a half, making it the oldest political party in the world. It has maintained a liberal tradition during most of that period. When it departed from liberalism, it usually got thoroughly defeated. Its defeats with liberal candidates, as in 1920 with that great American, Governor James M. Cox of Ohio, were incidents in its career, brought about by misunderstanding on the part of the public of many of the issues. And, even in 1920, Governor Cox lost hundreds of thousands of votes, in addition to an estimated two million that stayed away from the polls and a round million that voted for Eugene Debs, because of the issue of civil liberties arising from the activities of the Department of Justice, directed, ironically enough, by the man he defeated for the Party's nomination, Mitchell Palmer.

The hagiology of politics, likewise, must be considered. The Democratic Party possesses, through its fifteen decades of activity, heroes and martyrs, the remembrance of whom helps to cement the party's ranks and even, occasionally, to influence the trend of the platform.

Almost every State in the Union can boast of a great Democratic leader, Georgia possesses Crawford and Forsyth. Virginia, of course, is richest of all with Jefferson, Madison and Monroe. Michigan has Lewis Cass, and Tennessee and North Carolina dispute over Old Hickory. New York has a score of names, in the years between the Clintons and Franklin Roosevelt. Connecticut has Isaac Hill. With Sam Adams, even Boston has a remembrance of better days. Nebraska can remember the young Bryan with the golden voice. Missouri can take pride in Benton, victor over Clay and Webster in a battle of Titans.

Of course the Democratic Party is large, diffused over the whole Nation, filled with strange personalities of whom a few are somewhat disgusting; it is in constant disagreement within itself, sometimes without a definite policy or with a multiplicity of policies on many questions; and it frequently rides two horses at the same time with a pail of water on each shoulder. This is the admission of a Democrat; critics of the Party who feel no affection for it have had harsher things to say in the past and are thinking up more to say in their sparkling propaganda.

The very clumsiness that sometimes characterizes the methods of the Democratic Party is an argument in its favor. Its faults are the faults of our society, our people, and our way of life. It is genuinely representative of America, and Americans are human beings.

What makes the Democratic Party a majority party is that it consists of a large group of minorities. It is the party of the geographical minorities of the Nation, the South and the West. It is the party of the largest religious minority, the Catholic. It is the party of the largest racial minority, the Negro. It is the party of the largest minority of employed individuals, the industrial workers of the Nation. For those facts, it is not necessary to rely upon the testimony of a Democrat; every opponent of the Party from Hamilton to Hoover concurs; and so does every propagandist of the opposition from the friend of Blaine who coined the phrase "Rum, Romanism and Rebellion" to the friend of Colonel McCormick who coined the phrase "Second Louisiana Purchase."

The attraction of the Democratic Party for these minorities is its adherence to the fundamentals of civil liberty. The Democratic Party came into being to combat the Alien and Sedition Laws, under which Federalist police, as irresponsible as Boston graveyard wreckers, destroyed the printshops of Jeffersonian editors, and under which Federalist judges as irresponsible as the Massachusetts jurist who condemned the cobbler and the fishmonger, sentenced old soldiers of the Revolution to prison for talking too loudly of freedom in the taverns.

Every minority of that day welcomed the existence of a party that promised a government of law instead of a government by packed juries. Every successive minority has welcomed it. The Democratic Party has had its mad mullahs, its witch doctors, its Ploughboy Petes, its lunatics, its frauds, and its fools; but it has not stood sponsor for religious intolerance, as did the Know-Nothing Party of Jackson's day or the Republican Party of 1928. Precisely as the party of Henry Clay and Nicholas Biddle never recovered from the disease acquired by association with their Know-Nothing friends, so the party of Herbert Hoover and Claire Hoffman will never recover from the malignant fever contracted from the Ku Klux Klan.

It is difficult for a Democrat to phrase these simple, obvious, indisputable facts without an occasional lapse into the rhetoric of the campaign speech. It is even probable that I have engaged in a few minor overstatements about the glories of the Party, which, always, in Dixie, we accord capitalization; it is barely possible that I have been a trifle harsh about Republicans. One often speaks harshly of those things that are unfamiliar, and in my State the contact with a Republican Administration is remote; until the inevitable depression reminds Georgians that, through no fault of their own voting, the Nation has gone astray once again.

The Democratic Party is a cross-section of America. It contains a great many different economic, sectional, racial, and social groups, not all of whose members are in complete agreement upon every policy or upon every plan to carry out a policy. It is unavoidable that such a party should often be unwieldy, that its processes in arriving at agreement should often be slow as molasses on a winter day, and that it should have great difficulty in imposing any form of discipline within its ranks. But when some agreement is obtained, it represents an irresistible movement of an overwhelming majority of American citizens.

Laying aside party rhetoric reluctantly for a little while, the Democratic Party appears to have adhered rather tenaciously to certain basic tenets, accord upon which has enabled otherwise discordant elements to live within the same household:

The foremost obligation of government at every level is the protection of the civil liberties of the people.

Decentralization of government is desirable, wherever public services can be performed *effectively* upon the level nearest the people.

Enterprise shall be free from monopolistic interference.

America is a part of the world and not a colony for escapists.

The people have a right to experiment with their government and through their government.

Only men have rights; property, institutions, and government do not possess them.

This does not imply, or even suggest, that every individual enrolled as a Democrat on the voting lists or listed as a Democrat in the Congressional Directory believes in all or even one of these fundamental concepts. Nor does it follow that every Democrat with a big "D" is a democrat with a little "d." There have been Congressmen from every section of America who would regard these as dangerous, pernicious, Jacobin, revolutionary doctrines. But it is a general agreement upon these things that holds together the Democratic Party. It is a disbelief, among a group in the Nation, in one or more of these things that has led to the creation of the other parties.

Disagreement between Democrats usually arises out of the adoption of specific techniques for carrying out this general program under the conditions existing at the particular time. Moreover, there always have been conservative and liberal wings of the Party, and enough savoring of radicals to keep it alive and on its toes. In no other American party have all three been able to live with relative comfort. When agreements are eventually reached, the agreements generally mean definite advances in public policy. From the repeal of the Alien and Sedition Laws and the purchase of Louisiana, through the revocation of the charter of the Bank of the United States, the building of the Federal Reserve System, and the adoption of the New Deal guarantees of basic wages, secured bank deposits and old-age benefits, every important advance in America has first been advocated by some enthusiastic radical, who often saw it as a panacea for all national ills. Then it won gradual acceptance through the liberals within the Democratic Party and finally was passed by that party's efforts.

What is consequential to the America of today and the America of tomorrow is that the liberal majority within the Democratic Party retain control of the Party; make it the vehicle for acceptance of new ideas; and utilize it for that experimentalism required to solve our problems. Always it must be remembered that the leadership of any political party first dashes ahead enthusiastically for a time, then falls into step with those in the marching column, and then, growing a little tired, begins to lag behind. The dashing-ahead days not infrequently result in party defeats; the days when the march is united result in victory; the days when leadership falls behind its public result in party disintegration or, less frequently, in a change of leadership.

That party discipline among the Democrats is always relatively weak is widely recognized. That has always been the case, and unquestionably always will be the case. Greater discipline in the Party leadership, however, can be obtained. Jefferson obtained it, by the dropping of an able man and genuine democrat, with a little "d," from Party leadership in Congress because of persistent insubordination; John Randolph of Roanoke had immeasurable charm and exceptional brilliance, but lacked a concept of party responsibility. Jackson dismissed an entire Cabinet, and resorted to the effective expedient of obtaining instructions from the States, through their Legislatures, to their Senators upon their votes in the Upper Chamber, as measures to obtain discipline within the Party.

The distinction must be made between party discipline, as it applies to members of the Party, and party discipline as it applies to representatives of the people chosen through party methods. The first is an impossibility for a party with the basic philosophy of Jefferson; the second is a requisite to party responsibility.

The difficulty in obtaining a proper degree of party discipline in the national government, a difficulty not paralleled in most State governments, arises chiefly from the present organization of the Congress.

Many admirable studies have been made in the past four years of the needs for reorganization of Congressional procedure. Most of these have been directed at the problem of making it possible for the individual Representative or Senator to function effectively; most of them, including the extremely able study by Congressman Estes Kefauver of Tennessee, have failed to take into comprehensive consideration the aspect of party responsibility.

Except for the recommendation that special committees be eliminated, with which I cannot concur on principle, since that involves the greatest degree of abdication of the authority of a parliamentary body, most of the Kefauver recommendations, which were adopted in very large degree by the Joint Committee on the Organization of Congress, seem admirable. Certainly there is strong reason to adopt proposals to eliminate overlapping jurisdiction of committees, to set aside docket days when members can present arguments and witnesses in favor of their bills, to maintain complete records of committee proceedings, to require prompt report by the committee chairman of all bills approved, to limit the conferees of the two Houses to discussion of adjustment of differences and permit them no right to change subject matter on which there is agreement, and the preparation of nontechnical digests of all measures to accompany committee reports. There is reasonable objection to the suggestion that House and Senate committees hold joint hearings, and to proposals that all authority over the District of Columbia be relinquished in favor of a local municipal government, although it is necessary that something be done to give the residents of the District some representation in local affairs.

These reforms are excellent, but they do not reach the question of party responsibility. To attain that, three additional measures seem necessary. The first would permit the majority members of a committee to select the chairman of that body. The second would be to have the members of the Rules Committee of the House chosen by the party caucus and removable by a majority vote of such caucus; it would be desirable to eliminate from the Rules Committee all members of the minority party, and to facilitate the calling-up of a measure by action of the membership of the House. The third proposal is for a record vote upon all questions.

There is no actual novelty about any of these suggestions, except that of eliminating minority members from the Rules Committee. The seniority system of chairmanship is a modern engraftment upon Congress, without precedent in any of the States. The Rules Committee, as it exists today, was a creation of the insurgency of 1911 against Speaker Joseph Cannon. The requirement of a record vote has been demanded by most students of Congressional procedure for many years.

That the minority party should be represented on the steering committee of the House of Representatives is unreasonable. The majority party has the responsibility for the conduct of government; the minority party has the responsibility of subjecting the policies of the government to the most careful scrutiny and the most searching criticism, whenever it detects mistakes or weaknesses. Ample safeguards can be erected in the committee system for the protection of legislation introduced by a "private member," to borrow a term from British procedure to distinguish a measure presented independently and without Administration approval in advance. By the present status of the Rules Committee, the minority is invited into irresponsible alliance with recusant majority members.

Some reshaping of Congressional procedure, and some tightening of party discipline in that body, will be essential to the orderly conduct of government under our present system of checks-and-balances. Congressmen should receive better salaries, more adequate staffs for themselves and for their committees, and a special research body of technical analysts.

There is no vehicle through which the public can direct government, under a system of representative democracy, except party organization. The alignment within one party of all those sharing similar views on public questions, and the exercise of party discipline over the representatives chosen through party processes, must be effected if the government is to carry out popular mandates.

19

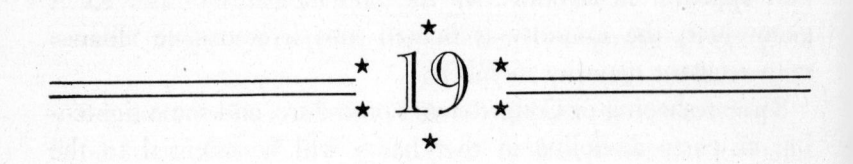

THE SHORE DIMLY SEEN

THE MEMBERS OF the Harris County delegation were discussing the needs at Pine Mountain Park when my telephone rang. Calls were supposed to be intercepted while I talked with the visitors, so I knew that my secretary, Grace Cannington, must think that the matter represented an emergency.

"John Trost is on the line," she said, betraying a little excitement. "He says it is important and wants to talk to you right now."

John Trost is agent-in-charge of the Federal Bureau of Investigation in Atlanta. I took the call.

"We have a man inside the Oakland City Klavern," the FBI agent began. "Last night the Klan had a meeting, and I thought you would be interested in what they decided." I waited.

"They proposed that each of five Klaverns select five men, and that the five Cyclops select five from this twenty-five, and send their names to the Grand Dragon, who would pick two of them to 'do a job on you.'"

"Thank you for telling me," I said. "Let me call you back in a little while and get the details."

"I thought you might like to know about it," he said. I hung up the phone and resumed my discussion with the Harris County delegation.

The Knights of the Ku Klux Klan, Incorporated, started a career of fantasy soon after the First World War. The shrouded order, with its weird rituals set forth in the "Kloran" and its outlandish hierarchy of Wizard, Titan, Dragon, Cyclops, Hydra, Kleagle, Fury and Kludd, was the invention of a rather harmless promoter of fraternal organizations, who wanted to go into business for himself with a secret order that would permit its members to play at something like Cowboys-and-Indians. He did not last long; another crowd of promoters, out after the money of suckers, took over. They were dethroned by a clique of politicians, who saw in the Invisible Empire a device to gain political control of many States; they gained control of more than one, including Indiana. Becoming entangled in the campaign of 1928, as an auxiliary of those dissident Democrats still labelled "Hoovercrat" in the South, the Empire collapsed in many States.

In its early days, the Ku Klux Klan, Incorporated had been more than a refuge for escapists; it had been the rallying ground for a good many hoodlums and thugs. People were beaten; "fiery crosses" were burned on the lawns of Catholics, Jews, Negroes and foreign-born Americans. After it was crushed in Indiana and driven underground in Georgia and Louisiana, the Klan chieftains devoted themselves mainly to politics on the State and local levels. Only occasional outrages occurred, such as the series of floggings near Atlanta, where one man was brutally beaten to death. Those convicted in the floggings received pardons from Governor Eugene Talmadge.

The Klan chiefs did well enough financially, even toward the end of the lush days. Its Imperial Wizard, Dr. Hiram Wesley Evans, was fined in the United States District Court for the Northern District of Georgia for operating an "asphalt monopoly" in Georgia.

During the era between the destruction of Warsaw and Pearl Harbor, the Klan became a refuge for native Fascists, an ally of the Bund and the Silvershirts. Some of its old leaders, who could stomach a few beatings or a little political graft, retired comfortably.

Perhaps they were nervous about sedition.

Finally, the Klan was dissolved. The Emperor of the Invisible Empire and Imperial Wizard of the Knights of the Ku Klux Klan, these being the titles of the chief of the order, suspended operations; possibly because the Federal Bureau of Internal Revenue became interested in a matter of unpaid income taxes.

Then in 1945, the Klaverns began again to function. The old regalia came out of hiding. The suckers began paying their Klatockens to the Kligrapp for distribution to the Kleagle and Titan and Dragon. The floggings recommenced. Lurid hate literature, attacking the Catholics, the Jews, the Negroes and the foreign-born Americans reappeared; some of the literature praised Adolf Hitler for his work in eradicating those in Germany who were less than one hundred per cent German.

The State corporation fees of the order were paid.

Georgia had no intention, however, of restoring the Knights of the Ku Klux Klan, Incorporated to the old status of power and profit and immunity. By my direction, Attorney General Eugene Cook brought *quo warranto* proceedings in the name of the State of Georgia against the Invisible Empire to forfeit its corporate charter. The petition to the Court asserted that the Klan had violated the terms of its charter not only by operating as a profit-making organization, as a political organization, and as a racket, but by beating people with five-foot thongs of rawhide studded with metal cleats and by promoting racial and religious hatred.

The members of the Oakland City Klavern were resentful of this interference.

Fascists are resentful of interference at all times. The native American Fascist is not different in ideology and aspiration from the German and Italian type; the Blackshirts, the Brownshirts and the Nightshirts are brothers in doctrine and methods.

Their ambition is to overthrow democratic government as we know it, under the pretense of preserving "order in an emergency." Their objective is to supplant the present national flag with one bearing a crooked cross.

I do not think that they will have their way in America. I doubt that they will have their way again soon in any part of the world. I think we will keep the flag we have.

Miss Maggie Brown had her difficulties with the first grade of Newnan public school. Not the least of her difficulties was persuading her pupils to reach some agreement about *The Star-Spangled Banner*. The agreement never was complete and never was lasting; it might have been the veritable model of international compacts.

I am inclined to think that I was the only member of the class ever to learn the second stanza. The others always dashed on to triumph in a just cause, while I lingered to puzzle out the identity of the banner that floated over the battered escarpments of Fort McHenry.

National anthems are hallowed by associations. That is fortunate, for thereby they are saved from the requirement of being good verse; but it always has seemed to me that there was great poetry in that second stanza of Francis Scott Key's. I did not know then what made it so; now I know that it is the autobiography of a man's heart in an infinitely long second, split off eternity.

My uncle, Alvan Freeman, who was the kindest man I have ever known and the gentlest and who had immeasurable patience with such things as time, and dogs, and children, explained it to me.

He made it live over again: the pacing of the alien quarter deck; the hideous hiss of the rockets and the earth-shaking burst of the bombs; the flash of the answering cannonade from the little fortress; the silence that came, and the dawn creeping bleakly over the Chesapeake; hidden in the half-darkness, a shore dimly seen, a shore much loved.

> On the shore dimly seen thro' the mists of the deep,
> Where the foe's haughty host in dread silence reposes,
> What is that which the breeze, o'er the towering steep,
> As it fitfully blows, half conceals, half discloses?

I always shared with Key his anxiety as the little breeze half-billowed the flag on its staff; my eyes followed his to the river below and the reflection mirrored there. I have never failed to share in his exultation when we discovered that the flag still was there; we wanted it to be there so much that it had to be.

Over the land of the free! Over the land where Roger Williams fled through the forests of New England in search of a place to worship God, and over the land where Jefferson lavished his affections upon poems in brick and marble. Over the land of the men of Gonzales, refusing to stir from the Alamo, and of Will Percy and Skillet tumbling in the tall grass by the banks of the Mississippi. Over the backwoods of Pennsylvania and Virginia where Abraham Marah plodded with a dangerous and seditious pamphlet called *Common Sense* in his peddler's pack, and over the pine forests where Dr. Charles Herty spent a lifetime developing a new industry that would not rob the land.

Over the home of the brave! Over the little Nebraska town where George Norris dreamed of rebuilding the hillsides of Tennessee, and over the Hermitage where Andrew Jackson buttoned his worn greatcoat around him before putting a flower on Rachel's grave and setting out for Washington to one last fight and it the best of all. The home of Horace Greeley tossing his old white hat into the race for President, and of Carl Schurz fighting to save the natural resources of the people, and of Clara Barton scolding for more bandages and more hot water after Gettysburg.

From such a land we must eliminate injustice and disunity and selfish greed. Into the mind of Jefferson, as he wrote his last letter, as into the mind of Sam Adams when he wrote the first of those to the Colonial Committees of Safety, recurred the words of that rigid old Puritan, Richard Rumbold, undaunted on the scaffold:

"I could never believe that Providence had sent a few men into the world ready booted and spurred to ride, and millions ready saddled and bridled to be ridden."

We can have security for all our citizens if we have the will to do so and the courage to do so. We can have an America in which none is hungry, or ill housed, or insufficiently clothed, or idle, or desperate with fear for his future and that of his children.

We can have peace with other nations if we discard the advice of the overwise and the cynical. The world is one world, not because the old relationships between time and distance have been altered by the triumph of man over the air, but because men are the same everywhere. Peace depends upon the relationship between men, not upon the dimensions of the physical world that they inhabit.

We can have freedom, if we make the freedom of other men our concern, because nowhere in all the world can some men be free, until everywhere all men are free. And they will be free on the shore dimly seen. . . .